Law and Religion in a Global Context

Volume 5

Series Editor

Frank S. Ravitch, College of Law, Rm 315, Michigan State University, East Lansing, USA

Law and Religion in a Global Context will focus on law and religion issues from a global perspective at a time when that field is of increasing importance and relevance around the world. Designed to be broad, the scope allows for books on the relationship between religion and government as well as on religious law. Focus will be placed on comparative law issues, but also on issues within single countries. Representative areas of focus will be:

- the relationship between government and religion ranging from laicete to theocracy
- religious freedom in pluralistic societies
- the relationship between religious freedom and other freedoms such as freedom of speech and sexual freedom
- regulation of religion by government
- original contributions on religious law

The series seeks to highlight up and coming voices in the field alongside those of established scholars. We encourage scholars from a wide range of geographic perspectives to apply. Purely doctrinal analysis of law and religion is not preferred. Nor is analysis of religious law issues without any original contribution or insights. The only exception to this rule might be books on legal doctrine from a region that has been under analyzed in English language literature.

Henrique Fernandes Antunes

Religion, Drug, or Cult?

Ayahuasca's Legal Path in Brazil, the United States, and France

Springer

Henrique Fernandes Antunes
Religions in the Contemporary World
Brazilian Center of Analysis and Planning (CEBRAP)
São Paulo, Brazil

ISSN 2946-5931 ISSN 2946-594X (electronic)
Law and Religion in a Global Context
ISBN 978-3-032-04367-2 ISBN 978-3-032-04368-9 (eBook)
https://doi.org/10.1007/978-3-032-04368-9

This Springer imprint is published by the registered company Springer Nature Switzerland AG
The registered company address is: Gewerbestrasse 11, 6330 Cham, Switzerland

To Beatriz Pizani Fernandes and
Márcia Araújo Estrada (in memoriam)

Acknowledgments

This book is the culmination of 15 years of research on the public presence of ayahuasca in Brazil and beyond. It weaves together insights from my master's and Ph.D. studies in anthropology, as well as postdoctoral fellowships in Brazil and abroad. Along this journey, I have been fortunate to receive the wisdom, support, and encouragement of many, to whom I am profoundly grateful.

First and foremost, I offer my deepest reverence to God, the Virgin Sovereign Mother, the Queen of the Forest, Jesus Christ, Saint Joseph, Saint John the Baptist, Saint Christopher, and the divine beings of the celestial court. This work would not have been possible without the presence and guidance of Mestre Raimundo Irineu Serra, my master, protector, counselor, and friend. Words cannot capture the magnitude of his influence on my life.

I am eternally thankful for the unwavering support of my family. To my grandmother Beatriz and my mother Vera, whose encouragement has shaped me in immeasurable ways. To my father Antônio Nedir and my brother Igor, whose presence has been a source of strength. To my aunt and second mother, Márcia (in memoriam), who remains in my heart. To my wife Paula, my love, partner, and dearest companion, thank you for your faith in me, your endless care, and your unwavering support. To my daughter Beatriz Maria, the light of my life and my greatest treasure.

I am also indebted to the friends and colleagues who have left an indelible mark on my intellectual and personal path. To the professors and peers from Unesp-Marília-FFC, Universidade de São Paulo, and Centro Brasileiro de Análise e Planejamento (CEBRAP), I extend my deepest appreciation. My heartfelt thanks to Paula Montero, who guided me through my master's and Ph.D. and whose mentorship left a lasting impact on my work. I am also grateful to professor Sérgio Domingues (Krahô) (in memoriam), a mentor and friend who challenged and inspired me during my undergraduate years, bringing a disruptive anthropological force into an intense Marxist environment.

I am especially grateful to professors Saba Mahmood (in memoriam) and Charles Hirschkind for hosting me at the University of California Berkeley. A special acknowledgment goes to Charles, whose guidance extended far beyond academic mentorship and grew into a cherished friendship. My sincere thanks go to professor Ronaldo Almeida, my supervisor and friend during my postdoctoral fellowship at CEBRAP, and to professors Maria Hermínia Tavares, Marta Machado, and Vera Coelho, who coordinated CEBRAP's International Postdoctoral Program. I am equally grateful to my postdoctoral supervisors, Daniel Cefaï at the Céntre d'Études de Mouvements Sociaux (CEMS/EHESS) and Lori Beaman at the University of Ottawa. To my colleagues in the research group *Religiões no Mundo Contemporâneo*, and those who shared the path of my undergraduate, master's, Ph.D., and postdoctoral studies, I deeply appreciate the debates, conversations, and camaraderie that enriched this journey.

To the Santo Daime community and dear friends, especially those at *Pronto Socorro Espiritual Raimundo Irineu Serra*, I extend my heartfelt gratitude. My sincere appreciation goes to padrinho Raimundo Nonato, madrinha Graça, Ramiro, Robson, Renato, Raimundo, Rejane, and Recislene and to all the Carneiro family. To my Santo Daime companions, Claude, Benjamin, Jeff, Julianna, Jason, Frederick, Clancy, Marcelo, David, Dylan, Nina, Anastasia, Emerson, Paulo Henrique, Saldanha, Alexandre, Rafael, Erika, Bruna, and Bruno, thank you for walking this path with me.

A special thank you to my colleagues and friends at the Chacruna Institute for Psychedelic Plant Medicines. In particular, my deepest appreciation to my friend Bia Labate, whose contributions to this work are immeasurable.

I also wish to express my sincere gratitude to Manuela Schwietzer and Rodrigo Vitorino at Springer for their confidence in this work, and to Peter Pushpanathan for his valuable assistance throughout the manuscript preparation.

I am deeply thankful to all who have contributed to this endeavor with their support, insight, and generosity. Your presence has been integral to the completion of this work.

This study was funded by the São Paulo Research Foundation (FAPESP) from 2010 to 2023 (Process Numbers: 2010/04228-8, 2013/24663-9, 2015/15855-7, 2019/11202-0, 2021/11399-8, 2022/11775-2), and by the Chacruna Institute for Psychedelic Plant Medicines in 2024 and 2025.

FAPESP
FUNDAÇÃO DE AMPARO À PESQUISA DO ESTADO DE SÃO PAULO

chacruna
Institute for Psychedelic Plant Medicines

Competing Interests The author has no competing interests to declare that are relevant to the content of this manuscript.

Contents

Chapter 1
Introduction

1.1 What Is Ayahuasca?

Is the use of ayahuasca a religious practice, a cultural expression, drug abuse, or a form of trickery by dangerous cults? The title of this book, framed as a question, suggests a quest for a definitive answer. However, my aim is not to categorize ayahuasca but rather to use this inquiry as a springboard for exploring the contested meanings and practices surrounding this Amazonian brew, particularly within legal and public policy contexts. In other words, rather than seeking to define what ayahuasca "is," this work examines how various actors—governments, ayahuasca groups, Indigenous peoples, legal institutions, non-profits, scholars, experts, activists, etc.—engage in disputes over its classification, legitimacy, and regulation.

Nevertheless, some context is necessary. Ayahuasca—known by various names such as Caapi, Kamarampi, Nixi Pae, Huni, Santo Daime, Hoasca, and Vegetal—is a brew prepared from a combination of two plants native to the Amazon rainforest: *Banisteriopsis caapi* and *Psychotria viridis*.[1] Historically, Indigenous peoples in countries like Bolivia, Peru, Colombia, Brazil, Venezuela, and Ecuador have utilized ayahuasca for various purposes (Luna, 1986). These practices are dynamic and have changed over time and, in recent years, ayahuasca has become a catalyst for political and cultural movements among Indigenous peoples of the Amazon (Antunes, 2023; Caicedo-Fernández, 2023; Labate et al., 2023).

In Brazil, since the first half of the twentieth century, one can find the development of three groups—Santo Daime, União do Vegetal (UDV), and Barquinha—that became commonly referred to in academic literature as the "Brazilian Ayahuasca Religions" (Labate & Araújo, 2002; Labate, 2004). These movements emerged in

[1] The composition of ayahuasca varies among different groups and contexts. While Banisteriopsis caapi is usually a common base ingredient, the admixture plants can differ. For instance, in some regions, Diplopterys cabrerana is used alongside B. caapi instead of Psychotria viridis.

H. Fernandes Antunes, *Religion, Drug, or Cult?*, Law and Religion in a Global Context 5, https://doi.org/10.1007/978-3-032-04368-9_1

the Amazon region between the 1930s and 1960s and centered their practices on the ritual use of ayahuasca. The term "Brazilian Ayahuasca Religions," developed in the early 2000s by anthropologist Beatriz Labate (2000), became a household category in anthropological studies, used to distinguish these groups from Indigenous and mestizo traditions found in other South American countries, such as Peru, Colombia, and Ecuador (Labate et al., 2008). Unlike those traditions, which are primarily associated with *vegetalismo*[2] and shamanic[3] practices, the Brazilian groups are described in the literature as a *sui generis* expression based on Christian influences alongside elements from Afro-Brazilian religions, Kardecist Spiritism, and European esotericism.

In recent decades, the consumption of ayahuasca has expanded into a diverse array of expressions, including neo-shamanism, psychotherapy, artistic, New Age, and others. These have been labeled as "urban neo-ayahuasqueiro" movements (Labate, 2004). This notion is used to describe a new moment, as ayahuasca gained popularity, which in turn led to diverse socio-cultural contexts, characterized by new ritual practices, and the insertion of a myriad of new actors, including neoshamans, life-coaches, therapists, facilitators, etc. The literature has framed these developments as part of a larger trend in which the use of ayahuasca has detached either from the Brazilian ayahuasca religions or from Indigenous settings, and transformed into a complex urban phenomenon, although these actors might frequently resort to some form of connection or alliance with religious or Indigenous groups in order to establish a source of legitimacy. In contrast, groups like Santo Daime and UDV, which present themselves as religious expressions, claim an Indigenous ancestral root through the use of ayahuasca, while some Indigenous groups dispute which of them introduced Mestre Irineu, the founder of Santo Daime, to ayahuasca (Labate & Coutinho, 2014). The symbolic disputes and historical genealogies tend to become blurry at this point.

Moreover, these developments are creating a vast and complex landscape that continues to diversify and expand, making this classificatory endeavor even more problematic. One example is the case of Indigenous groups that have been

[2] In her pioneering work, Dobkin de Rios (1972) examines the role of psychoactive plants, particularly ayahuasca, within the context of *vegetalismo*, a term that refers to the indigenous and mestizo Amazonian practices of shamanism. She explores how these practices, rooted in Amazonian cosmologies and healing practices, engage with the broader social and cultural dimensions of the Peruvian Amazon, drawing attention to the ways in which vegetalismo incorporates both therapeutic and religious elements of the ayahuasca experience.

[3] The notion of "shamanism" as a transcultural category has been widely criticized for oversimplifying diverse traditions and detaching them from their specific cultural contexts, instead reducing them to supposed universal motivations (Atkinson, 1992). Taussig (1989) provocatively described the term as a modern Western construct. More recently, scholars have drawn a distinction between shamanism, understood as Indigenous spiritual practices, and neo-shamanism, which adapts Indigenous traditions for purposes of personal transformation and self-exploration (Gearin & Sáez, 2021). However, I treat "shaman," "shamanism," and "neoshamanism" as native terms rather than fixed anthropological concepts. It should be noted that I have opted to translate the Portuguese word *pajé* as "shaman" for a lack of a better word.

introduced to ayahuasca through interactions with religious organizations such as Santo Daime and UDV (Rose, 2010). These interactions have led to new alliances and exchanges. The recent incorporation of the classical guitar, prominent in Santo Daime music, has influenced the creation of new musical genres among Indigenous peoples such as *haux* music (Bueno, 2017). This genre blends Indigenous chanting with new aesthetics and instruments, exemplifying the dynamic nature of contemporary ayahuasca practices. These developments highlight the multifaceted landscape of ayahuasca use in Brazil and beyond. Moreover, these varied contexts contribute to political disputes surrounding its use, as different actors seek to advance competing claims regarding tradition and legitimacy.

Another topic of growing interest, is the burgeoning industry of therapeutic retreats—a phenomenon often referred to as "ayahuasca tourism" (Stuart, 2002). This trend is particularly prevalent in countries like Peru and has increasingly expanded into Central America. Several factors have been attributed to this growth, including the rising global interest in alternative healing practices, the influence of psychedelic research, and the commodification of Indigenous practices within the wellness industry (Wolff, 2020). Participants in these retreats come from diverse backgrounds, seeking ayahuasca for spiritual growth, psychological healing, and even relief from mental health conditions. However, the rapid expansion of ayahuasca tourism has raised significant concerns regarding sustainability, commodification and safety (Fotiou, 2008, 2014, 2020).

Scholars have pointed to the ways in which the retreat industry often molds Indigenous rituals to meet Western expectations, sometimes at the expense of their practices. Additionally, there are concerns about the regulation of these spaces, as the influx of foreigners has led to a rise in the number of facilitators, increasing safety risks, and even cases of abuse (Kavenska & Simonova, 2015). As ayahuasca continues to become a global trend, the increased demand has also led to ecological implications. The harvesting of *Banisteriopsis caapi* and *Psychotria viridis* has intensified, raising environmental concerns regarding the impacts of its overexploitation and the broader implications of its commodification (Tupper, 2017).

When it comes to the legal challenges, their roots usually lie in the fact that *Psychotria viridis*, one of the constituent plants of ayahuasca, contains N,N-Dimethyltryptamine (DMT), a controlled substance under the United Nations' 1971 Convention on Psychotropic Substances. Despite this legal framework, in many countries, plants containing DMT are not subject to control, frequently placing ayahuasca in a legal gray area. While international treaties allow for exceptions concerning traditional and Indigenous uses, each nation determines its own regulatory approach, leading to a patchwork of legal interpretations (Labate & Cavnar, 2023). In some cases, ayahuasca is criminalized, leading to law enforcement actions and judicial disputes. Moreover, the legal challenges surrounding ayahuasca often raise complex issues such as the limits of religious freedom, the impacts of drug policies, and the reach of public health and public order, creating intricate scenarios that are not easy to navigate. These disputes highlight the tensions between different legal principles such as international drug control frameworks, national sovereignty, Indigenous rights, religious freedom, and human rights, resulting in diverse legal interpretations and enforcement approaches. In contrast, in some South American countries, including Peru and more recently Brazil, ayahuasca has been incorporated into affirmative cultural policies that recognize its historical significance as cultural heritage. These variations in legal treatment reflect broader debates about the intersection between the religious and Indigenous uses of ayahuasca and cultural heritage policies, and how to delimit and classify its traditional uses.

By comparing how different countries dispute and regulate the use of ayahuasca, one can contrast the processes through which certain practices attract public interest and become subject to state intervention. Given that ayahuasca use is documented in numerous countries, selecting specific cases for study is a crucial endeavor. In this particular case, I will focus on Brazil, the United States, and France. These countries provide distinct legal, cultural, and historical settings that allow for an examination of how ayahuasca is categorized, controlled, and contested. However, to fully grasp the relevance of these case studies and acknowledge potential biases, it is necessary to revisit a research and personal trajectory spanning 20 years, one that has navigated the intersections of law, religion, and psychoactive substances.

1.2 Why Brazil, the United States and France?

To understand my choice in contrasting these three countries, I must address my personal trajectory as an anthropologist and as a member of Santo Daime. I first encountered the word "ayahuasca" in 2004 during my second year as a Social Sciences undergraduate at São Paulo State University (UNESP-FFC). Someone described it as a hallucinogen used by Indigenous peoples of the Amazon and mentioned that a classmate was involved with an ayahuasca group. Shortly after, I visited him and asked whether he drank ayahuasca. He replied that he was a member of Santo Daime. I asked, "What's the difference?" He explained that the tea was the same but that Santo Daime was a Christian group. I remember seeing a copy of *O Uso Ritual da Ayahuasca* (*The Ritual Use of Ayahuasca*) (Labate & Araújo, 2002) at his house, the first edited volume published in Brazil on ayahuasca use. The book, over 700 pages long, is divided into three sections: Indigenous use, the "Brazilian ayahuasca religions," and biomedical studies on ayahuasca. Our conversation and my brief reading of the book's introduction were enough to spark my curiosity.

However, my interest in the use of psychoactive plants had begun earlier. One of the reasons I chose to study social sciences is related to the works of anthropologist Carlos Castaneda (1968, 1971, 1972). Initially, I had planned to pursue psychology, but Castaneda's narratives about Don Juan and his experiences with peyote, mushrooms, and datura captivated me so profoundly that I changed my major. To my surprise, the social sciences curriculum in Brazil bore little resemblance to Castaneda's accounts of "power plants." Later that year, I visited my friend several times in the Sorocaba region of São Paulo state, where I participated in three Santo Daime "*trabalhos*" (works, in the sense of labor). Just over a year later, I decided to become a member, or "*me fardar*" ("to get my star," as they say in the United States).

Initially, I had no academic interest in ayahuasca. Yet, 2 years after earning my Social Sciences degree, I began, in 2010, a master's in anthropology at the University of São Paulo.

My original research plan was to conduct a traditional ethnographic study, exploring concepts of self and embodiment within the Santo Daime tradition. However, several factors led me to change my research focus abruptly. During this time, I joined the research group "Religion in the Contemporary World," coordinated by my advisor, Professor Paula Montero. At the time, the group was focused on the increasing presence of religious actors in Brazilian public space. As part of this broader discussion, the concept of "public controversies" emerged as a key analytical category. Group members examined topics such as religious intolerance, spiritual abuse, debates on stem-cell research and abortion, and the participation of Pentecostal institutions in party politics, among other themes (Montero, 2015).

Coincidentally, 2010 was a particularly turbulent year in the public debate on ayahuasca in Brazil. In January, the *Conselho Nacional de Políticas sobre Drogas* (National Council on Drug Policies—CONAD) issued Resolution No. 1, which officially published the Final Report of the Multidisciplinary Working Group on Ayahuasca, originally drafted in 2006. The resolution reaffirmed the legitimacy of ayahuasca's religious use as a state-recognized cultural practice within Brazilian religious traditions and outlined recommendations for its "responsible use." The following month, *Isto É* magazine published the article *"A Encruzilhada do Daime"* (*The Daime Crossroads*), which criticized CONAD's decision and highlighted controversies surrounding ayahuasca, including allegations that certain religious groups were involved in illegal activities. Another significant event occurred in March 2010: the murder of cartoonist Glauco Vilas Boas, a leader of a Santo Daime church on the outskirts of São Paulo, and his son Raoni, by Carlos Eduardo Sundfeld Nunes, a former member of the group. In the wake of the killings, *Veja* magazine published *"O Psicótico e o Daime"* (*The Psycho and the Daime*), emphasizing that the perpetrator had been diagnosed with schizophrenia. The article questioned the safety of ayahuasca use among individuals with psychiatric disorders and scrutinized several aspects of CONAD's decision, fueling public controversy over the regulation of the religious use of ayahuasca.

The media coverage and reactions within academic and ayahuasca circles caught my attention just as I was seeking a new research topic. I then restructured my project to investigate the public controversy surrounding ayahuasca in Brazil. I collected and analyzed a wide range of materials—magazine and newspaper articles, television programs, documentaries, government documents (opinions, reports, and laws), institutional publications from ayahuasca groups, and anthropological scholarship. These materials formed the basis of my master's thesis, which examined the debates over definitions, regulatory frameworks, and the recognition of the use of ayahuasca as a legitimate religious and cultural practice in Brazil (Antunes, 2012).

For my doctoral research, I deepened my focus on ayahuasca regulation, undertaking a comparative analysis between Brazil and an international case where ayahuasca groups had secured legal religious exemptions. My two options at the time were the Netherlands, where a court granted a Santo Daime church legal protection in 2001, and the United States, where two groups had obtained religious exemptions, most notably the UDV, which won a landmark Supreme Court case in 2006. The language barrier and the need to translate Dutch legal documents posed a challenge. Conversely, the U.S. offered more extensive legal documentation, and I had contacts through an anthropologist friend familiar with U.S. Santo Daime groups who could assist my research. Additionally, my growing interest in the anthropology of secularism, particularly as developed in U.S. scholarship, influenced my decision to focus on this case.

I spent the year 2016 as a visiting scholar in the Department of Anthropology at the University of California, Berkeley, under the supervision of Professors Saba Mahmood and Charles Hirschkind. In the U.S., I gathered extensive material on the UDV and Santo Daime legal cases and conducted interviews with key figures involved in these disputes. This research formed the core of my doctoral dissertation, *O uso religioso da ayahuasca como um problema público: um contraponto entre os casos do Brasil e dos EUA* (The Religious Use of Ayahuasca as a Public Problem: A Counterpoint Between the Cases of Brazil and the USA) (Antunes, 2019).

After completing my doctorate, I turned my attention to the ongoing recognition process of ayahuasca as part of the Brazilian cultural heritage. The topic interested me because it marked a new chapter in Brazilian public policy on ayahuasca, moving away from drug policies and entering the realm of heritage policies. This shift was accompanied by the addition of new actors in the debate on ayahuasca use and an increased Indigenous political engagement. The First Indigenous Ayahuasca Conference held in 2017 underscored this shift, centering ayahuasca within the Indigenous political agenda in the Amazon from that point on.

A few years later, I became a postdoctoral fellow in the *Centre d'Études des Mouvements Sociaux* (CEMS) at the *École des Hautes Études en Sciences Sociales* (EHESS) in France. At the time, my research goals at the Cems were mainly theoretical and methodological. I wished to further understand the development and uses of the notion of "public problems" and also the contributions of French pragmatism to anthropology. Yet, some months after my arrival in the country, I was contacted by Claude Bauchet, leader of the Santo Daime group in Paris, who was awaiting his second trial for drug-related charges concerning ayahuasca. Despite the fact that my research in France was unrelated to the legal status of ayahuasca in the country, Bauchet's case piqued my interest. As I analyzed legal documents, government reports, and media coverage, I realized that his trial was not merely about drug-related issues but also about France's broader debates on "cults" and "sectarian movements" in the country.

My supervisor at the time, Professor Daniel Cefaï—who was aware of my intentions to write a book contrasting the regulation of ayahuasca in Brazil and the legal cases in the United States—suggested incorporating the French case into my analysis. The idea seemed very appealing considering the significant differences in each case. In Brazil, ayahuasca is regulated for religious use and is on the path to cultural heritage status. In the U.S., ayahuasca remains a controlled substance, but certain groups have secured legal exemptions for religious use. In France, ayahuasca is entirely prohibited, classified as a narcotic, and associated with dangerous cultish movements. The differences, however, go beyond specific drug policies and their stances on ayahuasca, as each country's position also reflects specific historical and cultural sensibilities shaping the relationship between religion and the state. As Talal Asad (2006) reminds us, modern national political cultures have never been homogeneous, static, or uncontested. Similarly, the concept of "religion" is not fixed but continually reshaped by legal, political, and social forces. Engaging with Asad (1993), my goal is to use ayahuasca as a lens to examine how public sensibilities define religion, delineate religious freedom, and determine the boundaries of state intervention.

These considerations help explain why I chose to contrast the cases of Brazil, the United States, and France. What remains less evident, however, is how my experience as a Santo Daime member in these three countries has influenced my understanding of the disputes surrounding ayahuasca. In Brazil, despite ayahuasca's legal recognition for religious use, social stigma persists, particularly due to its association with the notion of a "hallucinogenic drug." Nevertheless, ayahuasca groups operate with considerable autonomy, as the plants themselves are not subject to legal control. While occasional legal challenges arise for certain individuals or groups, regulatory directives and guidelines lack the force of law, allowing ceremonies to take place with minimal to no interference. Regarding the research, however, I faced limitations in accessing certain milieus. Most of my contacts were drawn from Santo Daime, making it difficult to engage directly with Indigenous communities who have increasingly voiced critiques of ayahuasca religions and also with the UDV which is historically known for having reservations regarding research conducted by nonmembers (Andrade, 2002). As a result, when it came to the Indigenous agenda on ayahuasca and to the UDV cases, I had to rely primarily on secondary sources, such as academic articles, theses, dissertations, institutional documents, interviews available online, and other sources.

In the United States, only a small number of churches have secured legal exemptions for religious use, yet a significant number of underground ayahuasca groups continue to operate. Most exist within a legal gray area, given that while DMT is classified as a controlled substance, the plants used to prepare ayahuasca are not. During my time at UC Berkeley, I had the opportunity to visit Santo Daime groups in California and became closely involved with a now-defunct church in Northern California. Despite the absence of formal regulation, there was little sense of fear regarding legal repercussions. Many participants assumed—though some experts dispute this—that the legal victories of the UDV and a Santo Daime church in Oregon extended implicit protections to other groups. Occasionally, individuals were instructed on how to deal with potential interactions with law enforcement, yet communication about ceremonies remained open, occurring freely through in-person discussions, phone calls, text messages, and emails. Not only was I able to attend ceremonies, but I also conducted formal and informal interviews with key actors, including Santo Daime members, lawyers and expert witnesses involved in legal disputes over ayahuasca, without any problems.

France, by contrast, presented an entirely different landscape, both in terms of research and personal experience. For the first time in my life, I was forced to suspend my Santo Daime practices due to the country's strict prohibition. This had a profound personal impact, as I had been attending ceremonies regularly in Brazil. The Santo Daime branch in Paris had ceased its activities following a second legal case, and I was repeatedly advised against discussing Santo Daime issues over the phone, text message, or email. For the first time, I felt the impact of living in a country that could put me in jail just for drinking ayahuasca. The climate of unease became so pervasive that, after a period of conversations and interviews with Bauchet, I began to wonder whether I was being surveilled. This experience reinforced a well-documented pattern in drug policies, from the criminalization of marijuana to the U.S. alcohol ban during Prohibition, illegality inevitably forces people and their practices underground.

Moreover, conducting research in France proved particularly challenging. Many individuals were reluctant to discuss the legal processes surrounding ayahuasca, and securing interviews was difficult. Despite reaching out to multiple individuals and agencies, I was only able to conduct a single interview with a former member of a state agency, who insisted on remaining anonymous due to concerns about potential professional repercussions. Some agencies directed me to contact other institutions or follow up at a later date, but these efforts ultimately did not yield any additional information or interviews.

These challenges compelled me to critically reflect on the limitations of my research and the potential biases that shaped by my personal trajectory. Engaging with these issues ultimately broadened my perspective on the complex disputes surrounding ayahuasca. In the Brazilian context, I was confronted with Indigenous critiques of ayahuasca religions, which required me to acknowledge and engage with diverse perspectives on legitimacy, appropriation, and tradition. In the French case, I often felt the need to temper my critique of government policies, despite perceiving them as potential violations of human rights. While recognizing these inherent tensions and biases is crucial, my goal is not to arbitrate questions of authenticity—determining who is "traditional" and who is not—nor to frame particular actors as victims or perpetrators. Rather, my aim is to offer an analysis that foregrounds the complexities of these ongoing disputes, encouraging readers to engage critically and formulate their own questions and conclusions.

1.3 On Secularism, Public Problems and Controversies

The anthropology of secularism has been a key source of inspiration in my research, particularly the works of Talal Asad (1993, 2001, 2003, 2006, 2018) and Saba Mahmood (2005, 2010, 2015), who provided a critical lens through which to examine the regulation of religious practices in different national contexts. Their analyses highlight how secularism functions not simply as a neutral doctrine ensuring the separation of religion and the state, but as a form of governmentality that imposes specific epistemological, ethical, aesthetic, and legal imperatives. This perspective has deeply shaped my approach to understanding the disputes surrounding ayahuasca in Brazil, the United States, and France.

Asad (2006) argues that the modern secular state is not characterized by an indifference towards religion or a rational ethic of political tolerance. Rather, it is an intricate arrangement of legal reasoning, moral practices, and political authority. Accordingly, the regulation of religion is central to the exercise of state sovereignty, wherein the law establishes the parameters within which religious practices can be recognized as legitimate. Asad underscores that secular law does not merely reflect preexisting social agreements; rather, it actively facilitates or obstructs different ways of life, responding to distinct sensibilities and authorizing particular forms of harm (Asad, 2003, p. 256). This insight is particularly relevant in understanding the legal frameworks that shape the status of ayahuasca in different national settings.

The anthropologist stresses that the way different religious traditions and their histories are politically perceived defines the sensibilities of secular citizenship and national belonging in a modern state (Asad, 2006, pp. 507–508). These sensibilities correspond to different forms of secularism. For Asad, the issue at stake is not merely the respect or accommodation of differences but the power to define and justify exceptions. Secularism, he contends, operates through particular structures of freedom and sensibilities within modern nation-states. According to Asad, all modern states, even those committed to promoting "tolerance," are built upon historical emotional legacies that shape relationships among their citizens. In this regard, secularism is invoked to prevent two forms of transgressions: the perversion of politics by religious forces, on the one hand, and state restrictions on religious freedom, on the other (Asad, 2006, p. 513). Mahmood (2010) extends Asad's critique by emphasizing that the classification of what is considered religious or secular is not merely descriptive but inherently normative, constituting an exercise of power that authorizes certain subjectivities while subordinating others. As a result, different forms of secularism do not simply tolerate religious diversity but actively reform and regulate religious practices according to their own norms and values (Mahmood, 2015).

These theoretical insights have been crucial in analyzing the differential treatment of ayahuasca across the three national contexts I explore. In Brazil, where ayahuasca enjoys legal recognition for religious use, its legitimacy is nonetheless conditioned by the state's governance of a religious practice through drug and heritage policies. In the United States, legal exemptions granted to a select number of churches underscore the role of the country's courts in defining which religious practices qualify for protection, while underground groups navigate a precarious legal gray area. In France, the strict prohibition of ayahuasca exemplifies the exclusion of certain expressions in the name of public health and order, and individual freedoms, a dynamic that mirrors Asad and Mahmood's analyses of how modern states invoke secular principles to curtail certain practices.

By engaging with these debates, my research moves beyond a purely legalistic or policy-oriented analysis of ayahuasca regulation to examine the broader mechanisms that shape its contested status. Rather than viewing the differences between

Brazil, the United States, and France as merely a matter of legal divergence, I approach them as distinct expressions of secular governance, each with its own configurations of power, moral sensibilities, and criteria for religious legitimacy. This perspective allows for a more nuanced understanding of how ayahuasca-related disputes are embedded within broader struggles over the boundaries of religious freedom, state authority, and the governance of practices and bodies in the contemporary world.

In addition to the anthropology of secularism, my research is also informed by French pragmatism, particularly the notion of "public problems." The pragmatist movement, which has gained momentum over the past decades, emerged in response to a broader crisis of paradigms in the social sciences. It represents a collective effort to reformulate theories of social action through a pragmatically oriented lens (Corrêa & Dias, 2016). According to Chateauraynaud (2016), while different scholars interpret pragmatist principles in varying ways, they share key commitments: an emphasis on empiricism, the centrality of action, and recognition of the plurality of logics that shape social life.

The sociology of public problems, in turn, offers valuable analytical tools for understanding how certain disputes become sites of public contention (Cefaï, 2002, 2009, 2017, 2018; Cefaï & Pasquier, 2003). This perspective emphasizes how public problems emerge, advance, and become institutionalized through the mobilization of different actors, institutions, and normative frameworks. Daniel Cefaï (2017, p. 189) argues that public problems take shape when a collective effort is made to delineate, control, and address a contested issue. This process involves negotiations among a range of actors—government agencies, non-profits, lawyers, scholars and experts, advocacy organizations, activists, the media, etc.—who seek to define the problem, assign causes, and offer possible solutions. In Cefaï's view, a problematic situation only assumes the form of a public problem when participants step beyond their habitual frameworks and engage in a process of inquiry, interrogating the causes, consequences, and social significance of particular events.

As ayahuasca-related disputes assume the characteristics assigned by Cefaï to public problems, they often acquire a degree of institutionalization, leading to state interventions in the form of legal adjudications, regulatory policies, or law enforcement measures. These disputes unfold within different arenas of contention, where various actors advance competing claims about the legitimacy, risks, and benefits of ayahuasca use. As Cefaï (2018, p. 5) notes, these processes generate sites of dispute, in which boundaries, stakes, and alliances are continually negotiated. More importantly, a pragmatist approach does not simply focus on actors but also considers the grammars of public life—the normative frameworks, repertoires of action, modes of justification and performances that shape how problems are formulated and addressed. Thus, the constitution of public problems must be understood within the constraints of legal systems, administrative discourses, scientific expertise, media representations, among other arenas, all of which delineate the terrain of what can be thought, judged, said, and done (Cefaï, 2002, p. 99). By integrating this approach to my research, I seek to examine the public disputes that shape ayahuasca's contested status in different national contexts.

My third influence connects the questions and insights from both the Anthropology of Secularism and the pragmatist approach to public problems, specifically the research conducted by the Religion in the Contemporary World research group, particularly its focus on public controversies. As stated earlier, at the time of my joining in early 2010, the group was interested in understanding the recent reconfiguration of the Brazilian public space and the significant role of religious actors and institutions in this process. At that time, dissent and critique began to emerge as increasingly frequent modes of action for religious actors in their interactions with each other and with the state. This development was intriguing, although there was difficulty in finding a systematic and comprehensive way to address it. The concept of "public controversy" provided a pathway for constructing an analytical tool through which we could analyze public disputes (Montero, 2015, p. 16). Instead of observing religious institutions and/or groups as empirical entities, the controversy-based approach led us to focus more on discursive practices and public performances than on institutional logics or values.

This new theoretical perspective allowed us to recognize that a particular tradition within religious studies—one that privileged the description of cosmologies, rituals, and institutions—was an active instrument in producing the very phenomena it sought to explain. As Montero states (2015, p. 18), the deontologization of religious groups appeared both timely and necessary, as empirical groups do not preexist the languages used to describe and categorize them. The same applies to the adjective "religious." As part of this research agenda, several works—including my own—focused on how categories were mobilized within the very contexts under observation. The aim was to examine how various disputes shaped the Brazilian public sphere, influencing what could be said, how it could be said, and by whom. In line with French pragmatism, another key contribution was the recognition that forms of regulation are the outcome of a series of disputes that bring together a heterogeneous array of actors. This heterogeneity underscored the impossibility of maintaining clear distinctions between "religious," "scientific," "legal," or "media" discourse. Instead, what emerged was a singular public discourse, whose configurations were contingent on the arenas in which it was articulated and dramatized. These insights served as inspiration to treat the category of "religion" and others not as a priori phenomena to be studied, but as the result of a set of interactions and disputes that take shape historically.

1.4 How to Do an Ethnography of a "Problem"?

Given the aims and theoretical framework of this book, it necessarily departs from conventional notions of anthropology and ethnography. Lila Abu-Lughod (1991) argues that anthropology had been and continued to be primarily the study of the non-Western "other" by the Western "self." She reminds us that the notion of the "other," opposed to the Western/anthropological self is key to anthropology's understanding of difference. As Trouillot (1991, p. 40) puts it, "the savage was the *raison d'être* of anthropology." Over time, however, anthropology has moved away from the idea of studying traditional societies and has begun to intersect with sociology and political science, exploring urban life, political movements, digital spaces, and other contemporary forms of sociality.

Despite the various transformations that anthropology has undergone, the idea that anthropological work takes place in an encounter with an "other," often spatially and culturally distant from the one who produces the ethnographic text, still prevails in the discipline (Narahara & Tavares, 2022, p. 1). In other words, anthropology has largely remained tied to the idea of studying a specific group or community culturally diverse from the anthropologist's background. If one were to ask graduate students in anthropology about their research, their responses would likely include statements such as, "I study the Yawanawá," "I study Umbanda," "I study skateboarders in São Paulo," or "I study the LGBTQIA+ movement." Despite its renewed interest in contemporary phenomena, there persists a widespread notion that anthropology must focus on particular groups, analyzing their characteristics, beliefs, practices, cosmologies, identity processes, and ways of inhabiting the world. Even in works in which the focus is a specific theme, such as urban violence or environmental activism, one is still usually restricted to the confinements of a specific group as the focus of the research.

My goal is to expand on the notion of anthropology beyond the conventional notion of ethnography, conceived as the household formula of fieldwork, interviews, and, most notably, participant observation. The discourse of participant observation was historically used to establish a researcher's bond with the studied group, reinforcing the idea that they were present—seeing, hearing, and sharing experiences—which, in turn, legitimized their authority to interpret and translate social interactions into anthropological knowledge. As James Clifford (1986) has pointed out, this rhetorical device consecrated a framework that granted ethnographers the authority to produce meaning through their firsthand experiences in the field.

But what happens when the subject of research is not a social group but a specific problem? One possible response is to expand the definition of ethnography beyond traditional notions of fieldwork and its associated methods. The reflexive turn in anthropology already challenged ethnography's status as a purely methodological tool, redefining it as a mode of writing as well. Several scholars have critiqued the notion of ethnographic authority, questioning the idea of the anthropologist as a privileged observer capable of deciphering hidden meanings within rituals, practices, and myths. This critique helped move ethnography beyond Malinowski's (1922) ethnographic realism and Geertz's (1973) interpretive approach, opening the door to more nuanced, negotiated forms of writing, such as dialogical and polyphonic ethnography (Clifford & Marcus, 1986). Nevertheless, even these methodological innovations continued to focus on the task of representing alterity. Despite methodological shifts, the primary objective remained: to research and present the "other," a category taken as a given rather than as a construct. As McGrane (1989) states, the ethnographic journey presupposes the existence of difference and everything happens as if the world (and the other) were there, given and ready to be observed.

In recent years, anthropological debates have expanded to include approaches such as a "native anthropology," which challenges traditional notions of ethnographic distance by incorporating the researcher's own practices and identity. This perspective questions the classic distinction between self and other, raising questions about the implications of being an anthropologist who studies a group to which he or she simultaneously belongs. A common concern within the field is that these anthropologists, inhabiting a hybrid position, do not experience the worlds they study as exotic or unfamiliar. For them, there is no process of adaptation to a foreign context, which complicates the conventional notion of fieldwork as a journey into otherness. As Gupta and Ferguson (1997) argue, this disorganizes the classic scheme of anthropological knowledge production, raising new methodological and epistemological challenges. Nevertheless, this discussion is still related to the broader issue of alterity, as it continues to revolve around the question of how to represent and engage with difference, even if one's own.

This book takes a different route. Rather than using ethnography to study the use of ayahuasca, or the practices of a specific group, I employ it as a tool to denaturalize and deconstruct categories such as "culture," "religion," "tradition," and "drug," historically embedded in legal, theological, and scientific discourses, and constantly contested by actors engaged in specific issues. The objective is not to define these terms in relation to people's lived experiences but to analyze how they become contested, how different actors negotiate their meanings, and how these negotiations shape possibilities for action, impose constraints, and determine legitimacy.

In this regard, it is important to note that this research investigates processes that date back 40 years in the case of Brazil and, as for the United States and France, 25 years. In addition, my primary research materials were documents: academic literature, laws, legal rulings, expert reports, public policies, newspaper articles, institutional records from Indigenous groups, ayahuasca communities, NGOs, and other organizations. While I conducted interviews with about 20 key figures—both formal and informal—the bulk of my research was bibliographical. I analyzed hundreds of documents, thousands of pages, from diverse sources, spending much of my ethnographic work not in a field site, but on my computer, scrutinizing an extensive array of materials.

The use of documents as primary ethnographic material is not new but has gained increasing recognition in anthropological research, particularly at the intersection of historiographic and ethnographic approaches (Castro & Cunha, 2005; Cunha 2004, 2005; Castro, 2008; Hull, 2012). The aim here is not to revisit debates on sources per se but rather to consider the archive not as a "deposit of past time" (Azoulay, 2011), static and sealed, but as a dynamic field of meanings, inquiries, tensions, ambiguities, silences, and gaps. By treating documents as active agents rather than inert records, we can apprehend how they constitute, hierarchize, separate, and connect actors and concepts. In the context of state and bureaucratic institutions, documents not only register reality but also create and legitimize categories and relationships recognized by the state, allowing for an analysis of how certain processes are constructed and responded to (Ferreira & Lowenkron, 2020).

My approach is to use documents not simply as sources of information but as lenses through which ethnographic narratives can be constructed about specific scenes, discourses, and disputes (Lowenkron & Ferreira, 2014). This methodological stance aligns with what Zeitlyn (2012) describes as reading archives against the grain, a strategy that reveals hidden structures of power, unspoken assumptions, and the contested nature of documentary production itself. Hence, my research does not treat documents as passive repositories but as sites of struggle where competing narratives are inscribed, negotiated, and contested.

By exploring these materials, I sought to understand how different categories are mobilized in public debates, how they shape regulation and policy, and how they frame the boundaries of permissible action. My ethnographic approach in this book, therefore, is not defined by the research techniques typically associated with ethnographic work. Instead, it is guided by the ways in which one poses and addresses a number of research questions, using anthropological knowledge to second-guess well-established notions and explore how certain issues become sites of contestation and regulation.

1.5 Book Outline

To explore these different case studies, the book is divided into seven chapters. The second chapter explores the historical process through which the use of ayahuasca in Brazil became recognized as a religious and cultural tradition. The chapter highlights how anthropological discourse played a critical role in redefining ayahuasca use from a stigmatized practice associated with drug use to an integral part of Brazil's religious and cultural landscape. Drawing on historical documents, government reports, media archives, and interviews, the analysis traces the interplay between state policies, legal frameworks, and academic classifications that ultimately enabled the formal recognition of ayahuasca use as a religious practice, distinguishing it from illicit substances. By focusing on the processes of regulation and legitimization, the chapter sheds light on the broader implications of defining religious and cultural heritage within the framework of public policy.

The third chapter examines the contested process of recognizing the religious use of ayahuasca as intangible cultural heritage in Brazil. While ayahuasca was historically subject to drug policies, the early 2000s marked a shift as heritage policies emerged as a new framework for legitimization. It explores how the process of defining the cultural status of ayahuasca generated both opportunities and conflicts. The chapter analyzes how indigenous groups increasingly asserted their role as original stewards of ayahuasca knowledge, challenging the legitimacy of ayahuasca religions as cultural representatives of the ayahuasca tradition. The chapter traces how these negotiations unfolded, revealing the complex interplay between religious identity, heritage policies, and state recognition. Ultimately, it highlights how heritage policies serve not only as legal and bureaucratic processes but also as sites of political struggle in contemporary Brazil.

The fourth chapter explores the legal battles that led to the recognition of ayahuasca use as a protected religious practice for some churches in the United States. It examines the legal disputes faced by the UDV and a Santo Daime church in Oregon, analyzing the cases that culminated in exemptions under the Religious Freedom Restoration Act (RFRA). The chapter contextualizes these legal battles within broader religious freedom jurisprudence, discussing landmark cases that influenced the legal framework for defining religious practices. Through the review of legal documents, court decisions, expert testimonies, and interviews, the chapter illuminates the regulatory complexities surrounding ayahuasca in the U.S., outlining the precedents set for religious groups seeking similar protections while raising questions about the broader implications of state intervention in religious practices.

Chapter 5 examines the evolving landscape of ayahuasca regulation in the United States following the legal victories of the UDV and Santo Daime churches. The chapter assesses the Drug Enforcement Administration's (DEA) exemption process for religious use of controlled substances under the RFRA, addressing the bureaucratic and legal challenges faced by new groups seeking protection. It also analyzes how scholars and experts have tackled notions of "sincerity" and "religion" as established by courts and government agencies, creating frameworks for churches that use psychedelic substances to navigate this intricate scenario. The chapter further examines the cases of Soul Quest Church of Mother Earth and the Church of the Eagle and the Condor as contemporary attempts to secure legal recognition for the religious use of ayahuasca, exploring the broader implications of state agencies determining religious legitimacy.

Chapter 6 analyzes the prohibition of ayahuasca in France, contextualizing it within broader European trends of criminalization and skepticism toward ayahuasca groups. Unlike other nations where ayahuasca is framed primarily as a public health or drug policy issue, France's ban is deeply intertwined with concerns about cults and sectarian movements. The chapter traces the legal history of ayahuasca in France, from early arrests of Santo Daime members in 1999 to pharmacological reports that reinterpreted ayahuasca use through the lens of "chemical submission," a legal category that gained a new meaning of "brainwashing" associated with the consumption of ayahuasca. Examining court decisions, media coverage, and expert analyses, the chapter reveals how the French state conflates ayahuasca use with sectarianism, further complicating the prospects of legal recognition for religious practices involving the brew.

The final chapter offers a comprehensive examination of the multifaceted journey of ayahuasca's recognition, or lack thereof, across different countries, highlighting the intersections of culture, religion, law, and state policies. Drawing on my analysis of case studies from Brazil, the United States, and France, this chapter sheds light on the complexities of classifying ayahuasca as a religious sacrament, cultural heritage, dangerous drug, or tool for cultish movements. It underscores the struggles faced by various groups and institutions in negotiating the legitimacy and regulation of ayahuasca use, ultimately offering insights into the broader implications of state intervention and the recognition of diverse uses of psychoactive plants in the context of the so-called "psychedelic renaissance."

References

Abu-Lughod, L. (1991). Writing against culture. In R. G. Fox (Ed.), *Recapturing anthropology: Working in the present* (pp. 137–162). School for American Research Press.

Andrade, A. P. (2002). Contribuições e limites da União do Vegetal para a nova consciência religiosa. In B. C. Labate & W. Araújo (Eds.), *O uso ritual da ayahuasca* (pp. 589–613). Campinas.

Antunes, H. F. (2012). *Droga, religião e cultura: um mapeamento da controvérsia pública sobre o uso da ayahuasca no Brasil*. Master's Thesis, Anthropology, University of São Paulo.

Antunes, H. F. (2019). *O uso da ayahuasca como problema público: um contraponto entre os casos do Brasil e dos EUA*. Doctoral Dissertation, Anthropology, University of São Paulo.

Antunes, H. F. (2023). "It is not solved just by writing it down on paper:" Patrimonialization policies and the religious use of ayahuasca as a Brazilian intangible cultural heritage. In P. Montero, C. Nicácio, & H. Antunes (Eds.), *Religious pluralism and law in contemporary Brazil* (pp. 111–140). Springer.

Asad, T. (1993). *Genealogies of religion*. Johns Hopkins University Press.

Asad, T. (2001). *Thinking about secularism and law in Egypt*. Isim.

Asad, T. (2003). *Formations of the secular modern: Christianity, Islam, Modernity*. Stanford University Press.

Asad, T. (2006). Trying to understand French secularism. In H. Vries & L. E. Sullivan (Eds.), *Political theologies: Public religions in a post-secular world* (pp. 194–215). Fordham University Press.

Asad, T. (2018). *Secular translations: Nation-state, modern self, and calculative reason*. Columbia University Press.

Atkinson, J. M. (1992). Shamanisms today. *Annual Review of Anthropology*, 307–330.

Azoulay, A. (2011). Archive. *Political Concepts: A Critical Lexicon*, 1. http://www.politicalconcepts.org/archive-ariella-azoulay/.

Bueno, D. (2017). *HAUXSTOCK: O festival indígena de Haux Music*. Crônicas Indigenistas. https://cronicasindigenistas.blogspot.com/2017/12/hauxstock-o-festival-indigena-de-haux.html

Caicedo-Fernández, A. (2023). Debates on the legality and legitimacy of yagé in Colombia. In B. C. Labate & C. Cavnar (Eds.), *Religious freedom and the global regulation of ayahuasca* (pp. 177–192). Routledge.

Castaneda, C. (1968). *The teachings of Don Juan: A Yaqui way of knowledge*. University of California Press.

Castaneda, C. (1971). *A separate reality: Further conversations with Don Juan*. Simon and Schuster.

Castaneda, C. (1972). *Journey to Ixtlan: The lessons of Don Juan*. Simon and Schuster.

Castro, C. (2008). *Pesquisando em arquivos*. Jorge Zahar.

Castro, C., & Cunha, O. M. G. (2005). Quando o campo é o arquivo. *Estudos Históricos, 36*, 3–5.

Cefaï, D. (2002). Qu'est-ce qu'une arène publique? Quelques pistes pour une approche pragmatiste. In D. Cefaï & I. Joseph (Eds.), *L'héritage du pragmatisme*. L'Aube.

Cefaï, D. (2009). Como nos mobilizamos? A contribuição de uma abordagem pragmatista para a sociologia da ação coletiva. *Dilemas, 4*, 11–48.

Cefaï, D. (2017). Públicos, problemas públicos, arenas públicas: O que nos ensina o pragmatismo (Parte 1). *Novos Estudos Cebrap, 36*(1), 187–213.

Cefaï, D. (2018). Público, socialização e politização: Reler John Dewey na companhia de George Herbert Mead. In D. S. Corrêa et al. (Eds.), *Crítica e pragmatismo na sociologia: Diálogos entre Brasil e França* (pp. 57–88). Annablume Editora.

Cefaï, D., & Pasquier, D. (Eds.). (2003). *Les sens du public: Publics politiques, publics médiatiques*. PUF.

Chateauraynaud, F. (2016). Pragmatique des transformations et sociologie des controverses: Les logiques d'enquête face au temps long des processos. *Raisons pratiques, 25*.

Clifford, J. (1986). The ethnographic effect. In J. Clifford & G. E. Marcus (Eds.), *Writing culture: The poetics and politics of ethnography* (pp. 1–26). University of California Press.

Clifford, J., & Marcus, G. E. (1986). *Writing culture: The poetics and politics of ethnography*. University of California Press.
Corrêa, D. S., & Dias, R. C. (2016). Crítica e os momentos críticos: De la justification e a guinada pragmática na sociologia francesa. *Mana, 22*(1), 67–99.
Cunha, O. M. G. da. (2004). Tempo imperfeito: Etnografia do arquivo. *Mana (Rio de Janeiro), 10*(2), 287–322.
Cunha, O. M. G. da. (2005). Do ponto de vista de quem? Diálogos, olhares e etnografias dos/nos arquivos. *Estudos Históricos (Rio de Janeiro), 36*, 7–32.
Dobkin de Rios, M. (1972). *Visionary vine: Psychedelic healing in the Peruvian Amazon*. Chandler Publishing.
Ferreira, L., & Lowenkron, L. (Eds.). (2020). *Etnografia de documentos: Pesquisas antropológicas entre papéis, carimbos e burocracias*. E-papers.
Fotiou, E. (2008). Shamanic tourism and the commercialization of ayahuasca. *Peripheria, 12*(15), 12–15.
Fotiou, E. (2014). On the uneasiness of tourism: Considerations on shamanic tourism in Western Amazonia. In B. C. Labate & C. Cavnar (Eds.), *Ayahuasca shamanism in the Amazon and beyond* (pp. 159–181). Oxford University Press.
Fotiou, E. (2020). Shamanic tourism in the Peruvian lowlands: Critical and ethical considerations. *The Journal of Latin American and Caribbean Anthropology, 25*(3), 374–396.
Gearin, A. K., & Sáez, O. C. (2021). Altered vision: Ayahuasca shamanism and sensory individualism. *Current Anthropology, 62*(2), 138–163.
Geertz, C. (1973). *The interpretation of cultures: Selected essays*. Basic Books.
Gupta, A., & Ferguson, J. (1997). Discipline and practice: "The field" as site, method, and location in anthropology. In *Anthropological locations: Boundaries and grounds of a field science* (pp. 1–46). University of California Press.
Hull, M. (2012). Documents and bureaucracy. *Annual Review of Anthropology, 41*, 251–267.
Kavenská, V., & Simonová, H. (2015). Ayahuasca tourism: Participants in shamanic rituals and their personality styles, motivation, benefits and risks. *Journal of Psychoactive Drugs, 47*(5), 351–359. https://doi.org/10.1080/02791072.2015.1094590
Labate, B. C. (2000). *A reinvenção do uso da ayahuasca nos centros urbanos*. Master's Thesis, Anthropology, University of Campinas.
Labate, B. C. (2004). *A reinvenção do uso da ayahuasca nos centros urbanos*. Mercado de Letras/FAPESP.
Labate, B. C., Antunes, H. F., & Antunes, I. F. (2023). 'Authorization? That's outrageous': Ayahuasca environmental legislation and Indigenous populations. In B. C. Labate & C. Cavnar (Eds.), *Religious freedom and the global regulation of ayahuasca* (pp. 160–176). Routledge.
Labate, B. C., & Araújo, W. S. (Eds.). (2002). *O uso ritual da ayahuasca*. FAPESP/Mercado das Letras.
Labate, B. C., & Cavnar, C. (Eds.). (2023). *Religious freedom and the global regulation of ayahuasca*. Routledge.
Labate, B. C., & Coutinho, F. (2014). "O meu avô deu a ayahuasca para o Mestre Irineu": Reflexões sobre a entrada dos índios no circuito urbano de consumo de ayahuasca no Brasil. *Revista de Antropologia USP, 57*(2), 215–250.
Labate, B. C., Rose, I. S. de, & Santos, R. G. dos (Eds.). (2008). *Religiões ayahuasqueiras: Um balanço bibliográfico*. Mercado de Letras.
Lowenkron, L., & Ferreira, L. C. M. (2014). Anthropological perspectives on documents: Ethnographic dialogues on the trail of police papers. *Vibrant (Florianópolis), 11*, 75–111.
Luna, L. E. (1986). *Vegetalismo: Shamanism among the mestizo population of the Peruvian Amazon*. Almquist and Wiksell International.
Mahmood, S. (2005). *Politics of piety: The Islamic revival and the feminist subject*. Princeton University Press.
Mahmood, S. (2010). Can secularism be otherwise? In M. Warner, M. Juergensmeyer, & J. Van Antwerpen (Eds.), *Varieties of secularism in a secular age* (pp. 282–299). Harvard University Press.

Mahmood, S. (2015). *Religious difference in a secular age: A minority report*. Princeton University Press.

Malinowski, B. (1922). *Argonauts of the Western Pacific: An account of native enterprise and adventure in the archipelagoes of Melanesian New Guinea*. G. Routledge & Sons.

McGrane, B. (1989). *Beyond anthropology: Society and the other*. Columbia University Press.

Montero, P. (Ed.). (2015). *Religiões e Controvérsias Públicas: Experiências, práticas sociais e discursos*. Terceiro Nome/Ed. Unicamp.

Narahara, K. L., & Tavares, I. N. (2022). Apresentação do dossiê – Quando o "Outro" é o antropólogo: Reflexões sobre produções etnográficas contemporâneas. *Mediações - Revista de Ciências Sociais, 27*(3), 1–20. https://doi.org/10.5433/2176-6665.2022v27n3e46766

Rose, I. S. (2010). *Tata endy rekoe – Fogo Sagrado: Encontro entre os Guarani, a ayahuasca e o Caminho Vermelho* (Doctoral dissertation, Universidade Federal de Santa Catarina, Florianópolis).

Stuart, R. (2002, Summer). Ayahuasca tourism: A cautionary tale. *MAPS Bulletin, 12*(2).

Taussig, M. T. (1989). The nervous system: Homesickness and dada. *Stanford Humanities Review, 1*(1), 44–81.

Trouillot, M.-R. (1991). Anthropology as metaphor: The savage's legacy and the postmodern world. *Review, 14*(1), 29–54.

Tupper, K. W. (2017). The economics of ayahuasca: Money, markets, and the value of the vine. In B. C. Labate, C. Cavnar, & A. K. Gearin (Eds.), *The world ayahuasca diaspora: Reinventions and controversies* (pp. 183–202). Routledge.

Wolff, T. J. (2020). *The touristic use of ayahuasca in Peru: Expectations, experiences, meanings and subjective effects*. Springer.

Zeitlyn, D. (2012). Anthropology in and of the archives: Possible futures and contingent pasts. Archives as anthropological surrogates. *Annual Review of Anthropology, 41*, 461–480.

Chapter 2
The Road from Drug to Religion and Culture: The Regulation of the Religious Use of Ayahuasca in Brazil

It would be far-fetched to say that the use of ayahuasca is a mainstream practice in Brazil. Although it is consumed by various Indigenous populations and there are state-recognized religious groups that originated in the north of Brazil, the use of ayahuasca is a relatively unknown practice among the majority of the population. One could argue, however, that its use is widespread in the country, given the urban ayahuasca scene that has been rapidly growing over the last decades (Labate, 2004). While it is impossible to determine a precise figure, there is an estimate of 50,000–150,000 regular consumers who drink ayahuasca at least twice a month in Brazil (Tófoli, 2022), which led researchers to proclaim it as the most psychedelic country in the world (Araújo, 2024).

Ayahuasca is consumed by over 40 Indigenous ethnic groups in Brazil (Tukano, 2022). While the majority of these populations have a history of using ayahuasca, some of them have been introduced to the brew over the last decades by religious and "neoshamanic" groups and through other Indigenous populations.[1] Moreover, ayahuasca has become a central element in the contemporary movement of the Indigenous peoples of the Amazon that has been gaining increasing visibility over the last decade, promoting a political and cultural agenda devoted to Indigenous rights. In addition, there are three groups, Santo Daime, União do Vegetal (UDV), and Barquinha, defined by the academic literature as the "Brazilian Ayahuasca Religions" (Labate & Araújo, 2002; Labate, 2004), that have emerged in the Amazon region. The first one, Santo Daime, was founded by Raimundo Irineu Serra, in the

[1] For an interesting study on the introduction of ayahuasca and other related practices by the Guarani from Southern Brazil, see Rose (2010). Her dissertation maps the network self-described "alliance of the medicines," formed in the early 2000s by the Guarani people, members of an international spiritual group called Sacred Fire of Itzachilatlan, and members of the Santo Daime community Céu do Patriarca São José in the city of Florianópolis. She focuses on the ways in which negotiations between these different groups have given rise to an intense circulation of people, substances, images, categories, rituals and aesthetics.

H. Fernandes Antunes, *Religion, Drug, or Cult?*, Law and Religion in a Global Context 5, https://doi.org/10.1007/978-3-032-04368-9_2

early 1930s in Rio Branco, the capital of the state of Acre. Barquinha was also founded in Rio Branco in the mid-1940s by Daniel Pereira de Matos. UDV, the last of the three groups to be created, was founded in the 1960s by José Gabriel da Costa in Porto Velho, the capital of the state of Rondônia, having no connection whatsoever with the Santo Daime or Barquinha.

According to Labate et al. (2008, p. 23), the anthropological category "Brazilian ayahuasca religions" first appeared in "O uso ritual da ayahuasca" [The ritual use of ayahuasca] (Labate & Araújo, 2002), referring to Santo Daime, Barquinha and UDV as religious movements of Brazilian origin based on the ritualized use of ayahuasca that incorporate elements from Christianity and other traditions. However, I found an earlier reference to the category in her master's thesis (Labate, 2000) on new modalities of ayahuasca consumption in urban centers. The term was born thus in the academic milieu to describe what was perceived as a particularity of the Brazilian context. As Labate (2004, p. 65) states:

> Although in several South American countries, such as Colombia, Bolivia, Peru, Venezuela and Ecuador, there is a tradition of ayahuasca being consumed by shamans and *vegetalistas*, it is curiously only in Brazil that there was the development of religions of non-indigenous populations that make use of this drink. These religions, such as the Bwiti religion in Gabon (which uses Iboga, Tabernanthe iboga) and the Native American Church in Mexico and the USA (which uses peyote, Lophophora williamsii), re-elaborate the ancient traditions of local systems through a reinterpretation influenced by Christianity. This re-reading, in the Brazilian case, is formulated through the heritage of ayahuasca consumption by the Amazonian systems of *curandeirismo* and folk Catholicism, as well as from other sources: the Afro-Brazilian tradition, Kardecist Spiritism and esotericism of European origin (above all, via the Esoteric Circle of the Communion of Thought).[2]

In her dissertation on the differences and similarities between Santo Daime, Barquinha and UDV, Goulart (2004) addresses the origins of the category. According to the anthropologist, the term "Brazilian ayahuasca religions" was inspired by the terms and definitions of the members of the groups themselves, appearing sparsely and indirectly in the earliest academic works, before later becoming consolidated as the main category in this field of study (Goulart, 2004, p. 8).

> After all, regardless of the line or division to which they belong, all these religions define themselves based on the use of ayahuasca, i.e., this is how they self-identify, as well as how they identify each other. At the same time, it is as ayahuasca religions that they are immediately known by other religious groups and in wider society. It is therefore a term that expresses the way in which these religious sects are recognized, either by themselves or by others. The notion still appears in the earliest works on these religions, even if it is defined or used in a tenuous and indirect way, and then has consolidated itself as a conceptual reference in this field of study (Goulart, 2004, p. 8).

Goulart recognizes, however, that the term "Brazilian ayahuasca religions" is predominantly an analytical category that often does not coincide with the perspective of the members of these groups. Her ethnographic research indicates that practitioners typically emphasize the distinctions and differences among their traditions over

---

[2] All translations of quoted material from Portuguese and French are my own.

shared elements. This can be illustrated by some of the media coverage. For instance, a 1995 newspaper article published in the *Jornal do Brasil* titled "A outra turma do chá: Confundida com o Santo Daime, a União do Vegetal sai do silêncio e busca imagem própria" (The Other Crew of the Tea: Mistaken for Santo Daime, the União do Vegetal Breakes the Silence and Seeks its Own Image) (Paiva, 1995) highlighted UDV's efforts to detach itself from the "trendy" image of Santo Daime and its celebrity followers:

> Lately, however, the discreet sister of Santo Daime—whose temples gained fame in the late 1980s through the artists who frequented them—has lost her fear of attracting attention. Tired of being confused with the daimistas, the UDV members embarked on an effort to create their own image, which culminated in the current conference [International Conference of Hoasca Research]—an event that cost 85,000 Brazilian reais and was supported by Telerj and Varig. "We want to show society what we are and what we do," says Dr. Glacus de Souza Brito, coordinator of the Center for Medical Studies of the UDV, located in São Paulo.

The article is a clear attempt by UDV to distance itself from Santo Daime and to claim its own narrative on the institution, especially focusing on promoting a dialogue with medical experts to legitimize the use of ayahuasca in Brazil. Regardless of the institutional aspirations of ayahuasca groups, however, the fact that they were part of the same socio-economic context, that they shared certain cultural practices and had a similar background, and that their founders were migrants from the northeast who were attracted to the Amazon region by rubber extraction in the first half of the twentieth century, made it possible for the academic literature to associate these groups as members of the same long-standing ayahuasca tradition (Antunes, 2011). As Goulart states, from the 2000s onwards, the use of the category "Brazilian ayahuasca religions" became a consensus and was widely present in the academic literature to refer to Santo Daime, Barquinha, and UDV. In a recent TV show, the anthropologist stated:[3]

> Religion is a more sociological, anthropological notion—let's put it this way—a concept used by specialists and scholars. In contrast, "doctrine" is a native term. As we say in anthropology, native and anthropological concepts. I mean, when I started studying these groups several years ago, in the early 1990s, when I started doing my first interviews with people from this group, from Santo Daime, many people said to me in the interviews: "Wait, you're talking about religion, but for me the Daime is not a religion." Several people told me that at the time. "So, what is it to you?" Then, it varied. The majority used the expression: "It's a doctrine, it's my spirituality, but it's not a religion".

From a term rarely used in the 1980s and 1990s, the category "Brazilian ayahuasca religions" has, over the last two decades, become widely recognized in academia, the media, and among ayahuasca groups. Initially, many practitioners rejected the label "religion," preferring terms like "doctrine" or "spirituality." However, as scholars, journalists, and policymakers began using the term to frame these practices within Brazil's religious landscape, leaders and representatives of ayahuasca

---

[3] "Santo Daime, religion or doctrine?" Boto Fé, History Channel Brazil https://www.youtube.com/watch?v=V44Anv-dx3U&t=65s

groups gradually adopted it, especially in legal and public contexts. As Goulart notes, this shift reflects an exchange between native and academic categories, with "religion" shifting from an external classification into a term now commonly used as a means of gaining legitimacy and recognition.

> In this process of dialogue, native notions and those of specialists, scholars, have, so to speak, exchanged. So nowadays, many leaders, many representatives of these religions use the term religion when they want to legitimize themselves publicly, when they want to publicly legitimize their sect, their group, their use of this drink. So nowadays the term religion is mainly used by leaders, by spokespeople, by representatives of these religions. So, from a specialist term, today it has also become a native term. They often use these expressions, "ayahuasca religions."[4]

Regardless of how the category is utilized within ayahuasca groups, it is crucial to highlight the significant impact it has had in the academic world. The term has become widely adopted in subsequent works, consolidating itself as a key framework to describe the Santo Daime, Barquinha, and UDV groups. It has reached a point where it is nearly impossible to find a recent work that does not either mention the category or employ this framework. However, the aim of this chapter is not to trace the genealogy of the term,[5] but rather to examine the process by which these groups came to be publicly recognized as "religions" in the first place. My interest lies not in the creation of a specific anthropological concept, but in the social process of recognizing the use of ayahuasca as a religious and cultural practice worthy of state recognition and protection. In the following pages, I will argue that the legitimization of the religious use of ayahuasca, along with the recognition of ayahuasca groups as "religions" through public policy development, cannot be separated from academic discourse. Scholars, particularly anthropologists specializing in ayahuasca, played a crucial role in classifying and defining the practices of ayahuasca groups as cultural and religious expressions of the Brazilian Amazon. As we will see, anthropological arguments and concepts played a prominent role in this debate, and some scholars even became key players in the regulation and legitimization processes of the brew in Brazil.

But when did ayahuasca become a subject of public interest and state intervention, and more importantly, how did this happen? Since the first half of the twentieth century, the use of ayahuasca has attracted the attention of public authorities in Brazil. There are records of incidents with local authorities, particularly in the early decades of Santo Daime and UDV in the Amazon region. However, these events did not gain national attention and were ultimately resolved at the local level. One well-known incident occurred in the 1940s, when Mestre Irineu's house was surrounded by around 40 police officers determined to arrest him. However, he successfully navigated the situation with the help of Colonel Fontenele, a local authority and close friend. As the persecutions grew, Mestre Irineu sought to cultivate a more

---

[4] "Santo Daime, religion or doctrine?" Boto Fé, History Channel Brazil https://www.youtube.com/watch?v=V44Anv-dx3U&t=65s

[5] For an analysis on how the academic literature presents the use of ayahuasca in Brazil through a historical perspective, see (Antunes, 2011).

orderly image for his community through the adoption of uniforms (*fardas*) during rituals, reinforcing his Christian faith, and fostering strong relationships with influential local politicians (Abreu, 2016).

The founder of UDV, Mestre Gabriel, was also targeted by local authorities. In 1967, he was arrested while leading a UDV session in Porto Velho. On that occasion, the local police chief, accompanied by several deputies, interrupted the session and took Mestre Gabriel to the police station to explain the gathering he was leading. He was detained until the following day, when he was released without charges (Souza, 2010, p. 42). This incident illustrates how these groups were frequently viewed with suspicion, attracting the attention of local authorities. In response, their leadership sought to cultivate good relationships with local powers and invested in processes of institutionalization, emphasizing their orderly conduct and Christian faith as a strategy for legitimization.

Ayahuasca also garnered some media attention in the 1960s and 1970s, with articles published in both local and national newspapers. However, despite these efforts, media coverage did not increase significantly during this period, and the use of ayahuasca remained a relatively marginal topic. In the 1960s and 1970s, only three and seven articles, respectively, were published in newspapers. In contrast, the number of articles grew substantially in the following decades, with approximately 140 articles published between the 1980s and 1990s (Lima, 2024, p. 49).

It is reasonable to suggest that it was only in the 1980s that ayahuasca became a subject of growing interest at a national level. It was during this period that the first anthropological and historical research were developed, focusing mainly on Santo Daime (Silva, 1983; Fróes, 1983; Couto, 1989). As Santo Daime and the UDV expanded, ayahuasca reached Brazil's major cities, gaining new followers among the urban middle classes, including TV personalities, renowned musicians, and other public figures. This growing interest in the media led to the publication of numerous articles on ayahuasca and the release of the first documentaries on the subject. Media coverage at the time often took on an exotic tone, a characteristic also seen in the initial articles of the 1960s and 1970s. However, the new development was the increasing association of ayahuasca groups with the social stigma surrounding drug use. It was also during this time that ayahuasca became a focus for federal government agencies, such as the *Divisão de Medicamentos* (Medicines Division of the Ministry of Health—DIMED) and the *Conselho Federal de Entorpecentes* (Federal Council on Narcotics—CONFEN).

Against this backdrop of social change, I analyze how the religious use of ayahuasca became an object to be defined and regulated in Brazil, emphasizing the role played by anthropological knowledge and anthropologists, who, alongside ayahuasca groups, worked with government bodies to legitimize both ayahuasca and its use. To this end, I have gathered a collection of documents published between the 1980s and 2020s, including institutional documents from ayahuasca groups, reports, and opinions issued by government bodies such as the now-defunct Federal Council on Narcotics (CONFEN) and the National Council for Drug Policy (CONAD). In addition to government documents, media coverage was also examined on a smaller scale, primarily in print media, including newspaper and magazine articles, and occasionally television programs and documentaries. I also resorted to the academic literature on the use of ayahuasca in Brazil, particularly works addressing the regulatory processes in the country. The primary aim is to understand the dynamics surrounding the framing of ayahuasca as a religious and cultural practice entitled to state recognition and protection. This chapter will explore how specific definitions and frameworks were put forward, shaping the regulation of ayahuasca use in Brazil.

2.1 Social Stigmas and the Increasing Visibility of Ayahuasca

The academic literature in Brazil has sought to trace the pathways through which ayahuasca became increasingly associated with the notion of a "drug." It is widely agreed that the use of ayahuasca gained significant visibility starting in the 1980s in Brazil, when it began to be classified as a hallucinogenic substance from the Amazon region. This classification sparked curiosity and fascination, while also creating new stigmas and categorizations. In exploring the growing visibility of ayahuasca in the 1980s, some researchers have attempted to link ayahuasca's drug stigma to historical factors and specific aspects of the trajectory of ayahuasca groups themselves. In a 2008 article, Goulart argues that, in their early decades, Santo Daime, Barquinha, and UDV had their practices associated with terms like "witchcraft," "quackery," and "charlatanism." Goulart associates the social stigmas surrounding Santo Daime in the first half of the twentieth century to the historical processes of persecution of popular therapeutic practices by local authorities, as well as the consolidation of medical science in Brazil (Goulart, 2008, p. 260–261). However, according to Goulart, there was also a racial stigma, as Mestre Irineu, the founder of Santo Daime, was a Black leader of a marginalized community on the outskirts of Rio Branco.

She states, however, that these accusations began to change by the 1970s, as new stigmas emerged and gained strength, contributing to characterize ayahuasca and its uses to notions such as "drug," "narcotic," "hallucinogenic," among others of this kind (Goulart, 2008, p. 261–262). To explain this change, the anthropologist addresses the Brazilian historical context of the late 1960s and mid-1970s, which involved a political upsurge and reformulation of the country's drug policies. Goulart associates the new "drug" stigma with a series of mechanisms for controlling and repressing drug use introduced in Brazil during that period. With regard to the Amazon region, the anthropologist argues that the 1970s were marked by the first federal initiatives to combat drug trafficking.

Goulart highlights the importance of the creation of a Federal Police (PF) office in the capital of Acre in 1973, which marked the beginning of relations between ayahuasca groups and federal agencies. According to the anthropologist, the PF quickly showed an interest in investigating these groups and especially the brew consumed in their rituals, summoning their leaders for questioning. Goulart also associates Mestre Gabriel's problems with the police with concerns that the tea used by him and his followers was actually a "drug" or "narcotic" (Goulart, 2008,

p. 262–265). She underlines that 2 years after the first raid against ayahuasca groups in Rio Branco, the PF began a new investigation, this time targeting the Centro Eclético da Fluente Luz Universal Raimundo Irineu Serra [Eclectic Center of the Flowing Universal Light Raimundo Irineu Serra] (CEFLURIS), currently Igreja do Culto Eclético da Fluente Luz Universal [Church of the Eclectic Cult of the Flowing Universal Light] (ICEFLU).[6] According to Goulart, the psychologist Paulo Roberto—founder of the first Santo Daime church outside the Amazon, located in the city of Rio de Janeiro—helped the institution in the investigations, providing clarification on the use of Santo Daime to the PF.

Another factor frequently linked to the classification of ayahuasca as a "drug" was the introduction of cannabis consumption by the ICEFLU, which later became known as "Santa Maria" [Holy Mary]. A pivotal episode, often referenced in the anthropological literature on the subject, is the use of cannabis by members of the group led by Sebastião Mota, which played a significant role in associating the use of ayahuasca with the notion of a dangerous "drug" and a social problem (Goulart, 2004, 2008; Labate, 2005; MacRae, 2005). In 1981, a regular visitor to Colônia Cinco Mil—the former headquarters of ICEFLU—was arrested by local police for carrying a small quantity of Santo Daime and cannabis. Following the arrest, the police raided Colônia Cinco Mil and discovered a cannabis plantation with 18 plants (MacRae, 2005, p. 475). MacRae notes that, in response to the raid, Padrinho Sebastião and other ICEFLU members approached local authorities to clarify their practices with Santo Daime and their use of cannabis (MacRae, 2005, p. 475). Undoubtedly, the use of cannabis by ICEFLU led to increased media visibility of the group's ayahuasca practices, with the police raid on Colônia Cinco Mil becoming the subject of one of the first national media articles on ayahuasca groups.[7] This event prompted a series of government actions to investigate ayahuasca use in Acre. Notably, MacRae (2005) and Labate (2005) highlight the Ministry of Justice's initiative, in 1982, to form a commission to investigate the practices of ICEFLU, which included a historian, a sociologist, an anthropologist, and a psychologist.

The period marked the onset of national media attention, with several magazines and newspapers publishing articles on ayahuasca and its potential risks. Labate (2005) emphasizes that it was common to encounter sensationalist headlines, categorizing ayahuasca as a "hallucinogen" and referring to ayahuasca groups as "cults" from the Amazon region. Some of these headlines were particularly striking, such as "Cult in Acre uses drugs in ceremonies" (Folha de São Paulo, 08/17/1982),

[6] The ICEFLU was founded by Sebastião Motta de Melo in 1975, 5 years after the death of Mestre Irineu. The institution was the first dissidence from the original Santo Daime, as well as the main group responsible for expanding Santo Daime, creating branches in various regions of Brazil and internationally.

[7] MacRae is referring to the article from August 1982, "Seita no Acre usou drogas em cerimônias" (Cult in Acre Uses Drugs in Ceremonies), published by Folha de São Paulo, which mentions a mobilization on the part of the Federal Police in Acre to investigate complaints about the existence of a mysterious sect, the "marijuana cult," whose adherents would consume hallucinogens on a large-scale during services (Folha de São Paulo, 08/17/1982).

"Santo Daime cult uses Amazonian hallucinogen in rituals" (Jornal do Brasil, 11/06/1983), and "Santo Daime: The Drug of the Amazon" (Manchete, 14/01/1984; Labate, 2005). Despite these eye-catching titles that linked ayahuasca to the notion of a new "drug" from the Amazon, some articles also emphasized its religious and cultural significance. For instance, the article "Santo Daime cult uses Amazonian hallucinogen in rituals" (Jornal do Brasil, 11/06/1983) describes Santo Daime as a "socio-religious expression" and a "cultural phenomenon." It also includes a quote from Clodomir Monteiro da Silva, an anthropologist and author of the first master's thesis on Santo Daime:

> The professor of University of Acre, anthropologist Clodomir Monteiro da Silva, [...] observes that "the hallucinatory experiences are not simply imaginary manifestations, psychopathological, without sense or social strength. While lived in a ritual framework which involves the body, art and mind, these experiences interact with economic and social aspects of the environment in which they exist." In a macrocosmic perspective—states the anthropologist—the Daime is seen as "a yeast that leavens the dough," that contaminates the profane and transforms it in sacred, pure (Jornal do Brasil, 11/06/1983).

Another article of great repercussion at the time was published by *Veja* magazine, titled "Divine Trip: A Hallucinogen that Leads to a Religious Trance" (Veja, 11/09/1983). Interestingly, the article also quotes Silva, describing Santo Daime as a "hallucinogen" widely consumed in the Amazon region, but one that "unlike other drugs, seen as socially disruptive, […] has a religious and social function in the Acre communities that consume it. 'Dispersed in the forest, the people from Acre found in the Daime ritual a form of social cohesion,' says […] anthropologist Clodomir Monteiro da Silva." The article further highlights that Santo Daime members experience "intermittent hallucinations that can last up to 4 hours after drinking it. During the trance, the members feel transported to other worlds and at times go through the 'supreme vision' (suprema miração)" (Revista *Veja*, 11/09/1983). Given its national impact, "Divine Trip" is one of the most frequently cited articles by scholars exploring the media focus, stressing its role in associating the use of ayahuasca with the concept of a drug (Labate, 2005; Goulart, 2008). The goal, however, is not to determine the extent to which media coverage contributed to the stigmatization of ayahuasca use, but rather to emphasize its role in increasing the visibility of the phenomenon in Brazil. Despite the exoticizing tone of some articles, which emphasized intense trips with a new Amazonian hallucinogenic drug, they also highlighted the anthropological insights, with parts of the articles dissociating Santo Daime from drug stigmas, emphasizing its cultural and social importance and its role in fostering social cohesion within the group.

The late 1970s and early 1980s thus marked a period of growing public interest in the use of ayahuasca in Brazil. Still, it is important to note that my focus is not on the specific causes behind the shift in the social stigma of ayahuasca use from witchcraft and charlatanism to a potentially harmful drug. Instead, the emphasis is on how the use of ayahuasca, as it spread beyond its cultural and geographical origins into Brazil's major cities, gained visibility and attracted the attention of new social groups, including the urban middle class, and entered new arenas such as academia and the media, becoming an object of public scrutiny. An additional consequence of this growing public interest in ayahuasca was its eventual incorporation into federal drug policies.

2.2 The Ban of Ayahuasca and the Federal Council on Narcotic Drugs

The 1980s was also a key moment for the use of ayahuasca in the country in terms of public policy. For the first time at the national level, the issue of banning or possibly regulating ayahuasca was at stake. It was then that a series of key actors—among them, members of the CONFEN, professionals from various fields of knowledge, such as sociology, anthropology, philosophy, medicine, psychiatry, psychology, as well as members of some of the most important ayahuasca institutions in the country—addressed the possibility of regulating its use. Unquestionably, the ban of ayahuasca in March 1985 was an important milestone. The measure was an initiative of the DIMED of the Ministry of Health, which issued Ordinance No. 2, with instructions on the prohibition, supervision and control of substances that cause physical or psychological addiction and products that contain them (Dimed, 1985). The ordinance had important consequences as it included *Banisteriopsis caapi*—one of the plants that make up ayahuasca—on the list of controlled substances, immediately making illegal the practices of ayahuasca groups that had been carried out for decades.

A few months later, the UDV sent a petition to the CONFEN asking for the measure to be reviewed (Labate, 2005, p. 409). In response, the CONFEN issued Resolution No. 04 of 1985, appointing a working group[8] to "examine the question of the production and consumption of substances derived from plant species [that make up ayahuasca]" (Confen, 1985). The document stated that the plants in question were not on the international list of the Economic and Social Council of the United Nations (ECOSOC), that there were no CONFEN records on studies of the plants and that the issue should be assessed taking into account sociological, anthropological, chemical, medical and health issues. According to the resolution, the purpose of the working group was to examine the request for a provisional suspension of the inclusion of *B. caapi* on the DIMED list, and it was given powers to request technical examinations, carry out research, take depositions and set up commissions to analyze the use and production of ayahuasca, and to present a report within 3 months (Confen, 1985).

[8] The working group was made up of Antônio Carlos de Moraes, vice-president of CONFEN and representative of the Ministry of Finance, who acted as chairman of the WG, Suely Rozenfeld, representative of the National Health Surveillance Division (DIMED), Isac Germano Karniol, representative of the Brazilian Medical Association, Sérgio Dario Seibel, representative of the Ministry of Social Security and Assistance, and Paulo Gustavo Magalhães Pinto, representative of the Federal Police Department's Narcotics Repression Division (Confen, 1985).

Initially, two members of the WG, Isac Germano Karniol and Sérgio Dario Seibel, traveled to Rio Branco, the capital of Acre, to gather information that could support the group's efforts. According to a subsequent report, their visit was prompted by the fact that Acre was home to several communities that practiced the use of ayahuasca. This initiative led to the presentation of a report to the CONFEN plenary in late 1985.[9] Karniol and Seibel observed that the groups utilizing ayahuasca upheld "moral and ethical standards of conduct" similar to those of mainstream Brazilian society, and in some cases, even stricter. Regarding the ceremonies, they noted that the outcome of the ritual was not solely dependent on the tea but also on the surrounding environment, including the music and dance. Furthermore, they emphasized that once the ceremonies concluded, participants returned to their homes in a disciplined manner. Overall, they described the members of such "sects" as calm and joyful individuals, adding that many attributed positive transformations, such as the revitalization of family life, renewed engagement in work, and a "reconnection with oneself and with God, etc., through their faith and the tea" (Report by Isac Germano Karniol and Sérgio Dario Seibel apud Confen, 1987, p. 7).

The report also pointed out that the preparation of ayahuasca is labor-intensive and lengthy, occurring within a ceremonial context, which makes it unlikely that production levels would increase to a degree that could lead to "misuse" or consumption outside ritualized settings by the general public. Finally, they noted that in some cases, individuals from urban centers in Brazil, in their "search for a meaningful lifestyle," seemed to have found these spiritual practices, and that such people "appear [...] to be well integrated with themselves and the work they are doing" (Report by Isac Germano Karniol and Sérgio Dario Seibel apud Confen, 1987, p. 7).

In its subsequent action, the WG met at the end of January 1986 and, by unanimous agreement, opted to temporarily remove B. caapi from the DIMED list until the final report was completed (Confen, 1986). The WG justified this decision by stressing that the inclusion of B. caapi on the DIMED list had occurred without prior consultation with CONFEN, the body responsible for providing normative direction and supervising activities within the National System for the Prevention, Supervision, and Repression of Narcotics in Brazil (SISNAD). Furthermore, the resolution referenced the investigations conducted by Karniol and Seibel of the "religious communities practicing the ritual use" of ayahuasca, observing that the long-standing use of 'daime' had not led to any known societal harm (Confen, 1986). Lastly, the resolution reiterated "the necessity for additional research in sociological, anthropological, medical, chemical, and public health fields, continuing the work already carried out on the issue" (Confen, 1986). The group reconvened in June 1986 to brief the newly appointed president of the WG, Domingos Bernardo

[9] To date, it has not been possible to obtain a copy of the report developed by Karniol and Seibel. We did, however, have access to parts of the report that were cited in the 1987 Final Report of the WG.

da Silva Sá,[10] on the progress of their activities and the stages that had been completed.

From the onset, the primary focus of the research was the ceremonial and religious use—considered synonymous by CONFEN—by Santo Daime, the Barquinha, and the UDV. At this early stage, it was clear that the aim was to conduct studies on the matter that would encompass various disciplines, especially the humanities. Another significant aspect of the approach was the establishment of a working group consisting of experts from diverse fields, tasked with generating knowledge to guide the decisions of the federal agency. Additionally, a recurring theme in the initial stages of policy development is evident in the early resolutions: the depiction of the religious use of ayahuasca as a practice that does not produce the societal harms typically associated with drug abuse. Rather, ayahuasca consumption was framed as a socially integrating activity that fostered moral and ethical standards, contributing positively to the community life of the groups involved.

2.3 "Hallucinogen" or "Culture": The Working Group's Final Report

The Working Group (WG) released its final report in June 1987, following nearly 2 years of research. The report was authored by the jurist and WG coordinator, Domingos Sá. As outlined in the document, the purpose of the WG was to examine the production and consumption of ayahuasca in the communities that used the "daime" or "vegetal," the terms for the drink employed by the Santo Daime, Barquinha, and UDV groups (Confen, 1987, p. 5–6). To achieve this objective, several activities were conducted, which are briefly outlined in the report. Among these, members of the WG made multiple visits to ayahuasca communities, including participation in ceremonies where they consumed the tea. The first of these visits was carried out by Karniol and Seibel, culminating in the earlier mentioned report. Later, in April 1986, Sá and Sérgio Seibel traveled to the "Céu do Mar," a Santo Daime community in Rio de Janeiro, which was the first church outside the

[10] Domingos Bernardo da Silva Sá was a lawyer and a full member of the Brazilian Lawyers Institute (IAB). Sá taught as an adjunct professor at the Law Faculty of the Catholic University of Petrópolis, and also served as a member of the Federal Council of the Brazilian Bar Association (OAB), as an advisor to the Council for Public Policies on Drugs (CONAD), and as a jurist and advisor to the Federal Council on Narcotics (CONFEN). In addition, he was president of the State Council on Narcotics—CONFEN-RJ and Undersecretary of State for Justice of Rio de Janeiro (http://silvasa.adv.br/advogados.html). Sá is described by many scholars as one of the most important actors in the regulation process of ayahuasca, having also written on the subject (Sá, 1996). In a 1995 interview with Folha de São Paulo, Sá was questioned about the fact that he had two sons that were part of ayahuasca religions. He replied that "It wasn't because my children are part of the Daime or because they had any experience with ayahuasca that I gave a favorable opinion. It was because I gave a favorable opinion that my children once took part or came close to or had some kind of experience" (https://www1.folha.uol.com.br/fsp/1995/10/22/cotidiano/15.html).

Amazon region. Sá and Seibel provide details about the community and describe the ritual they took part in.

> The "church" is located in a place that provides the necessary conditions to enable this true "rite of expiation" (through vomiting or diarrhea, or both, cumulatively). It can therefore be said that a "work" [Santo Daime ceremony] does not fail to include, in its planning, the "rite of expiation," with spaces and places that enable the purging (vomiting or diarrhea) of the possible suffering participant. The hymns evoke the forces of nature, the power of God, the Virgin Mary and all the saints. They praise human virtues, exhort people to love, humility and repentance for their faults. They proclaim the joy and strength of those who have faith in divine power and do good (Confen, 1987, p. 10).

Sá also addressed the account of anthropologist Regina Abreu, who stated that "the Santo Daime Community is close to the model of society described by French anthropologist Louis Dumont as holistic" (Confen, 1987, p. 8). There was a clear emphasis on describing the community setting, seeking to establish comparisons between the environment, the symbols, the Santo Daime rituals—with candles, rosaries, images of the Virgin Mary, the evocation of the power of God and human virtues, or rites of expiation—and the symbolism and liturgy present in the Catholic Church. The members of the WG highlighted, among other characteristics, the ritual similarities between the two Santo Daime communities in Acre and Rio de Janeiro, arguing that the differences "were like the distinctions observable between two Catholic masses celebrated in two different parishes" (Confen, 1987, p. 14). The description of the visit to the ICEFLU headquarters in Céu do Mapiá, located in Amazonas, once again referred to Catholic imagery:

> We were able to see that people from various regions of Brazil (Brasília, Bahia, the city of Rio de Janeiro, Visconde de Mauá) crossed paths with us along the way. The impression made on the rapporteur of this study was that many of those people were like true pilgrims, on a pilgrimage to the center of the "Santo Daime doctrine", in search of sacred contact with the old man with the apostolic beard—"Padrinho Sebastião." All of this, combined with the search for integration with nature, seems like very rich material to be recorded for further analysis by social researchers. In addition, seeing the interaction between members of human groups from different regions and cultures in different parts of Brazil is fundamental for a correct assessment of the issue and the final considerations of this work (Confen, 1987, p. 16).

In addition to references to Catholic practices, it is crucial to highlight the emphasis that shapes the tone of the report. In the passage above, as well as throughout the document, Sá aims to portray the interaction between individuals from Brazil's major urban centers and the *caboclo*[11] population of the Amazon region as a cultural exchange that encompasses not only the movement of people but also goods, practices, symbols, rituals, and ways of life. The WG sought to emphasize the ritual similarities between the Santo Daime churches in the southeast and those based in the Amazon, reinforcing the notion of a migration of Amazonian culture itself,

[11] The term "*caboclo*" refers to individuals of mixed Indigenous and European ancestry in Brazil, often used to describe the descendants of Indigenous peoples and Portuguese colonizers. In the context of Brazilian religious and cultural practices, *caboclo* is also used to refer to spirits of Indigenous ancestors invoked in certain Afro-Brazilian religions, such as Umbanda and Candomblé.

transcending geographical boundaries and introducing a community-oriented lifestyle to members in large urban centers. In this context, it is worth mentioning a passage cited in the report from the book *História do Povo Juramidam* by historian Vera Fróes (1983), one of the first academic works on Santo Daime in the country. This passage describes the relocation of the ICEFLU headquarters from Rio Branco to the Rio do Ouro rubber plantation and, later, to Céu do Mapiá, its current base in the state of Amazonas.

> The move from the rural community of Colônia Cinco Mil to the interior of the Amazon rainforest has a meaning on a material and spiritual level: the Daime will protect its children—the *Midam*—who heed the call to return to their origins, to the rubber plantations where many were born and raised. It is also a return to the time when Mestre Irineu worked in the forests cutting rubber and met the Daime (Fróes, 1983, p. 121 apud Confen, 1987, p. 20).

The drive towards the forest started by the ICEFLU is described as a process of retraditionalization, in which the return to the origins, to the community life of the rubber plantations, to the time of Mestre Irineu, was not only a physical move to the interior of the Amazon rainforest, but a spiritual journey, along the lines of a Catholic pilgrimage, as described in the report. The report also draws on Fróes' study when describing the trajectory of Padrinho Sebastião, whose introduction to spiritual paths is compared to Mestre Irineu's initiation process with ayahuasca. According to Fróes, "just like Mestre Irineu, Padrinho Sebastião had his initiation guided by a healer, Mestre Osvaldo, a black man born in São Paulo, also called '*cumpade* Osvaldo', because he was the godfather of his son, Pedro Mota" (Fróes, 1983, p. 42 apud Confen, 1987, p. 19). These passages are proof that the G.T. based a large part of its conclusions on information and arguments found in the emerging literature on the use of ayahuasca in Brazil, incorporating historical and anthropological analyses into the report.

The document also dedicated a section to analyzing ayahuasca's effect on the body. The report highlighted Karniol's stance that psychotropic drugs are classified in particular ways by different specialists. The psychiatrist chose to prioritize ayahuasca pharmacological action as a marker, classifying it as a "hallucinogen."

> Thus, hallucinogenic drugs are those that predominantly cause alterations in sensory-perception, most often hallucinations, i.e. perceptions without an external object. Characteristically, visual hallucinations are provoked by these substances, which differentiate them from alterations normally present in certain mental syndromes, such as schizophrenia, where auditory hallucinations are found. Some hallucinogenic drugs are used as pure substances, such as LSD. More common is the use of a plant or, rarely, a mixture of plants, as is the case with ayahuasca (Confen, 1987, p. 25).

Following this statement, the report concluded, after a brief discussion of the active ingredients that compose the drink, that "it is indisputable that Ayahuasca, as a whole, has a hallucinogenic effect" (Confen, 1987, p. 26). Regarding its physical effects, the report noted that ayahuasca induced a hallucinogenic effect, along with other secondary reactions such as vomiting, diarrhea, and so on. However, Sá emphasized that, concerning the chronic clinical or mental consequences of prolonged ayahuasca use, there were no sufficient elements to make a thorough assessment at that time. The WG thus concluded that, based on observations made during visits to communities where ayahuasca is used ritually, no abnormalities had been observed. The WG stressed that, at the time of the Final Report, there were no records or objectively proven evidence that conclusively demonstrated any social harm resulting from the use of ayahuasca in the studied communities (Confen, 1987, p. 27). A central aspect of the report's conclusion pertains to the hallucinogen/culture tension, a recurrent theme in the 1980s discourse surrounding the use of ayahuasca.

> There are, however, untouched but not untouchable concepts that, in fact, are much more like prejudices, since they are so often the result of ideas that have simply been inherited and accepted, without ever having been subjected to any critical analysis. [...] These questions have most often revolved around two words: "hallucinogen" and "cultures." Is ayahuasca a "hallucinogen?" Is it possible to admit its use by city residents, given the different "cultures," urban and rural? (Confen, 1987, p. 28–29)

In response to this questioning, the conclusion presented two main arguments. On one hand, it engaged with the biomedical discourse, challenging the classification of ayahuasca as a "hallucinogenic drug." On the other hand, it drew from anthropological perspectives, emphasizing the notion of "culture." Regarding the label of ayahuasca as a "hallucinogen," the WG, despite Karniol's position, opted for a semantic deconstruction and a conceptual critique of the term. They argued that this categorization carried inherent biases tied to biomedical and pharmacological determinism. The report contended that the altered states sought by ayahuasca users in their ceremonies did not resemble "hallucinations" in the clinical sense of "madness" or "insanity." Instead, they framed it as "a project, rigorously common to all of them: the search for the sacred and for self-knowledge" (Confen, 1987, p. 29).

Sá emphasized that it was not the WG's role to determine whether the experience of the sacred or the pursuit of self-knowledge through ayahuasca was an illusion, daydream, or fantasy. Furthermore, from the WG's perspective, the moral and ethical standards of the ayahuasca groups were similar to those of broader Brazilian society, often even stricter, and they were law-abiding communities. The WG frequently described ayahuasca users as "calm" and "happy" individuals, stressing that "the use of tea does not seem to hinder or have adverse consequences on the social life of the followers of the various sects. On the contrary, it seems to guide them towards the pursuit of social happiness, within an orderly and hard-working context" (Confen, 1987, p. 29). The WG also argued that the frequent "pilgrimages" and exchanges between ayahuasca users made it impossible to draw a strict divide between Amazonian culture and the rest of the country. They viewed the expansion of ayahuasca throughout Brazil as a process of cultural exchange, one that enriched both urban and rural ways of life. Reflecting on this cultural exchange between urban groups and rural communities of the Santo Daime, anthropologist Regina Abreu noted:

> There are still other considerations to add to the issue we pointed out earlier, regarding the conversion to the doctrine of segments of urban-industrial society, a fact that generates fears on the part of religious groups, civil and military authorities and sectors of civil society. The adoption of the Santo Daime Doctrine in large cities obviously has characteristics that are

peculiar to urban life. Clearly, we will not find in it the typical works of rural areas, such as hunting and large-scale agriculture. But the conversion to the [Santo Daime] doctrine can lead converts to ritual and lifestyle practices that retain the basic characteristics of rural religious communities. There is a similar project in both cases. [...] As a result, these communities, whether in the countryside or in the city, which adopt the Santo Daime Doctrine, may appear to many to be exotic groups, but living with this diversity can only be enriching for individuals and for society as a whole (Confen, 1987, p. 31–32).

The anthropologist characterized the expansion of Santo Daime and União do Vegetal to Brazil's major urban centers as part of a legitimate social process of expansion and dissemination of rural religious phenomena which, in a process of exchange, were able to present an alternative way of life and new forms of social relations based on community practices from the Amazon. Notably, the final quote in the report is an excerpt from Claude Lévi-Strauss's *Race and History*:

No culture is alone, it is always capable of coalitions with other cultures, and this is what allows it to build cumulative series. The probability that a longer series will emerge from these naturally depends on the extent, duration and variability of the coalition system. [...] The only loss, the only tare that can afflict a human group and prevent it from fully realizing its nature, is that of being alone (Lévi-Strauss et al., 1970, p. 262–263 apud Confen, 1987, p. 32).

Considering the ways in which the WG portrayed the use of ayahuasca, the choice to quote Lévi-Strauss' work at the conclusion of the report was not random. It upholds the WG's framework, addressing cultural diversity from a political standpoint, converting a possible fear of the unrestrained expansion of ayahuasca use to Brazil's major urban centers into a legitimate historical process of cultural exchange. The use of the notion of "culture" to refer to ayahuasca was strategic insofar as it allowed the legitimation of the expansion of ayahuasca use—described in the document as a cultural expression from the Amazon—to Brazil's big cities.[12]

Resorting to anthropological discourse, the WG presented the use of ayahuasca and its widespread presence in Brazilian cities as part of Brazilian cultural and religious diversity in its various expressions. It was highlighted multiple times throughout the report that the religious use of ayahuasca did not present the characteristics of drug abuse. On the contrary, it was often described as a socio-integrative practice and the groups were frequently portrayed as communities with ethical and moral standards that met the basic principles of Brazilian society, presenting a balanced lifestyle. Based on this stance, the WG stated the legitimacy of the religious use of ayahuasca, maintaining its previous decision to exclude B. caapi from DIMED's list of controlled substances.

Ultimately, anthropological discourse and categories played a pivotal role throughout the development of the report, portraying the use of ayahuasca as a

[12] In a later work Sá (1996, p. 1) reaffirmed his emphasis on the cultural aspects that revolve around the use of psychoactive substances, stating that "from the outset, I affirm my conviction that the cost-benefit equation when it comes to drugs is essentially a cultural one. Otherwise, how could we explain, from an exclusively medical or pharmacological point of view, for example, the full assimilation of alcohol and tobacco use in our society?". He reiterated that "the historical expression of these [ayahuasca] sects is closely linked to 'a certain culture'—the Brazilian one. More than that, to the Indigenous people, to the *caboclo*, to the Amazon" (Sá, 1996, p. 6).

legitimate religious and cultural expression from the Amazon. Not only was the anthropological work important to affirm the legitimacy of the use of ayahuasca, but it was vital to question the notion of "hallucinogen" and to establish that different modes of perception are culturally informed. Moreover, the WG also resorted to research techniques consecrated by anthropology. The research team engaged in fieldwork, which included taking part in ayahuasca ceremonies on multiple occasions and recording detailed accounts of these experiences. In addition to maintaining field reports, the WG members observed the everyday interactions and social dynamics within the Santo Daime and União do Vegetal (UDV) communities. They interviewed both members and leaders of these communities, looking for additional insight into the groups' dynamics. This integration of anthropological notions and some of its classical methods into the policymaking process enabled the WG to produce a 35-page report that guaranteed the freedom of religious use of ayahuasca in Brazil.

2.4 Self-Regulation and New Developments on Public Policies

The years following CONFEN's Final Report were marked by the first attempt to self-regulate and create guidelines for the religious use of ayahuasca in Brazil. In November 1991, representatives of some of the main UDV, Santo Daime and Barquinha groups in the country developed the "Charter of Principles of the Religious Entities that Use the Hoasca Tea." The idea for the charter was proposed by the UDV. Their aim was to create ethical principles and common procedures for the consumption of ayahuasca in Brazil. The charter established a set of recommendations regarding preparation, consumption and ritual procedures for ayahuasca groups.[13] The document stressed that the tea should be "restricted to religious rituals, in places authorized by the respective leaders of the institutions, and its use in association with drugs or any psychotropic plants is forbidden" (Acre, 1991, p. 1).

In addition to these recommendations, the charter presented some restrictions. These included a commitment not to commercialize ayahuasca and a restriction on any practice of quackery. Its potential benefits should be considered exclusively from a spiritual point of view, without advertising hysteria that could mislead public opinion and government bodies. Furthermore, the document recommended that people under the influence of any drugs, licit or illicit, should be denied access to religious rituals with ayahuasca (Acre, 1991, p. 1). Finally, the signatory groups declared a commitment to seeking the regulation of the use of ayahuasca in Congress, stipulating legal mechanisms that would avoid future controversies over the inappropriate use of the tea (Acre, 1991, p. 2). The Charter of Principles marked

[13] The document was ratified at the First International Ayahuasca Conference in Rio Branco, when the organizations met to sign the document in common agreement. According to Labate (2005, p. 409), throughout the event, the groups presented aspects of their structure, history and rituals, as well as debating issues such as the drug policy situation in the country.

an important development for the public debate on the use of ayahuasca in Brazil, given that it was the first initiative to establish common principles and parameters for regulating the religious use of ayahuasca in the country. It was the initial attempt by the ayahuasca groups to seek legitimacy and recognition from public bodies at a national level by developing a set of guidelines and principles that aimed to standardize and typify their practices, creating control mechanisms and restrictions, something unheard of in the country at the time.

The document also raised concerns similar to those expressed by public authorities and academic literature. It emphasizes the image of ayahuasca as portrayed in the mainstream media, with a clear effort to dissociate it from recreational psychoactive substance use, highlighting the "religious," "ritual," and "spiritual" aspects of ayahuasca consumption. It is worth noting that some of the guidelines and recommendations regarding the production, consumption, and dissemination of information in the charter would later reappear, nearly unchanged, in the National Council for Drug Policy's (CONAD) 2006 report on ayahuasca, and were formally incorporated into the regulation process of the religious use of ayahuasca 15 years later.

In addition to the Charter of Principles, the early 1990s saw the first biomedical study on ayahuasca in the country, the Hoasca Project. In 1993, at the invitation of the UDV, a group of biomedical experts from the United States, Finland and Brazil began an examination of the biochemical and psychological effects of ayahuasca. The research selected 15 UDV members who had been affiliated with the institution for more than 10 years and 15 people who had never consumed ayahuasca. The aim of the project was to undertake a comparative study to assess the past and current physical and psychological conditions of the two groups. Among the main results, the research concluded that the long-term consumption of ayahuasca in a ceremonial context showed no evidence of toxic effects or psychological damage to its users. The UDV members obtained results that were on average or slightly better than those of the control group. Even though the study highlighted the benefits of consuming ayahuasca in a controlled environment, it did not rule out the possibility of the drink itself having therapeutic potential.[14]

Despite the significance of the study, biomedical discourse did not play a central role in shaping the initial public policies on ayahuasca use. Although the UDV sought to establish partnerships and projects in the biomedical field as a strategy to legitimize ayahuasca use and counter claims that it posed risks to individual and public health, the dominant framework in CONFEN and CONAD initiatives was culturalist, drawing on anthropological knowledge and aligned with constitutional principles safeguarding Indigenous and Afro-Brazilian cultural heritage. This approach is evident in another key measure taken by CONFEN in 1992, 1 year after the development of the charter. The council issued a new resolution to reassess the

[14] The results of the Hoasca Project's research were presented for the first time in 1995, at the 1st International Conference of Hoasca Studies, in the capital of Rio de Janeiro. In 2008, Jace Callaway, Denis McKenna and Charles Grob also presented their experience during the II International Hoasca Congress, in Brasília (DF) (https://udv.org.br/pesquisas-cientificas/projeto-hoasca/). According to Callaway (2011, p. 80–81), nearly 15 scientific articles [in the biomedical field] have been published directly from the results of the Hoasca Project since 1994.

religious use of ayahuasca in response to an anonymous complaint filed in 1988 with the Federal Court of Rio de Janeiro, the State Secretariat of the Civil Police of Rio de Janeiro, and CONFEN. The complaint alleged that ayahuasca groups had over "ten million fanatics" among their followers, that many of their leaders were "drug addicts and former guerrilla members," and that 80% of Acre's population was consuming the tea. It further claimed that ayahuasca use induced a state of mental torpor, leading individuals to neglect their physical lives and families, and that followers were coerced into forced labor and excessive financial donations (Confen, 1992, p. 1).

Ayahuasca groups were also accused of burning incense behind closed doors that allegedly contained cannabis, and the UDV specifically was accused of mixing ayahuasca with LSD. Regarding children, the complaint claimed they were forced to stay awake for more than 72 h, "totally distressed by horrifying visions." The document concluded that ayahuasca use in Brazil posed a threat to national security and was part of a counterattack by urban guerrillas (Confen, 1992, p. 1–2). Given the gravity of these accusations, the then-president of CONFEN, Ester Kosovski, tasked Domingos Bernardo da Silva Sá with updating the information from previous reports and conducting new research on the matter. This new round of investigations culminated in CONFEN's 1992 report on ayahuasca. Sá contacted leaders of Santo Daime and UDV, arranging new visits to gather information and documents on their activities. In total, he conducted eight visits to ayahuasca groups in Rio de Janeiro, Rio Branco, and the municipality of Pauini in Amazonas. He met with representatives of various groups at a meeting held at Rio Branco City Hall, where he collected a series of documents on their practices, statutes, and "testimonies from followers of various sects, with accounts of healing, family reunions and positive redirections of life" (Confen, 1992, p. 5–6). Sá also consulted specialists and professors in anthropology, psychopharmacology, and psychiatry who had prior experience studying ayahuasca.[15]

According to anthropologist Edward MacRae, his role as a consultant was to emphasize the significance of the socio-cultural context and the formal and informal control mechanisms established by ayahuasca groups themselves. At the time, he explained, the goal was to examine the religious use of ayahuasca through the lens of "harm reduction." This approach sought to move away from a purely biomedical perspective that focused solely on ayahuasca's effects on the body and psyche while also critiquing the prevailing prohibitionist paradigm, which had contributed to the spread of social stigmas surrounding psychoactive substance use (MacRae, personal communication 2019). However, CONFEN's arguments extended beyond a

[15] The specialists consulted by Sá were: Dr. E.A. Carlini, professor of psychopharmacology at the Escola Paulista de Medicina; psychiatrist Dr. Isac Germano Karniol, who took part in the WG that developed the 1987 report; Dr. Edward MacRae, anthropologist, visiting researcher at the Addiction Guidance and Care Program of the Psychiatry Department at the Paulista School of Medicine and member of the São Paulo Institute of Social Medicine and Criminology (IMESC); Dr. Clod, visiting researcher at the Department of Psychiatry of the Escola Paulista de Medicina; and Dr. Clodomir Monteiro da Silva, anthropologist and director of the Philosophy and Social Sciences Department at the Federal University of Acre (Silva, 1983).

critique of the biomedical model, frequently emphasizing ayahuasca's cultural and social significance as well as its historical value. Drawing on Silva's work (1983), the report underscored the "clear social and ritual nature of ayahuasca," noting that "the use of Santo Daime is almost exclusively social, which always implies frequently a kind of sequence of acts or rites" (Confen, 1992, p. 16). To further support this argument, the jurist cited an excerpt from MacRae's statement:

> By the way, it is appropriate to check what MacRae says: "The various anthropological and historical studies carried out on this use of drink have highlighted [that…], far from leading to an abusive and destructive use of psychoactive substances, the most noticeable tendency is to promote modest and austere lifestyles, focused on the cult of spirituality and family, and community values" (Confen, 1992, p. 12–13).

Sá repeatedly affirmed the legitimacy of ayahuasca use as a cultural and religious expression, emphasizing its crucial role in fostering social cohesion within local communities. Additionally, he underscored the necessity of the expansion of ayahuasca groups beyond the Amazon rainforest as an essential measure for their protection and continuity.

> Once again it should be remembered that the use of ayahuasca has been considered legitimate until now, and that a large number of people have invested their lives in these sects, making them central to their social, individual and spiritual identities. […] Bearing in mind the importance of the socially integrating aspects of these sects, the corollary is that weakening them would only contribute to weakening social cohesion, arousing feelings of revolt and returning many of those who have found meaning in these sects in their lives to anomie. Thus, it is important to reiterate that arbitrarily restricting the celebration of ayahuasca sects to a certain geographical region would mean denying the notion that Brazil is a legally and culturally integrated whole, and would be as unwise and counterproductive as trying to confine *Candomblé* to Bahia, Lutheranism to the German colonies of the South or Pentecostalism to the descendants of Americans. (Confen, 1992, p. 26–27)

The jurist's statement highlights the socio-integrative role of ayahuasca's religious use, emphasizing its capacity to foster social cohesion within communities and families while shaping their "social, individual, and spiritual identities." According to Sá, their ceremonies and cultural activities stood in stark contrast to the destructive patterns often linked to psychoactive substance abuse, which the report—drawing on Durkheim's terminology—characterized as a form of social "anomie."[16] The

[16] Since the 1980s, anthropologists have highlighted the significance of ayahuasca in the social life and dynamics of these communities, questioning the alleged reductionist view of ayahuasca as a "drug." The literature suggests that this framework confined ayahuasca to the pharmacological realm, overlooking its broader socio-cultural importance. In his master's thesis in anthropology on the ritual use of ayahuasca on Santo Daime, Couto posited that "the use of the drink within established ritual patterns, instead of leading the system towards anomie, towards anti-structure, strengthens its structure, if we bear in mind Turner's thinking, which sees social life as the tension between anti-structure (communitas) and structure (societas). It is important to clarify our understanding of the drink. Certainly, the view of the drink as a narcotic is very poor and is certainly far from helping us to understand its use, which involves socio-symbolic components corroborated by collective approval" (Couto, 1989, p. 27–28). In a later work in which he revisits his thesis, Couto emphasized that the drink "is a material element with great symbolic power and social cohesion, because a ritual is structured around it, and rituals are moments of order, leading the system as a whole to structure, to cohesion" (Couto, 2004, p. 393).

comparison between the stigmatization of ayahuasca's religious use and the repression of Afro-Brazilian practices in the first half of the twentieth century is particularly significant. This parallel reinforces the legitimacy of ayahuasca as a religious and cultural expression, which became eligible for state protection after the 1988 Constitution. Sá also reiterated the criticism of the terms "hallucinogen" and "hallucination," already present in the 1987 report. He argued that what was once considered madness, absurd, heretical, or fanciful had since been incorporated into scientific and doctrinal frameworks, emphasizing that the history of perceptions is a history of conflicts, favoring certain perspectives over others. From Sá's perspective, accusations of madness primarily revealed the inability of various segments of Brazilian society to coexist with different ways of perceiving reality.

Quoting Stanislav Grof, Sá highlighted the problems of diagnosing someone as psychotic based solely on the content of their experience, arguing that the notions of "normal" or "pathological" should be based on how the individual integrates their perceptions into their life experiences. Beyond the question of pathology, Sá drew on Mircea Eliade's work to argue that adjectives are insufficient to define human experience and that images, symbols, and myths are not random creations of the psyche but respond to specific needs, functioning to elucidate different "modalities of being." The jurist emphasized that concepts such as hallucination, delirium, and illusion had limited applicability for describing ecstatic experiences, being "far from translating the reality of these spiritual states" (Confen, 1992, p. 22–23).

In hindsight, it is clear that the use of academic literature was strategic in establishing the legal framework for ayahuasca consumption at this early stage of policy-making. While physicians and psychiatrists were consistently involved in the first reports and statements, the recurrent critique of biomedical discourse and what was termed "pharmacological determinism," the problematization of the category "hallucinogen" and its implications, as well as the framing of ayahuasca group practices as legitimate cultural manifestations, shaped the categorizations and classifications adopted by the Brazilian government for the use of ayahuasca.

The 1990s therefore witnessed the recurrence of a series of dynamics around the issue of the religious use of ayahuasca in the country. The period was marked by the unprecedented initiative of self-regulation by the main ayahuasca groups at the time, which established a set of common parameters and principles regarding the religious use of ayahuasca. At the same time, the work of researchers and the incorporation of arguments from the academic literature played a fundamental role in the initial development of public policies in Brazil, helping to define the institutional agenda of the use of ayahuasca in the country. Although the association of ayahuasca use with the notion of "drug" did not disappear over the following decades, the anthropological arguments prevailed in the institutional arena, paving the way for the consolidation of the notion of ayahuasca institutions as religious groups and cultural expressions of Amazonian origin. This framework was fundamental for the shaping of public policies on the use of ayahuasca for religious purposes in Brazil over the following decade.

2.5 The Safeguard of Ayahuasca as a Religious and Cultural Practice

After the 1992 report, the regulation of ayahuasca's religious use by federal agencies was revisited in the 2000s[17] by CONAD.[18] In Resolution No. 26, issued on December 31, 2002, CONAD declared that "the ritualistic use of 'ayahuasca tea' constitutes a regional cultural and religious expression that has long been recognized by Brazilian society" (Conad, 2002). The resolution also reaffirmed that ayahuasca groups were aware of the prohibition of its commercialization, as its use must remain strictly religious. Additionally, CONAD opposed the drink's export, citing its exclusive ritualistic function within a Brazilian cultural tradition, as well as legal restrictions imposed by Brazilian law and international agreements (Conad, 2002). Finally, the resolution established a Working Group tasked with presenting:

> [...] a proposal for social control measures and other suggestions that may be appropriate, in view of the need to be brought into practice by society, within the principle of shared responsibility, norms and procedures that preserve consecrated religious cultural expressions, observing the objectives and norms established by the National Anti-Drug Policy and the pertinent legal statutes. (Conad, 2002, p. 2)

The resolution was issued on the final day of Fernando Henrique Cardoso's administration as president of Brazil, but his successor, Luiz Inácio Lula da Silva, did not directly request the formation of the Working Group. However, Lula's administration (2003–2010) ushered in a shift in public policy, emphasizing affirmative actions for ethnic, racial, and gender minorities (see Chap. 3). In 2004, anthropologist Edward MacRae was invited to collaborate with CONAD as a representative of the Ministry of Culture (MinC). That same year, CONAD decided to revisit the regulation of ayahuasca's religious use. To this end, Paulina Duarte, a representative of the National Anti-Drug Secretariat (SENAD) and a member of the Office of Institutional Security of the Presidency, invited a group of researchers to join CONAD's Scientific and Technical Advisory Chamber (CATC). On March 24, 2004, CONAD tasked the CATC with preparing a new study and technical-scientific report on various aspects of ayahuasca use (MacRae, 2008, p. 295). The CATC held a series of meetings on the subject, with the participation of anthropologists Sandra Lucia Goulart, Beatriz Caiuby Labate, and MacRae, all experts in the field. These discussions led to a new report that reaffirmed key points from previous resolutions.

Among the issues addressed was the position of the United Nations International Narcotics Control Board (INCB) on ayahuasca, which stated that "since the plant is

---

[17] In the mid-1990s, CONFEN took a stance on the consumption of ayahuasca by minors under the age of 18. In June 1995, the institution approved an opinion recommending that the tea should not be given to people with mental disorders, or to minors under the age of 18, even if accompanied by their parents. In May 1997, at CONFEN's third ordinary meeting, the decision in question was ratified. This was later overturned by CONAD.

[18] In the 2000s, the National Council for Drug Policy (CONAD) replaced the now defunct Federal Council on Narcotics (CONFEN).

used practically in natura, there is no need for any control, adding that there will be no control of plants used in tea form, according to the INCB's opinion, since there is no purification, concentration, or isolation of substances"[19] (Conad, 2004a, p. 1). The report also underscored the importance of a bioethical approach, emphasizing the role of informed individual decision-making. It asserted that individuals have the right to access a broad range of information provided by professionals from various fields, public institutions, and civil society. According to the document, "it is the right of the person to be informed for safe individual decision-making or by their family circle" (Conad, 2004a, p. 2).

The CATC examined the use of ayahuasca by children and pregnant women, emphasizing the fundamental right to informed individual decision-making. It argued that understanding the perspectives of the communities that consume ayahuasca is essential, as well as considering individuals' specific circumstances and the historical contingencies surrounding its use. The document also referenced Article 1.634 of the Civil Code, which governs parental authority, noting its broad scope: "committing parents to the proper upbringing and education of their children, subjecting them to the loss of this power in the event of abuse of authority or failure to fulfill the duties assigned to them by law" (Conad, 2004a, pp. 2–3). Additionally, it addressed the Statute of the Child and Adolescent (Bill No. 8.069, enacted on July 13, 1990), which guarantees children and adolescents the right to freedom, including freedom of belief and religious practice (Art. 16, III). The document cited an excerpt from the statute, emphasizing that the educational process must respect "the cultural, artistic, and historical values specific to the social context of children and adolescents, guaranteeing them freedom of creation and access to cultural sources" (Bill No. 8.069, Art. 58, apud Conad, 2004a, pp. 2–3).

In summary, the CATC determined that the participation of children and adolescents in religious practices should be left to the discretion of legal guardians, taking into account their physical and psychological development, as well as the cultural values of their social context. The report concluded that families, while respecting individual autonomy, should be responsible for making such decisions, and that direct state intervention would be both impractical and undesirable. This reasoning was also applied to pregnant women, who were deemed responsible for safeguarding the development of the unborn child.

Another key aspect of the report was the therapeutic use of ayahuasca. The agency emphasized the importance of encouraging research on the brew, including clinical studies. Citing MacRae's work, the document highlighted the immense botanical diversity of the Amazon rainforest and the increasing interest of pharmaceutical companies in its potential applications. It underscored the ritualistic dimension of ayahuasca as a fundamental component of folk healing systems and argued that harnessing this botanical wealth would be impossible without scientific investigation. Consequently, the Chamber proposed studying the therapeutic use of

[19] This statement was made through the request of the Santo Daime church in the Netherlands in the early 2000s.

ayahuasca on an experimental basis. The report also affirmed that there should be no direct or indirect restrictions on the religious practices of ayahuasca communities. It reiterated the right to religious freedom, referencing previous rulings by CONFEN and CONAD and stressing "the inviolability of conscience and belief and the guarantee of state protection for manifestations of popular, Indigenous, and Afro-Brazilian cultures, based on Articles 5, 6, and 7 of the Brazilian Constitution, thus avoiding any form of prejudice" (Conad, 2004a, p. 6).

Shortly afterward, CONAD issued Resolution No. 5, formally recognizing "the legal legitimacy of the religious use of ayahuasca" and stating that "the process of legitimization began more than 18 years ago, with the provisional suspension of the plant species that make up the brew from the lists of the Division of Medicines (DIMED), by Resolution of the Federal Council of Narcotics (CONFEN)" (Conad, 2004b, p. 1). The resolution reaffirmed the constitutional right to freedom of worship and individual decision-making, emphasizing that choices regarding the religious use of ayahuasca should be made with access to the broadest possible range of information. Finally, CONAD established a Multidisciplinary Working Group (MWG) tasked with conducting a survey on the religious use of ayahuasca, monitoring its practices, and assessing the feasibility of research into its therapeutic applications. The MWG was also responsible for creating a national registry of ayahuasca-using entities and drafting a document outlining ethical guidelines for its use, including measures to prevent misuse (Conad, 2004b, p. 2).

2.6 The Final Report of the Multidisciplinary Working Group—Ayahuasca and Recent Developments

The members of the Multidisciplinary Working Group on Ayahuasca (MWG) were selected following discussions at CATC meetings. During one such meeting on the formation of the MWG, MacRae proposed including representatives from ayahuasca religious groups. He argued that this approach aligned with harm reduction principles, which prioritize collaboration with the people directly affected by policies rather than imposing top-down measures without consulting user communities. According to MacRae (personal communication, 2019), his suggestion aimed to foster dialogue and develop policies that genuinely reflected the needs of ayahuasca groups. CONAD accepted the proposal.

As a result, in May 2006, the MWG was officially established by Jorge Armando Felix, the Chief Minister of the Office of Institutional Security of the Presidency of the Republic and President of the National Anti-Drugs Council. The group comprised specialists from various fields, including anthropology (Dr. Edward John Baptista das Neves MacRae), pharmacology and biochemistry (Dr. Isac Germano Karniol), social work (Dr. Roberta Salazar Uchoa), psychiatry (Dr. Dartiu Xavier da Silveira Filho), and law (Dr. Ester Kosovski). In addition to these researchers, six representatives from religious organizations that use ayahuasca were also included, having been elected during a seminar held in Rio Branco on March 9–10, 2006.

According to MacRae, electing representatives from ayahuasca groups was not an easy task. To facilitate the process, the CATC commissioned anthropologists Beatriz Labate and Sandra Goulart to map the country's major ayahuasca groups and help determine appropriate representatives. Following their recommendations, seats were allocated to representatives from Brazil's main ayahuasca institutions at the time: Barquinha, UDV, and the Santo Daime branches of Alto Santo and ICEFLU. MacRae noted that there was internal pressure to exclude ICEFLU due to its controversial association with cannabis use. However, the institution retained its representation, as it was one of Brazil's largest ayahuasca groups with a significant national and international presence. Due to ongoing disputes and tensions among different ayahuasca groups, the Barquinha representatives ultimately decided not to participate in the MWG. As a result, the Alto Santo branch of Santo Daime ended up with two representatives.[20]

The MWG received support from the National Anti-Drug Secretariat, represented by Dr. Paulina do Carmo Arruda Vieira Duarte, Director of Prevention and Treatment Policies, and CONAD's Executive Advisory, represented by Dr. Domingos Bernardo da Silva Sá, a Full Member of CONAD and rapporteur of CONFEN's reports on ayahuasca (Conad, 2006, pp. 2–3). Between August and November 2006, the MWG held seven meetings at the National Anti-Drug Secretariat headquarters, addressing various topics, including the registration of ayahuasca institutions, legal frameworks for regulating its religious use, the protection of freedom of worship, guidelines for the production, consumption, and shipment of ayahuasca, procedures for admitting new members, and the definition of ayahuasca's therapeutic applications. A broader discussion also explored the relationship between ayahuasca, culture, and Brazilian society.

According to MacRae, despite tensions and differences among the groups, efforts were made to foster dialogue and mutual respect between ayahuasca representatives and other MWG members. The discussions culminated in a report summarizing the key points addressed in the meetings (Conad, 2006, p. 3). In the introduction to the *Final Report—Ayahuasca*, the MWG reaffirmed the previous decisions of CONFEN and CONAD, emphasizing that no direct or indirect restrictions should be imposed on the religious practices of ayahuasca communities.

[20] MacRae (2008, p. 297) highlights the tensions that surfaced during these meetings: "During this event, the deep rivalry and animosity between various ayahuasca groups once again became evident. [...] Thus, the members of the daimist groups known by the name *Alto Santo*, who maintain their practices and conceptions closer to the original teachings of their founding *Mestre* Raimundo Irineu Serra, and the followers of the groups known by the designation *Barquinha* made a series of accusations against the organizers of the meeting, claiming that they had favored the daimist group *Centro Eclético Fluente Luz Universal Raimundo Irineu Serra* (CEFLURIS) [now ICEFLU] by reserving a place on the MWG specifically for a representative of this controversial but prominent Santo Daime *line*. [...] In 2006, the major accusations raised, especially against followers of *Padrinho* Sebastião, focused mainly on allegations of "commercialization of the sacrament" and its use in association with drugs or psychotropic plants, such as *Cannabis sativa*. The *Barquinha* churches ended up refusing to take part in the MWG, and ironically, their place was taken by a member of *Alto Santo*, a *line* which, although a minority, ended up having two representatives."

> The freedom of religious use of Ayahuasca should be reiterated, [...] considering the inviolability of conscience and belief and the State's guarantee of protection for expressions of popular, Indigenous and Afro-Brazilian cultures, based on Articles 5, 6 and 215 of the Brazilian Constitution, thus avoiding any form of manifestation of prejudice (Conad, 2006, p. 1–2).

The report also outlined the key decisions, opinions, and reports developed by CONFEN and CONAD over the past decades. The MWG reiterated the constitutional responsibility of the Brazilian state to protect the religious use of ayahuasca as a legitimate national tradition. The document further emphasized "the culmination of the process of legitimizing the religious use of Ayahuasca in the country, which began more than twenty years ago with the creation of the 1st CONAD (then CONFEN) Working Group" (Conad, 2006, p. 4).

Thus, from the 2000s onwards, the regulatory process concerning ayahuasca shifted from addressing concerns about the alleged risks of the brew to emphasizing its recognition as a legitimate cultural and religious practice deserving protection by the Brazilian state. Consequently, the association of ayahuasca with the concept of "drug" became increasingly irrelevant within the context of public policy, eventually disappearing from the MWG's Final Report on ayahuasca. With this shift in focus, the working group concentrated on developing a deontological framework to establish standards and guidelines for the "responsible use of ayahuasca." In this regard, it is important to highlight the passage from the report that underscores the significance of preserving the religious use of ayahuasca.

> The correct identification of what is the religious use, according to the concepts and practices dictated by the institutions themselves that use Ayahuasca, will ensure the protection of freedom of belief guaranteed by the Federal Constitution. [...] It is therefore a question of ratifying the legitimacy of the religious use of Ayahuasca as a rich and ancestral cultural expression, which, precisely because of the relevance of its historical, anthropological and social value, is worthy of state protection (Conad, 2006, p. 7).

The report emphasized the need to define the religious use of ayahuasca in terms that align with the beliefs and practices of the groups themselves. The MWG explained that its goal was to consolidate the guidelines for the religious use of ayahuasca, a process that had begun two decades earlier with the "Charter of Principles." This effort culminated in the creation of a code of ethics aimed at establishing clear standards and best practices to protect what CONAD recognized as a valuable cultural and religious tradition. Among the key points was a strong opposition to the commercialization of ayahuasca. The report argued that selling ayahuasca was not an "act of faith" but a "business" endeavor, which compromised the integrity of the traditional use upheld by religious communities. The MWG stressed that every aspect of the making of ayahuasca—from gathering the plants to preparing and consuming the brew—must be understood as an act of faith. In contrast, seeking profit was framed as incompatible with the genuine and responsible practices that these groups deem legitimate.

The MWG also highlighted that the "culture of religious use of ayahuasca," grounded in faith and rooted in plants from the Amazon Rainforest, inherently involves environmental stewardship in the extraction of the species (Conad, 2006,

p. 9). As a result, it emphasized that responsible spiritual use also requires sustainability in plant cultivation, encouraging groups to grow and prepare ayahuasca for their own consumption rather than for sale. The MWG further recommended that tourism and commercial ventures be avoided, stating that as religious organizations, ayahuasca groups should not exploit the effects of the brew for profit. At the same time, the report affirmed that the Federal Constitution guarantees the right to religious freedom, which includes the right to promote one's faith through legitimate exchanges among members.

> What we want to avoid is that a responsible, serious religious practice, legitimately recognized by the State, is transformed, by virtue of noncompliance with ethical principles, into commercialism of psychoactive substances, enriching people or groups, who find in the argument of faith only the protection for inappropriate practices (Conad, 2006, p. 9).

Another issue addressed by the MWG concerned advertising practices and the dissemination of information. It was pointed out that advertising around the use of ayahuasca has been the target of misrepresentation and abuse, especially on the internet, where it was common to find offers of all kinds of paid courses and workshops, associating ayahuasca with promises of transformative experiences unrelated to religious rituals. The MWG stated that the responsible religious use was incompatible with advertising or offering promises of miraculous healings, or of sweeping personal transformations, agreeing "that those who make responsible religious use do not disclose information that could induce people to have a fanciful image of Ayahuasca and deal with the subject discreetly, without making a fuss about the effects of the substance" (Conad, 2006, p. 10).

The issue of the therapeutic use of ayahuasca was also mentioned in the report. According to the MWG, "'therapy' is understood as an activity or process aimed at healing, maintaining or developing health, which takes into account scientific ethical principles" (Conad, 2006, p. 10). The report highlighted that some institutions carry out healing ceremonies in which ayahuasca is used. The MWG stressed, nevertheless, that the therapeutic use traditionally attributed to religious rituals with ayahuasca "is not therapy in the sense defined above, it is an act of faith and, as such, it is not up to the State to intervene in the conduct of people, groups or entities that make use of the drink in a strictly religious context" (Conad, 2006, p. 10). The CONAD reaffirmed that it had limited itself to authorizing the use of ayahuasca in religious rituals, determining that the therapeutic use of the drink without professional qualification and the backing of scientific research was not only illegal but a reckless professional practice. It was thus decided that:

> Any practice that involves the use of Ayahuasca for strictly therapeutic purposes, whether the substance alone or in association with other substances or therapeutic practices, should be prohibited until its effectiveness has been proven through scientific research carried out by research centers linked to academic institutions, following scientific methodologies. In this way, the legitimacy of Ayahuasca's therapeutic use will only be recognized once research has been completed to prove it. Based on the reports of the representatives of the user entities, it was found that the healings and solutions to personal problems should be understood in the same religious context as other religions: as acts of faith, with no necessary cause and effect relationship between the use of Ayahuasca and cures or solutions to problems (Conad, 2006, p. 11).

Moreover, the document pointed out that the spread of ayahuasca consumption and increased access had led to the emergence of new groups that were not equipped with the necessary experience to deal with the brew and its effects and were no longer practicing the responsible use of ayahuasca by associating it with practices that are not related to religious use. The report expressed concern regarding the possibility of an increase of the use of ayahuasca for recreational purposes. It was established thus that the responsible use of ayahuasca presupposed the presence of experienced people, capable of dealing with the various aspects surrounding its religious use. In addition, the MWG recommended that the "groups should be constituted into formal organizations, with legal personality, consolidating the idea of responsibility, identity and social projection, enabling users to practice religion in an environment of trust" (Conad, 2006, p. 11–12).

The procedures for welcoming new members were also a point of discussion. While each group follows its own traditions for integrating newcomers, the MWG suggested additional precautions. It advised that individuals' psychiatric history and emotional state at the time of participation be taken into account, ensuring they are not under the influence of alcohol or other psychoactive substances. Furthermore, prospective participants should be fully informed of all conditions required for ayahuasca use before joining a ritual for the first time. To this end, the MWG recommended conducting a preliminary interview to assess medical and psychological suitability, as well as to clarify the ritual's procedures and effects. The document stipulated that each organization should provide guidance and support to participants throughout the entire ceremony (Conad, 2006, p. 12). Finally, the report examined the use of ayahuasca by pregnant women and minors. Given the lack of scientific evidence on potential harm and in consideration of existing practices within ayahuasca communities, the MWG upheld the terms of CONAD Resolution 05/04. As a result, the decision regarding ayahuasca use by minors under 18 remained a matter for parental discretion, while pregnant women were entrusted with personal responsibility for their participation (Conad, 2006, p. 12).

The document concluded by reaffirming human dignity as a core national principle, emphasizing that freedom of conscience and belief are inviolable rights. However, beyond the notion of individual liberty, it underscored that the legitimation of ayahuasca use stemmed from its recognition as a religious and cultural expression rooted in the Amazon. Thus, rather than focusing primarily on safeguarding personal freedoms, the scope was to protect what had, over the decades, been established by academia and public policy as a legitimate spiritual and cultural tradition. Four years after the publication of the MWG's *Final Report—Ayahuasca*, CONAD issued Resolution No. 1 on January 25, 2010, seeking to further public awareness and reinforce the official framework for the religious use of ayahuasca in Brazil. The resolution mandated the full dissemination of the *Final Report of the Multidisciplinary Working Group* (Conad, 2010).

It is important to address some of the guidelines presented by CONAD and how they portray a specific notion of "religion." According to the institution, religion is neither commerce nor tourism, and religions should avoid practices associated with those activities, such as advertising and sales on the internet. Moreover, not only ayahuasca groups should distance themselves from practices that might associate them with business enterprises, but they were recommended to avoid any form of proselytism. The CONAD also established a clear and definitive boundary between religion and therapy, with scientific standards serving as the line of demarcation. While this ensured the protection of ayahuasca groups' freedom to conduct their ceremonies as "acts of faith," it also required them to concede that these rituals did not qualify as therapeutic in the formal, scientific sense outlined by the agency. This distinction raises an important issue central to the book: the way ayahuasca practices and the discourse surrounding them involve intersecting domains—such as drug use, religion, culture, and therapy. The complexity of these intersections challenges the normative frameworks and classificatory efforts of governmental agencies, highlighting the difficulties of imposing rigid categories on practices that span across such diverse fields. In order to legitimize and protect what was defined as the "religious use of ayahuasca," the latter had to conform to a number of principles that put it in a specific realm of activities commonly associated with religious phenomena, specifically with Catholicism, such as gratuity, charity, and the repudiation of any form of healing as a therapeutic practice.

In 2020, congresswoman Jéssica Sales from *Movimento Democrático Brasileiro* (MDB) of Acre authored Bill 179/2020 PL 179/2020, which aimed to turn into law the CONAD's resolutions that regulated the use of ayahuasca in Brazil.[21] The bill proposed by Sales was shelved in 2022 due to the lack of political support, as some ayahuasca groups feared that, if implemented, the bill could create additional hurdles for them. The shelving of the bill is a testament to the fact that initiatives for increasing regulation of ayahuasca are not consensual and sometimes they are seen as possible risk and an overreach by government bodies. As Sávio Dellano, the coordinator of ICEFLU's legal department, stated in an online event on the ban of ayahuasca by the French government: "Regulations themselves put a strain on us. It also puts us under greater surveillance by the state. And that is not interesting for us either. If the state thinks there should be regulations, we will comply because we have nothing to hide".[22]

In 2025, the *Agência Nacional de Vigilância Sanitária*—Anvisa *(National Health Surveillance Agency)* banned the sale and advertising of ayahuasca and its derivatives, raising significant concerns within the ongoing debate about the regulation of the drink, particularly in relation to the intersections of religion, commerce, and therapy (Minuano, 2025). While Anvisa's actions reaffirm the protection of ayahuasca's ritualistic and religious use, as enshrined by previous rulings, they also underscore the tension between maintaining ayahuasca restricted to the religious context and its increasing commercialization, particularly in urban contexts. The decision to ban the sale of ayahuasca on digital platforms, despite the growing

[21] CONAD's resolutions are considered normative acts. A normative act refers to a legal instrument that sets out norms, standards, or regulations. While laws are created by legislative bodies, normative acts are generally issued by executive authorities or agencies. In most legal systems, laws have a higher authority and broader scope than normative acts.

[22] https://www.youtube.com/watch?v=MNNRxW2NJnM&t=3584s

global interest and market, reflects a broader concern with protecting public health. However, it also points to the complex dynamics at play, where ayahuasca is simultaneously framed as both a religious sacrament and a potentially harmful substance, complicating its legal and cultural status.

The regulation of the religious use of ayahuasca in Brazil can be seen thus as a two-sided coin. On the one hand, it guaranteed the safeguard and protection of ayahuasca groups from criminalization as drug users and traffickers. On the other hand, it created a set of guidelines that compelled them to conform their practices to the characteristics of other historically recognized religious expressions by stating that "religion" is not "commerce," "tourism," "therapy," nor "drug use." In a similar fashion to the historical categorization that portrayed the wine in the Catholic Church as the blood of Christ, ayahuasca had to be understood as a religious sacrament, now completely dissociated from the notion of drug use and abuse. In order for that to happen, however, ayahuasca groups had to abide by a normative framework that, despite being constructed through a dialogue with scholars and government bodies, put forward a number of recommendations and a set of restrictions to the use of ayahuasca in the country.

2.7 Between Drug, Religion and Culture

The Brazilian government's recognition of ayahuasca groups as legitimate religious and cultural expressions did not eradicate certain arguments and notions from the public debate, particularly those surrounding the category of "drug," which remained a recurring point of contention throughout the 2000s and 2010s. An example was the television program "MTV Debate," broadcast in March 2010, which focused on the issue of ayahuasca use in Brazil. Titled "Daime: drug or religion?," the program featured professionals from the fields of psychoanalysis, psychiatry, psychology, anthropology and toxicology, some of them members of ayahuasca groups or experts on the subject. As the title shows, one of the central issues of the debate was the contrast around two basic themes: drugs and religion. The legitimacy of the freedom of worship was underlined, but it was pointed out that the regulation of ayahuasca could set precedents for the legalization of other psychoactive substances, such as cocaine. Some of the measures adopted by CONFEN and later CONAD in relation to ayahuasca were highlighted, as well as the implications for institutional control mechanisms over psychoactive substances, underlining that the regulation process included investigations by legal and medical bodies, among others. Questions about the possibilities of therapeutic use, as well as the effects of ayahuasca on the body, its psychoactive compounds and contraindications from a pharmacological point of view were also discussed. Despite the drug controversy, the majority of the guests recognized the use of ayahuasca as a tradition and cultural expression, whether in the Indigenous context, or in the context of Santo Daime, Barquinha and UDV.

In February of the same year, *Isto É* magazine published an article—shortly after the publication of CONAD's 2010 resolution No. 1—titled *A encruzilhada do Daime* [The Daime Crossroads], addressing the recommendations of MWG Ayahuasca and problematizing the regulation of ayahuasca for religious purposes in Brazil. According to the report:

> It all started at the beginning of the last century, in the heart of the Amazon. Caboclos from the northeast, attracted by rubber extraction, immersed themselves in the centuries-old culture of the forest peoples, inevitably absorbing much of its essence. Soon the so-called ayahuasca religions were born, mostly Christian groups that incorporated the consumption of a hallucinogenic tea used by the Indigenous people into their rituals. Today, these same cults are at the center of a controversy that involves delicate and dangerous issues, such as religious freedom, drug trafficking and death. (Isto é, 05/02/2010).

Similar to the MTV show, the article highlighted the possible risks of the regulation of ayahuasca setting precedents for the establishment of religions that incorporate illicit drugs such as marijuana and cocaine, creating a public health problem. The article also addressed the groups' history, emphasizing that Santo Daime gained notoriety in the 1980s when it arrived in the urban centers of the southeast and south of Brazil, a time when there was a change in the profile of the followers, especially with the adhesion of artists, celebrities, college students and the urban middle classes. Finally, it reported on two recent deaths allegedly related to ayahuasca use: a young man who drowned hours after drinking the tea at an "independent cult," and the case of a young man, who supposedly had a history of using psychoactive substances, who died of a heart attack in the middle of an ayahuasca ceremony.

Another crucial incident at the time was the assassination of cartoonist Glauco, leader of a Daime church in Osasco, *Céu de Maria*, and his son by a person who used to attend the church. Given the fact that Glauco was a public figure and one of the main Brazilian cartoonist as the time, the news of his assassination had major impacts in media outlets, in academic circles and, of course, among ayahuasca groups, creating a huge buzz around the risks of ayahuasca. The incident led to the publication in March 2010 of high-profile article by Veja magazine, one of the biggest media outlets in the country. Titled "O psicótico e o Daime" (The Psycho and the Daime), the article focused mainly on the risks of people with mental disorders ingesting the brew, also pointing out the risk of drug interactions between DMT with other psychoactive substances. It also highlighted the fact that DMT is a controlled substance but stressed that plants with small amounts of the substance are not. The article underscored that CONFEN's decision to remove ayahuasca from DIMED's list of proscribed substances, allowing its religious use in 1987, was "the first in a succession of errors that culminated in the tea being consecrated as a 'sacred drink,' a title granted to the hallucinogenic substance by the Brazilian state last January" (Veja, 24/03/2010).

In contrast, some scholars spoke out, questioning the media's approach regarding the regulation of ayahuasca. Three articles by Labate (2009, 2010a, 2010b) addressed the media coverage on ayahuasca and highlighted supposedly gross errors in the *Isto É* and *Veja* magazines' reports. The first one focused exclusively on the treatment given by media outlets to the issue of drugs and the dilemmas of anthropology in face of the press (Labate, 2009). In the other articles, Labate (2010a, 2010b) denounces the sensationalist and misleading coverage of ayahuasca by Brazilian media outlets *Isto É* and *Veja*. She argues that both magazines reinforced prejudice and misinformation, using alarmist narratives to discredit ayahuasca-using religious groups such as Santo Daime and União do Vegetal. In *Isto É*'s *"As Encruzilhadas do Daime"* (2010), she highlights factual inaccuracies, including the false claim that the Brazilian government recently "legalized" ayahuasca, the unsubstantiated association of the brew with recent deaths, and erroneous assertions about addiction and trafficking. Similarly, in *Veja*'s *"Alucinação Assassina" (Assassin Hallucination)*, which links the murder of cartoonist Glauco to ayahuasca use, she exposes the magazine's alleged long-standing editorial bias, pointing out its failure to provide a balanced analysis of the case. She criticizes both articles for distorting facts, misrepresenting legal frameworks, and reinforcing negative stereotypes rather than engaging in a nuanced discussion about the regulation and cultural significance of ayahuasca. Labate warns that such media portrayals not only mislead the public but also threaten religious freedom and the right to cultural diversity.

This clash between media and academia underscores a broader struggle over who has the authority to define ayahuasca's use, legitimacy, and legality. While scholars like Labate emphasize cultural and religious rights, media portrayals often challenge state policies, fueling criticism of ayahuasca regulation. This tension became particularly evident in legislative efforts such as Bill 2491/10, introduced by Congressman Paes de Lira, which sought to overturn CONAD's resolution and prohibit ayahuasca in Brazil. According to the Bill project presented by Paes de Lira:

> The broad right to religion is of paramount importance, but all the constitutional provisions listed make it clear that the Constitution aims to extirpate the misuse of drugs from society. In view of the apparent conflict between constitutional norms, namely the broad right to religion and the prohibition of drug use and trade, the following reasoning must be made: which one is in the interest of society or of the community? The core of this reasoning is the principle of the supremacy of public interest over private interest. The use of a drug, even if it is a religious one, in this case "santo daime tea" or "ayahuasca," must be prohibited when it causes harm to the individual's health; this is the reason for banning drugs: the right to health, to life. These [rights] are unavailable and it is known that not only the user is a victim of their use, but society as a whole (Câmara dos Deputados, 2010, p. 3–4).

After facing strong criticism from scholars involved in the discussions on ayahuasca regulation in Brazil, the Bill was shelved in January 2011. The following year, the NatGeo Channel series *Tabu* dedicated an episode to ayahuasca, which aired in March 2012. The episode opens with a montage of Amazon rainforest imagery, Indigenous people, Santo Daime practitioners, and the brewing of ayahuasca. As the scenes shift rapidly, the narrator introduces the theme:

> Indigenous wisdom transformed into religion. For some, a path to spirituality, for others, just a drug consumed by fanatics. Ayahuasca, a drink with hallucinogenic properties, is said to have the power to open the doors of perception. [...] Proponents of ayahuasca believe that the tea has the power to open new frontiers of the mind. But some people consider the tea to be a dangerous narcotic, which can drive people out of control and even cause tragedies. A powerful drink, a controversial one, a taboo (Tabu, Ayahuasca, broadcast on the NatGeo Channel on March 28, 2012).

Despite the formal recognition of ayahuasca as a legitimate cultural and religious expression by government bodies in Brazil, it remained a topic of controversy. The portrayal of ayahuasca groups as dangerous organizations consuming a hallucinogenic brew persisted in public discourse. However, recent studies have highlighted a shift in the media's portrayal of ayahuasca. In his dissertation, Lima (2024) analyzed over 700 news articles about ayahuasca, revealing that, over the past decade, the media has increasingly associated the brew with the potential therapeutic benefits of a new pharmaceutical treatment for conditions like depression, anxiety, PTSD, and substance abuse. Lima attributes this shift to two main factors: the rise of a psychedelic niche in media outlets, driven by professionals specializing in psychedelics, and the growing body of research into ayahuasca's therapeutic potential, such as studies by the neuroscientists at the Instituto do Cérebro (Brain Institute) of the Federal University of Rio Grande do Norte.

Notwithstanding Lima's findings indicating a recent shift in media coverage, there are still articles that question the legitimacy of ayahuasca's religious use, labeling it as a dangerous substance. One such example is the media coverage surrounding the drowning death of Nizo Neto, the grandson of famed Brazilian comedian Chico Anysio. In several outlets, Nizo's parents linked his death to the "abuse" of ayahuasca and his involvement with a neoshamanic group, *Porta do Sol*. In the article "Chá de ayahuasca pode, sim, causar psicose e até matar" [Ayahuasca Tea Can, Indeed, Cause Psychosis and Even Kill], Giulia Vidale (2024) adopts a critical stance, arguing that ayahuasca consumption can lead to psychosis and even death. Published by *Veja*, the article cites Nizo Neto's case, suggesting that ayahuasca may have played a role in his death. The journalist quotes experts who state that "the substance is hallucinogenic and, like any other drug with such an effect, it can cause permanent psychiatric disorders and even kill" (Vidale, 2024).

These cases highlight that the debate over the legitimacy of ayahuasca use is far from settled. Rather than reaching a consensus, the issue remains mired in complex symbolic disputes that span political, academic, and media spheres. While concerns about its potential for abuse and harm continue to surface, they have not yet succeeded in undermining the Brazilian government's position on the matter. Despite the ongoing criticisms, the government's recognition of the use of ayahuasca as a culturally and religiously significant expression has remained largely intact, with these opposing narratives failing to alter the established cultural and legal framework supporting its religious use.

2.8 The Regulation of the Religious Use of Ayahuasca in Brazil

The emergence of the religious use of ayahuasca as an object of public interest began to take shape in the 1980s, as the phenomenon gained increasing visibility, becoming a major media story, the subject of academic production, and the object of public policies, especially after the banning of ayahuasca in 1985, with the inclusion of *B. caapi* on DIMED's list of controlled substances. This scenario encouraged ayahuasca groups to question the government's decision. Meetings were held and working groups formed to investigate, analyze, collect data, interview members of ayahuasca groups, and assess health risks. These involved professionals and experts from various fields of knowledge, and in some occasions, representatives of ayahuasca groups themselves. Opinions, reports, articles, resolutions, newspaper and magazine articles, documentaries, and television programs were created within this landscape. At the same time, academics and ayahuasca groups organized congresses and scientific events on the subject. The first psychiatric and psychological evaluations and medical studies began in the country. Meanwhile, a growing number of dissertations, theses, and books, mainly in the humanities, were produced.

In the midst of this historical process, a series of actors engaged in disputes over the possibility of banning or regulating ayahuasca, which eventually culminated in processes to establish parameters and define the acceptable uses of the drink in the country. Between 1980 and 2010, physicians, psychiatrists, psychologists, anthropologists, sociologists, philosophers, social workers, journalists, representatives of government bodies, and members of ayahuasca groups have been involved in the definition of the acceptable parameters for the use of ayahuasca in the country.

In hindsight, the analysis of the disputes surrounding the process of regulating ayahuasca for religious use in Brazil has shown how anthropological frameworks, methods, categories, and arguments were progressively incorporated into the drafting of public policies, to the detriment of a biomedical discourse that associated ayahuasca with the notion of a drug and hallucinogen. The anthropological discourse was crucial for the development of the framework that portrayed the religious use of ayahuasca as a socio-integrative religious and cultural expression from the Amazon region, associated with Indigenous and Afro-Brazilian ancestral traditions. As a result, the use of ayahuasca in Brazil has shifted from a relatively unknown phenomenon to a practice regulated by government bodies. Despite pressure from some segments to associate its use with the practice of drug abuse and trafficking, the religious use of ayahuasca in Brazil has become worthy of state protection and safeguarding as part of the traditional religious and cultural expressions of the country. This process culminated in the public recognition of ayahuasca groups as legitimate representatives of the Brazilian religious pantheon. In contrast, this recognition was accompanied by a process of standardization of what was understood as the responsible use of ayahuasca, creating guidelines and recommendations for the practices of ayahuasca groups.

It should be noted that, although the process of regulating ayahuasca presents an important and relatively recent case study of the processes of the making of a "religion" in the public arena, this phenomenon is not new in the Brazilian context. As Montero (2006, 2009) argues, historically, the formation of the Brazilian state as an autonomous political sphere was marked by intense conflicts over the autonomy and freedom of non-Christian practices. The conflicts in question centered mainly on the repression of certain practices and groups in the name of a public order based on the hygienist scientific framework of the time and fostered debates that involved a series of social actors, including jurists, journalists, physicians, scholars, and members of the Catholic Church (Montero, 2006).

The situation intensified through the enactment of the Penal Code of 1890, when a series of practices were classified under the labels of "quackery," "charlatanism," and "illegal practice of medicine" (Schritzmeyer, 2004, p. 76). The public acceptance of these expressions as religions was a direct reaction to the medical-legal repression of a series of practices perceived as threats to public morality, such as trance mediumship, possession, and unconventional therapeutic practices. As Montero points out, the new Brazilian Republic was faced with the challenging question of defining what could be considered "religion," a phenomenon that had the right to legal protection from the state, and what should be classified as "magic acts," understood as an antisocial practice that needed to be repressed. Consequently, the ways in which the practices present in Umbanda, Candomblé, and Kardecist Spiritism have been re-signified as religious are largely the result of a process of reframing popular expressions into the notion of religion. In light of this, Kardecist mediums and *pais de santo*[23] had to create new repertoires based on Catholic cultural codes to escape the constraints of the new legal framework developed by the Brazilian state.

One can argue thus that the characterization of the religious use of ayahuasca in Brazil as a public issue is also related to the ways in which popular expressions that emerged at the margins of the state have been dealt with in the country. These processes encompassed the domains of the Brazilian state, but they also surpassed them, by comprising a myriad of actors mobilized to construct a framework that portrayed these practices as legitimate cultural and religious expressions. While in the cases of Umbanda and Kardecism, the shift referred to the transformation from "quackery," "witchcraft," and the "illegal practice of medicine" to "religion," in the case of ayahuasca, the main shift was the passage from "drug" to "religion" and, as we will see in the next chapter, to "cultural heritage."

Historically, the formation of the Brazilian state and the organization of civil society imposed the invention of religions. In a similar fashion to African Brazilian religions and Kardecist Spiritism in the passage from the nineteenth to the twentieth century, there was a historical and political process that started in the 1980s, whose end result portrayed ayahuasca groups in all their complexities and differences within the well-established notion of "religious organizations." The recognition process as religions allocated these institutions in a particular place with specific access to the Brazilian state and participation in civil society. Within the realm of religions, however, it is noteworthy that the legal space that ayahuasca groups were able to occupy was, as in Candomblé and Umbanda, relegated to the protection of cultural traditions of African Brazilians and Indigenous peoples, portrayed as a vital element of Brazilian religiosity. The use of ayahuasca was thus understood as religious because it was first conceived as part of an Amazonian cultural tradition. And it was

[23] "Pai de Santo" is a term used in Brazil to refer to the spiritual leader in Afro-Brazilian religions, particularly Candomblé and Umbanda.

through the framework of culture and the anthropological discourse that the recognition as religions was envisioned. To become recognized as a religion, the use of ayahuasca first had to be conceived as a cultural phenomenon, and what field was better suited for this task than anthropology and its practitioners?

References

Abreu Jr, J. S. (2016). *A cura no Santo Daime: Concepções de saúde e doença nas linhas do Alto Santo*. Master's Thesis, Anthropology, Federal University of Bahia.

Acre. (1991). *Carta de Princípios das entidades religiosas usuárias do chá Hoasca*. Rio Branco. http://udv.org.br/wp-content/uploads/2016/12/carta_p.pdf

Antunes, H. F. (2011). A literatura antropológica e a reconstituição histórica do uso da ayahuasca no Brasil. *R@U: Revista de Antropologia Social dos Alunos do PPGAS-UFSCAR, 3*(2), 76–103.

Araújo, D. (2024, July 10). Dráulio Araújo: "O Brasil é o país mais psicodélico do mundo". *Breeza*. https://breeza.com.br/2024/07/10/draulio-araujo-o-brasil-e-o-pais-mais-psicodelico-do-mundo/

Callaway, J. C. (2011). Projeto Hoasca: Um depoimento pessoal 15 anos depois. In J. Bernardino-Costa (Ed.), *Hoasca: Ciência, sociedade e meio ambiente* (pp. 75–82). Mercado de Letras.

Câmara dos Deputados. (2010). *Projeto de Lei n.° 2491/2010* [Bill No. 2491/2010]. Câmara dos Deputados.

Conselho Federal de Entorpecentes (CONFEN). (1985). *Resolução no 04/85*. Brasília. https://www.bialabate.net/pdf/texts/Resolu%C3%A7%C3%A3o%20n%C2%BA04%20de%201985.htm

Conselho Federal de Entorpecentes (CONFEN). (1986). *Resolução no 06/86*. Brasília. https://www.bialabate.net/pdf/texts/resolucao_06.pdf

Conselho Federal de Entorpecentes (CONFEN). (1987). *Relatório Final do Grupo de Trabalho 1987*. Brasília. http://www.bialabate.net/wp-content/uploads/2008/08/Relatório-Final-GT-Confen-1987.pdf

Conselho Federal de Entorpecentes (CONFEN). (1992). *Parecer do Dr. Domingos Bernardo de Sá – 02/06/1992*. Brasília.

Conselho Nacional de Políticas sobre Drogas. (2002). *Resolution No. 26 of 12/31/2002*. Brasília. https://www.bialabate.net/pdf/texts/resolucao_26.pdf

Conselho Nacional de Políticas sobre Drogas. (2004a). *Opinion of the Technical-Scientific Advisory Chamber – 08/17/2004*. Brasília. https://www.bialabate.net/pdf/texts/parecer_catc.pdf

Conselho Nacional de Políticas sobre Drogas. (2004b). *Resolution No. 05 – 11/04/2004*. Brasília. https://www.bialabate.net/pdf/texts/resolucao_05.pdf

Conselho Nacional de Políticas sobre Drogas. (2006). *Final Report – Multidisciplinary Working Group on Ayahuasca*. Brasília. https://www.bialabate.net/pdf/texts/gmt_conad_port.pdf

Conselho Nacional de Políticas sobre Drogas. (2010). *Resolution No. 01 – 01/25/2010*. Brasília. https://www.bialabate.net/wp-content/uploads/2008/08/Resolucao-Conad-_1_25_01_2010.pdf

Couto, F. L. R. (1989). *Santos e Xamãs – Estudos do uso ritualizado da ayahuasca por caboclos da Amazônia, e, em particular, no que concerne sua utilização sócio-terapêutica na doutrina do Santo Daime*. Master's Thesis, Anthropology, University of Brasília.

Couto, F. L. R. (2004). Santo Daime: Rito da Ordem. In B. C. Labate & W. S. Araújo (Eds.), *O uso ritual da ayahuasca* (2nd ed., pp. 177–205). Mercado das Letras/FAPESP.

Divisão de Medicamentos (DIMED). (1985). *Portaria no 02/85*. Brasília. https://www.bialabate.net/wp-content/uploads/2008/08/Portaria-02-de-marco-de-1985-da-DIMED.pdf

Folha de São Paulo. (1982, August 17). *Seita no Acre usaria drogas em cerimônias*.

Fróes, V. (1983). *História do povo Juramidam: A cultura do Santo Daime*. Suframa.

Goulart, S. L. (2004). *Contrastes e continuidades em uma tradição amazônica: As religiões da ayahuasca*. Doctoral dissertation, Anthropology, Universidade de Campinas.

Goulart, S. L. (2008). Estigmas de grupos ayahuasqueiros. In B. C. Labate et al. (Eds.), *Drogas e cultura: Novas perspectivas* (pp. 251–288). EDUFBA.
Isto É. (2010, February 5). *A encruzilhada do Daime.*
Labate, B. C. (2000). *A reinvenção do uso da ayahuasca nos centros urbanos.* Master's Thesis, Anthropology, University of Campinas.
Labate, B. C. (2004). *A reinvenção do uso da ayahuasca nos centros urbanos.* Mercado de Letras/FAPESP.
Labate, B. C. (2005). Dimensões legais, éticas e políticas da expansão do consumo da ayahuasca. In B. C. Labate & S. L. Goulart (Eds.), *O uso ritual das plantas de poder* (pp. 397–458). Mercado de Letras.
Labate, B. C. (2009). As encruzilhadas da imprensa: Uma análise da reportagem de capa da revista IstoÉ sobre a ayahuasca. *R@U: Revista de Antropologia Social dos Alunos do PPGAS-UFSCar, 1*(2), 105–115.
Labate, B. C. (2010a). Notas sobre a pseudo-reportagem de capa da revista IstoÉ sobre a ayahuasca. *Casa Amarela.* http://neip.info/novo/wp-content/uploads/2015/04/notas-sobre-a-pseudo-reportagem-de-capa-da-revista-isto-sobre-a-ayahuasca.pdf
Labate, B. C. (2010b). A lamentável reportagem da revista Veja sobre a morte de Glauco. *Casa Amarela.* http://neip.info/novo/wp-content/uploads/2015/04/lamentavel_veja_glauco_labate.pdf
Labate, B. C., & Araújo, W. S. (Eds.). (2002). *O uso ritual da ayahuasca.* FAPESP/Mercado das Letras.
Labate, B. C., Santana de Rose, I., & Guimarães dos Santos, R. (2008). *Ayahuasca religions: A comprehensive bibliography & critical essays.* MAPS.
Lévi-Strauss, C., et al. (1970). Raça e história. In *Raça e ciência.* São Paulo: Perspectiva.
Lima, V. M. (2024). *Da floresta amazônica aos laboratórios: Dinâmicas sociotécnicas na legitimação e deslegitimação da ayahuasca entre as décadas de 1960 a 2010.* Doctoral Dissertation, Social Sciences, Federal University of ABC.
MacRae, E. (2005). Santo Daime e Santa Maria: Usos religiosos de substâncias psicoativas lícitas e ilícitas. In B. C. Labate & S. L. Goulart (Eds.), *O uso ritual das plantas de poder* (pp. 459–487). Mercado de Letras.
MacRae, E. (2008). A elaboração das políticas públicas brasileiras em relação ao uso da ayahuasca. In B. C. Labate et al. (Eds.), *Drogas e cultura: Novas perspectivas* (pp. 289–314). EDUFBA.
Manchete. (1984, January 14). *Santo Daime: a droga da Amazônia.*
Minuano, C. (2025). *Anvisa bans the selling and advertising of ayahuasca in Brazil.* Chacruna Institute for Psychedelic Plant Medicines. https://chacruna.net/anvisa-bans-the-selling-and-advertising-of-ayahuasca/
Montero, P. (2006). Religião, pluralismo e esfera pública no Brasil. *Revista Novos Estudos, 74*, 47–65.
Montero, P. (2009). Secularização e espaço público: a reinvenção do pluralismo religioso no Brasil. *Etnográfica, 13*(1), 7–16.
Jornal do Brasil. (1983, November 6). *Seita do Santo Daime usa em rituais alucinógeno amazônico.*
Paiva, A. (1995, November 5). A outra turma do chá. *Jornal do Brasil, B*, 12.
Rose, I. S. (2010). *Tata endy rekoe – Fogo Sagrado: Encontro entre os Guarani, a ayahuasca e o Caminho Vermelho* (Doctoral dissertation, Universidade Federal de Santa Catarina, Florianópolis).
Sá, D. B. (1996). A consciência da expansão: Discursos sediciosos. *Crime, Direito e Sociedade, 1*(2), 145–174.
Schritzmeyer, A. L. P. (2004). *Sortilégios de saberes: Curandeiros e juízes nos tribunais brasileiros (1900-1990).* IBCCRIM.
Silva, C. M. (1983). *O Palácio de Juramidan: O Santo Daime, um ritual de transcendência e despoluição.* Master's Thesis, Anthropology, Federal University of Pernambuco.
Souza, V. M. (2010). *Ayahuasca, identificando sentidos: O uso ritual da bebida na União do Vegetal.* Master's thesis, Social Sciences, Federal University of Maranhão.

Tófoli, M. (2022). Quantas pessoas consomem ayahuasca no Brasil? *Chacruna Institute* for Psychedelic Plant Medicines. https://www.chacruna-la.org/artigos-pt/quantas-pessoas-consomem-ayahuasca-no-brasil

Tukano, D. (2022). Ayahuasca e os desafios dos conhecimentos indígenas diante da globalização. https://www.daiaratukano.com/post/ayahuasca-e-os-desafios-dos-conhecimentos-ind%C3%ADgenas-diante-da-globaliza%C3%A7%C3%A3o#:~:text=No%20Brazil%20seu%20uso%20tradicional,%2C%20Makuna%2C%20Manchinery%2C%20Matis%2C

Veja. (1983, September 11). *Divine Trip: A Hallucinogen that Leads to a Religious Trance.*

Veja. (2010, March 24). *O psicótico e o Daime.*

Vidale, G. (2024). *Chá de ayahuasca pode, sim, causar psicose e até matar.* https://veja.abril.com.br/saude/cha-de-ayahuasca-pode-sim-causar-psicose-e-ate-matar

Chapter 3
Who's Heritage Is It? The Patrimonialization of the Religious Use of Ayahuasca in Brazil

Since the mid-1980s, the use of ayahuasca in Brazil had been framed within the confines of drug policy. Yet, in a remarkable twist, from the mid-2000s onwards, the Brazilian government began to shift its stance, not only regulating its use but embracing it as a symbol of cultural heritage. This transformation was part of a broader movement, fueled by the rise of heritage policies aimed at preserving a specific set of cultural expressions. The notion of "intangible heritage"—an idea that had taken root in Brazil since the late 1970s—finally gained legal recognition in the 1988 Constitution. This landmark document, crafted in the wake of a long military dictatorship, declared pluralism as the cornerstone of the Brazilian state, setting the stage for the government's eventual recognition of ayahuasca as part of the nation's diverse cultural tapestry.

While the inclusion of diversity as a fundamental right set the stage for a wave of groups and associations to adopt the language of social rights promotion as a means of public advocacy (Montero, 2018), the recognition of "intangible cultural heritage" in the Brazilian Constitution expanded the scope of cultural heritage policies, enabling a wider range of practices and traditions to gain legal recognition. This shift spurred various institutions and communities to assert their cultural legacies, seeking acknowledgment for their rituals, celebrations, and knowledge as valuable national assets. The reach of this new framework has proven extensive, encompassing a broad spectrum of cultural expression (Antunes, 2023).

This new framework emerged with the establishment of a normative mechanism by the Instituto do Patrimônio Histórico e Artístico Nacional (Institute of National Historical and Artistic Heritage - IPHAN, 2000) in the 2000s, marking the creation of the National Inventory of Cultural References (INRC), led by anthropologist Antônio Arantes. According to Arantes, the development of the INRC was driven by the need to establish a democratic understanding of cultural heritage, providing a tool for identifying, documenting, and preserving intangible cultural expressions. He emphasizes that the scope of the INRC was grounded in the tools and methodologies of the social sciences, especially anthropology, reflecting the need for a

H. Fernandes Antunes, *Religion, Drug, or Cult?*, Law and Religion in a Global Context 5, https://doi.org/10.1007/978-3-032-04368-9_3

specific approach to intangible heritage in response to evolving heritage policies.[1] Regarding the INRC methodology, Arantes states (2009, p. 7–8):

> This methodology considers, above all, that the identification of significant cultural practices must start from the values attributed by the social groups involved. [...] And it was not us who conceived things this way; it's the new constitutional text that links the expressions that make up the nation's cultural heritage to the references that are important to the identities of the social groups that are part of the Brazilian nation. Now, the almost unsolvable problem faced by the policymaker is to identify the social groups that make up the nation. This is a serious issue that requires very complex decisions. Not just decisions of a technical nature, but basically decisions of a political nature.

One can see thus that the parameters stipulated by the Brazilian government regarding intangible heritage policies focus on the actors themselves, their values, practices and knowledge, identifying them as "cultural assets" of the Brazilian nation. The undeniable emphasis placed on the values and knowledge of social groups did not exclude, however, the need for experts to take an increasing role in developing methodologies and categories to identify intangible cultural expressions. As Arantes points out, perhaps the most pressing and difficult challenge was the fact that these identification processes frequently involved decisions of a "political nature."

This complexity is evident in the ongoing process of recognizing the religious use of ayahuasca as intangible cultural heritage. It highlights the disputes surrounding heritage policies, which frequently transcend policy boundaries and intersect with academic, political, and legal realms. These disputes involve a variety of actors who work in collaboration or opposition, forging alliances, developing and contesting categories. These ongoing tensions are not only influencing the future direction of heritage policies on ayahuasca but, in some cases, are questioning the capacity and legitimacy of the Brazilian state to produce policies that can truly reflect the diverse visions and aspirations of the groups involved in this multifaceted process.

3.1 The Religious Use of Ayahuasca as Intangible Cultural Heritage

In September 2006, the facilities of the *Centro de Iluminação Cristã Luz Universal* (Center of Illumination Universal Christian Light—CICLU-Alto Santo), the church founded by Mestre Irineu in the outskirts of Rio Branco, were listed as historical and cultural heritage in Acre by a decree issued by Governor Jorge Viana and the mayor of Rio Branco Raimundo Angelim (Labate 2010d, p.1). This initiative marked an important achievement for the Santo Daime church, solidifying its relationship with both state and local governments. It represented a significant historical

[1] According to IPHAN's INRC Application Manual, the goal was to identify and document "cultural assets to meet the demand for recognition of assets that represent the cultural diversity and plurality of the groups that make up society" (Iphan, 2000, p. 8).

shift, heralding the beginning of a crucial change in which ayahuasca moved beyond the scope of drug policies to be recognized as regional and national cultural heritage.

The following year, the Câmara Temática das Culturas Ayahuasqueiras (Thematic Chamber of Ayahuasca Cultures) was established within the Municipal Council on Cultural Policies of the Fundação Garibaldi Brasil (Garibaldi Brazil Foundation) in Rio Branco. The committee was composed of members who had played an active role in the development of the cultural heritage field in the region. Its primary objectives were to address the challenges and propose solutions in areas such as culture, health, education, and the environment, fostering dialogue between various government bodies and non-governmental institutions (Neves, 2011). A decade later, on July 30, 2018, the Governor of Acre, Tião Viana, signed Bill 3399, officially establishing Ayahuasca Culture Day in the state, to be celebrated on November 24. This date was chosen to commemorate the signing of the "Charter of Principles of the Religious Entities that Use the Hoasca Tea" in 1991.[2] Despite the undeniable significance of these initiatives, their impact was initially confined to the local and state levels.

In 2008, thanks to the efforts of local groups and Acre state authorities, ayahuasca gained national attention as a subject of heritage policy. This was sparked by a formal request submitted to the IPHAN, seeking the recognition of the religious use of ayahuasca as an intangible cultural heritage of Brazil. The request stemmed from a collaborative effort involving representatives from Santo Daime (CICLU-Alto Santo), Barquinha, UDV, and cultural foundations in Acre, such as the Fundação de Cultura e Comunicação Elias Mansour (Elias Mansour Culture and Communication Foundation) and the Garibaldi Brazil Foundation. Marcos Vinicius Neves[3] addressed the discussions that led to the request:

> This process basically started three years ago [2006], when we had a meeting with the cultural foundations, both the State Foundation and the Municipal Foundation, and the office of congresswoman Perpétua Almeida (PCdoB—Communist Party of Brazil), as well as the leaders and representatives of the more traditional centers here in Acre, specifically Alto Santo, Barquinha and União do Vegetal. So, we decided that the time had come [...] to start an affirmative action in a completely different direction, a new approach, which is to recognize traditional ayahuasca cultures, [...] affirming not only the cultural expression, but also the historical trajectory of these pioneer and traditional communities that brought hope to the national culture as a whole.[4]

---

[2] https://udv.org.br/blog/estado-do-acre-institui-dia-da-cultura-ayahuasqueira/

[3] A historian and archaeologist, he was one of the key proponents of the patrimonialization request submitted to IPHAN. Neves played a significant role in the public sector's cultural heritage efforts in the State of Acre, working for 2 years at the Fundação Garibaldi Brasil and later spending 6 years at the Department of Historical Heritage of the State Government and the State's Cultural Foundation. Since 2005, he has served as the Director-President of the Municipal Culture Foundation of Rio Branco. Interview with Beatriz Labate, July 10, 2009. Available at: https://www.bialabate.net/texts/ayahuasca-como-patrimonio-imaterial-da-cultura-brasileira

[4] Interview with Beatriz Labate held on July 10, 2009. https://www.bialabate.net/texts/ayahuasca-como-patrimonio-imaterial-da-cultura-brasileira

According to Neves, it was a matter of setting new guidelines for public policies on ayahuasca in Brazil, no longer focusing strictly on the religious aspect, but on affirmative policies to safeguard the history of ayahuasca communities and recognize the use of ayahuasca as a traditional Amazonian cultural expression. The request should be understood from the background of a specific political moment in Acre, in which several key players close to ayahuasca groups of Rio Branco were inserted in strategic government sectors.[5] Together, they marked the beginning of a different approach regarding public policies on ayahuasca, no longer related to drug policies, and inserted in the cultural heritage field (Assis & Rodrigues, 2017). Santo Daime member and local journalist, Antônio Alves, also addressed the primary scope of the request:

> The initial request's goal was to recognize the passage of ayahuasca—which is an indigenous heritage, not only in Brazil but in several countries, especially those closest to the Andes—to the Brazilian culture. This passage took place through the work of those ayahuasca practitioners who learned from the Indigenous people and who systematized religious doctrines—Mestre Daniel, Mestre Gabriel and Mestre Irineu. [The focus was on] their work, the initial formulation, their history and the systematization of ayahuasca as a Christian, spiritist, popular, northeastern religiosity based on all the inheritances they brought from Brazilian culture, and how this religiosity incorporates Indigenous culture and reworks this culture.[6]

From the beginning, there was a clear effort to dissociate the religious use of ayahuasca from the indigenous traditions, portrayed not as a specific Brazilian cultural expression, but as part of a larger cultural and geographical landscape that encompassed other South American countries. Although Alves recognized the role of Indigenous traditions for the urban religious use of ayahuasca, the Indigenous use of ayahuasca was not portrayed as particularly Brazilian per se. According to his statement, the initial request's goal was to identify and register the specific contributions and cultural expressions of ayahuasca religions, presented as part of Brazil's syncretic religious landscape.

Despite the intentions of its proponents, the IPHAN refused the initial request to register the use of ayahuasca as intangible heritage of Brazilian culture, based on the argument that food or drinks, as well as philosophies, theologies and beliefs were not subject to registration. Still, there was also an understanding on the part of the Department of Intangible Heritage (DPI) at the IPHAN that the agency could face external pressures or future claims, due to the fact that the request did not include some ayahuasca groups, nor the several Indigenous ethnic groups that consume ayahuasca. There was, above all, a concern that Indigenous peoples could claim that

[5] Among these actors, it is worth mentioning congresswoman Perpétua Almeida; journalist Antônio Alves, from CICLU-Alto Santo, and a member of the *Partido dos Trabalhadores* (Workers' Party—PT) and president of the Elias Mansour Culture and Communication Foundation (FEM); historian Marcos Vinícius Neves (cited above), the federal judge Jair Facundes, a friend of CICLU, among others (Assis & Rodrigues, 2017).

[6] https://bialabate.net/mp3/toinho.mp3

the request was a usurpation of their knowledge, given that the registration was exclusively linked to certain religious groups[7] (Iphan *apud* Neves, 2017, p. 163).

Notwithstanding the initial refusal, the IPHAN designated the creation of the National Inventory of Cultural References (INRC). In September 2011, the institution started a bidding process to select the organization responsible to carry out the inventory. The company that won the bid, whose managers are members of a UDV church in Rio Branco, set up a research team that included the participation of several scholars, including anthropologists experts in ayahuasca such as Wladimyr Sena Araújo, Sandra Goulart and Edward MacRae (Labate & Goulart, 2016, 7–8). According to Edson Lodi—journalist, poet, and UDV member—who was involved in the process, the research team met in Rio Branco in February 2012. At that time, the members of the group participated in a training course which was attended by the IPHAN superintendent in the state and technicians from the institution, representatives of Indigenous communities, and officials from the *Fundação Nacional dos Povos Indígenas* (Indigenous Peoples National Foundation—FUNAI). As attested by Lodi, one of the researchers' primary aims was to make it possible for ayahuasca groups to be informed of the research group's activities and to encourage them to take part in the inventory.[8]

Three years later, in March 2015, representatives of Alto Santo, Barquinha and UDV presented a new request, signed jointly with the then Governor of the State of Acre and the Mayor of Rio Branco, to the IPHAN proposing to advance the recognition of the practices already researched by the agency. In response, in June 2015, the IPHAN reaffirmed the importance of including Indigenous uses of ayahuasca in the registration process, along with the need to expand the research to other communities. Hence, an executive project was developed to gather data on Indigenous practices linked to ayahuasca. The Department of Intangible Heritage pointed out, however, that the execution of the project, in the terms in which it was drawn up, required complex logistics and high costs, which made its implementation unfeasible (Dias, 2024, p. 2). It should be noted that in the previous year, the IPHAN had established several recommendations for the research team, which proceeded to elaborate their report. This was the first of the three stages of the register process. The Final Report of this stage, with an analysis that addressed the social, pharmacological, legal and religious aspects of the use of ayahuasca, was completed in 2015, and presented in Rio Branco in August 2017. According to Labate and Assis (2018, p. 224), the cultural assets that would be registered as intangible cultural heritage were not identified by then.[9]

---

[7] According to IPHAN: "The Advisory Board called for clarification regarding the cultural expression in question and the inclusion of Indigenous peoples in the process, considering that ayahuasca tea is knowledge originating from Indigenous communities. Therefore, they expressed concerns that the registration of the tea by other groups could be seen as a usurpation of their knowledge" (Iphan *apud* Barros, 2016, 248).

[8] https://udv.org.br/blog/inventario-cultural-da-ayahuasca/

[9] The content of the report has not yet been made public by the IPHAN.

Since then, despite the multiple efforts of the actors involved, the administrative process for registering the ritual use of ayahuasca as an intangible cultural asset on a federal level has not advanced. In 2024, Attorney General Lucas Dias started a procedure to investigate the paralysis of the process of registering the ritual use of ayahuasca and the IPHAN's possible failure to adopt the necessary measures for the protection and promotion of cultural assets related to the ritual use of ayahuasca in the state of Acre. According to Dias, the slowness of the administrative procedure had a significant impact on the Amazonian states of Brazil, where its use is widespread among both Indigenous and urban populations. Despite acknowledging the need to recognize Indigenous practices and those of other groups involved in the use of ayahuasca, Dias stressed that the cultural expression that was initially proposed for registration had particularities that justified a more circumscribed recognition process. He argued for the possibility of registering cultural assets related to the use of ayahuasca progressively by recognizing cultural practices with specific characteristics such as the religious use of ayahuasca by Santo Daime, UDV and Barquinha, without impeding the subsequent expansion of the research activity to cover other groups and Indigenous peoples (Dias, 2024, p. 3–5).

Despite institutional hurdles, the nearly decade-long standstill in the process illustrates the intricate disputes that have complicated the cultural inventory. Interestingly, while the institutional process has faltered, the ongoing debate surrounding ayahuasca's heritagization has sparked broader dynamics. Over time, new actors—who were not part of the initial request—have increasingly entered the conversation, questioning the underlying assumptions of the process and advocating for their inclusion in dialogues with state agencies.

3.2 Tensions and Disputes Surrounding the Recognition Process

In addition to the patrimonialization request, the ayahuasca religious groups in Acre have developed other strategies to strengthen their demands, such as organizing the "Seminar: Traditional Ayahuasca Communities," held in 2010 in Rio Branco. The seminar was proposed by the Thematic Chamber of Ayahuasca Cultures of Acre and the Municipal Council for Cultural Policies, with representatives from local ayahuasca religious groups, the Ministry of Culture (MinC), IPHAN, and the cultural foundations of Acre in attendance. During the event, the organizers called for the involvement of the Legislative Assembly and Acre's representatives in the National Congress, as well as municipal, state, and federal public authorities, to support the development of public policies for "ayahuasca cultures." Their main concerns were the recognition of their practices and the fight against religious intolerance and the stigma associated with ayahuasca[10] (Acre, 2010, p. 1).

While these groups' initiative to present ayahuasca as a shared cultural tradition in order to demand recognition from state agencies is noteworthy, it does not imply a consensus or a unified project among the groups that consume ayahuasca. On the contrary, the process of recognizing the religious use of ayahuasca as an intangible cultural heritage of Brazilian culture has been marked by tensions and disputes. The early 2010s, in particular, were characterized by negotiations and conflicts between ayahuasca groups and public institutions regarding their participation in IPHAN's cultural inventory. These disputes largely centered on defining the cultural references that would form the common ground among the different ayahuasca branches (Labate & Coutinho, 2014).

These tensions were particularly evident at events such as the I Encontro da Diversidade Ayahuasqueira (First Meeting on the Cultural Diversity of Ayahuasca), held in Rio de Janeiro in 2011. The meeting was organized by groups that had been excluded from the initial recognition request, including ICEFLU, as well as other ayahuasca groups and representatives of Indigenous ethnic groups from Acre. The event was supported by MinC and IPHAN and is often described as a reaction to the "Seminar: Traditional Ayahuasca Communities" held in Acre the previous year (Assis & Rodrigues, 2017). According to the organizers, the purpose of the meeting was to identify and register the "diversity of ayahuasca," expanding the patrimonialization request initiated by the ayahuasca groups in Acre. The event was notably critical of the initial request to IPHAN, particularly for its failure to include Indigenous peoples who use ayahuasca (Labate & Goulart, 2016, 8–9).

The conflicts can be illustrated by two documents that resulted from the meeting: the Manifesto da Diversidade Cultural Ayahuasqueira (Ayahuasca Cultural Diversity Manifesto) and the Carta para o Encontro da Diversidade Cultural Ayahuasqueira (Letter to the Ayahuasca Cultural Diversity Meeting) signed by Alex Polari, member of the ICEFLU doctrinal council. The "Manifesto"—signed by Santo Daime groups, independent ayahuasca organizations, and representatives of Indigenous peoples—reaffirmed the importance of the religious use of ayahuasca in Brazilian religiosity and culture, highlighting the need for broadening the diversity that characterizes the ayahuasca universe. According to the document:

> What we call the ayahuasca field nowadays went beyond the Amazon forest during the twentieth century, since its beginnings, being inserted in the capitals of practically all Brazilian states. They are the most diverse symbolic expressions that, beyond their immediate cataloging, express the Brazilian religious and cultural ethos, whose cradle can be found in the miscegenation of the Brazilian people, in its indigenous, Afro-descendant, Eastern and European expressions and manifestations. [...] The I Ayahuasca Cultural Diversity Meeting is the expression of the richness of this movement (Rio de Janeiro, 2011, p. 1–2).

[10] It is not uncommon for policies on intangible heritage to involve processes of social legitimation through the symbolic positivization of stigmatized practices, such as the production and selling of *acarajé* in Bahia. Historically persecuted and marginalized until the mid-twentieth century, it has become a Brazilian intangible cultural heritage, and a symbol of Bahian cuisine and traditional culture (Reinhardt, 2018).

The Manifesto also stressed the religious rights of the use of ayahuasca, emphasizing the need for more affirmative actions, such as those developed by the Minc. The document highlighted the importance of initiatives that give visibility to the cultural expressions based on the use of ayahuasca, expressing the willingness of the groups that attended the event to participate and contribute to the recognition of these cultural expressions as intangible heritage by IPHAN. In contrast, the letter sent by the ICEFLU representative presented a harsher tone regarding the ways in which the patrimonialization process was being conceived at that time. The initial criticism mentioned the non-inclusion of representatives of Indigenous peoples, ancestral holders of this heritage according to Polari, and condemned the exclusion of groups considered relevant to the tradition of the religious use of ayahuasca without any prior consultation or debate. Furthermore, Polari rejected the categorization given to ICEFLU, classified under the rubric of "eclectic."[11] According to the ICEFLU representative, it was not a matter of affirming the position of "traditional" or denying the classification of "eclectic," but problematizing the way in which the construction of "a 'theory of the 3 fields' (originators, traditional and eclectic) represents mainly an attempt at a political solution, instead of properly raising a rigorous methodological debate that could address the difficult issue of ayahuasca diversity" (de Alverga, 2011).

For the ICEFLU, the Brazilian state should have begun by inventorying the indigenous and pan-Amazonian ancestral origin of ayahuasca, moving on to contemporary developments, "covering both traditionalist and eclectic elements contained in the urban and genuinely Brazilian religious phenomenon of the Santo Daime Christian religions." According to Polari, ICEFLU considers "the sacramental brew the primary fact of the ayahuasca culture" and "along with its ritualized nature, authentic sacred alchemy, with an elaborate system of symbolic prescriptions and the beauty of its ceremonial, as the core of 'designating it as historical heritage'" (de Alverga, 2011).

In the following year, the Thematic Chamber of Ayahuasca Cultures and the Garibaldi Brasil Municipal Culture Foundation held the 1st Sectorial Forum of Ayahuasca Cultures of Rio Branco. According to the organizers, the aim of the forum was to update and resume the discussions of the Seminar "Traditional Ayahuasca Communities," held in 2010, and to inform the general public about their

[11] As stated by Labate and Goulart (2016, p. 7) the creation of a new classification arrangement is an important novelty in this debate, initiating a distinction between "originators," "traditional" and "eclectic" segments. The category "originators" encompasses the various indigenous ethnic groups that consume ayahuasca. The "traditional" category concerns the "three founding masters" of the three "ayahuasca branches," *Santo Daime* (CICLU-Alto Santo), *Barquinha* and UDV, which express traditional Amazonian culture, however, adopting a markedly Christian stance. The "eclectic" category, on the other hand, refers to the *Santo Daime* group ICEFLU—which vehemently rejects such a notion—and also includes other expressions, such as institutions classified under the "neo-ayahuascans" rubric. According to Marcos Vinícius Neves, the idea of this classification emerged in a meeting in 2007, in which leaders of the ayahuasca groups of Acre discussed with Federal Deputy Perpétua Almeida (PCdoB) about the possibilities of creating public policies focusing on ayahuasca (Neves, 2011, p. 176).

actions. During the event, there were several discussions on issues such as historical and cultural heritage, environmental preservation, socio-economic development, education, health, culture, leisure, urbanization, and security. Through the "2nd Letter from the Ayahuasca Communities of Rio Branco," the Forum approved a series of proposals to be forwarded to municipal, state and federal public bodies, with the aim of implementing policies and actions that promote ayahuasca cultures as a representative segment of Acre's culture. According to the document:

> All of us who sign this Charter publicly assume the commitment to work collectively for the development of Public Policies for Ayahuasca Traditional Communities, centered on democracy (in the commitment of public power with society), in citizen participation (which represents the permanent construction of an active citizenship), in the right to diversity, the affirmation of people and collectivities, and the strengthening of local cultural identities (Acre, 2012, p. 2).

Among the proposals approved for the cultural sector was support for the registration of the religious use of ayahuasca as State and National Intangible Heritage at the state and municipal levels. Beyond the national scope, they encouraged discussions to enable the future recognition, by UNESCO, of the religious use of Ayahuasca as an Intangible World Heritage, considering its Pan-Amazonian presence. The letter declared the support for carrying out the Inventory of Ayahuasca Cultures in partnership with the IPHAN, as well as reinforcing its interest in promoting research on the knowledge of "Traditional Ayahuasca Communities and Indigenous Peoples." The document also suggested the development of policies to value ayahuasca's masters and other keepers of the memories of traditional communities, as well as campaigns to raise awareness and combat prejudice against ayahuasca groups. It also highlighted the need for a compromise between Ayahuasca communities and Indigenous peoples, as well as the regulation and the right to transport ayahuasca for Indigenous peoples.

Despite declaring the need to establish a dialogue with Indigenous peoples regarding the recognition of the religious use of ayahuasca and the formal support to the Indigenous agenda, the tensions between the latter and the ayahuasca groups from Acre lingered. They were especially related to the non-inclusion of Indigenous peoples in the original request. In response, the actors who elaborated the request argued that they did not require the consultation of Indigenous peoples, because the Indigenous use of ayahuasca constituted a distinct phenomenon, associated with international Pan-Amazonian identity and culture, while the use made by ayahuasca religions was part of the national culture. Regarding the excluded groups classified as "eclectic," they stated that the request sent to IPHAN focused solely on the cultural traditions associated with the founding masters of the three Brazilian ayahuasca religions, but not on later developments.[12] Other disagreements about

[12] MacRae (n.d.) argues that this categorization is an arbitrary attempt by the Acre groups, who claim the title of "traditional," to exclude ICEFLU from the patrimonialization process. According to MacRae, ICEFLU is portrayed as a rupture with the original church founded by Raimundo Irineu Serra, despite its founder, Sebastião Mota de Melo, having been a direct follower of Irineu Serra and a member of the CICLU-Alto Santo between 1965 and 1975.

possible projects for ayahuasca patrimonialization can be observed in Marcos Vinícius Neves' speech, when interviewed by anthropologist Beatriz Labate about the specific focus of the request developed by the ayahuasca religious groups of Acre. According to Neves:

> Our focus is cultural, our focus is historical, not religious. [...] We cannot forget that the founding masters of the most traditional branches of ayahuasca had a common historical project. [...] They were very successful in inserting it into the local society, making an impressive transposition of expressions that were traditionally Indigenous [...] to Brazilian society. This is the project, this is the focus. It is an affirmative action that does not seek to deny anything that exists today [...] only to affirm the more precise delimitation of the social phenomenon that happened in the western Amazon, and the recognition of this as part of national culture. [...] And it seems to us, to all who participate in this movement, that this is what was relegated to the background, as ayahuasca began to be discussed in other areas.

One can see thus that there was an obvious disagreement regarding the possible paths for the patrimonialization of ayahuasca between the ayahuasca religious groups themselves. Other tensions were manifested at the II World Ayahuasca Conference, held in Rio Branco, in October 2016. As in the first conference, the event was organized by the Spanish NGO *International Center for Ethnobotanical Education, Research, and Service* (*ICEERS*) and was attended by representatives of various Indigenous ethnic groups of Acre, of ayahuasca religious groups, IPHAN representatives, as well as therapists, sociologists, anthropologists, physicians, politicians and local authorities (Labate & Assis, 2018). Regarding the IPHAN's position, there were questions concerning the intentions and expected outcomes for the process. According to Gusmão, who works at DPI/IPHAN-Brasília, the suggestion of registering ayahuasca with the INRC did not fit in any of the existing records in Brazil.

> The registration of ayahuasca is not possible. What we can do, considering the registration process, is register some cultural expression related to what we call a cultural system linked to the use of ayahuasca. A celebration? That would be possible! A specific knowledge that is suddenly related to preparing the brew or preparing the ceremony? We can register it. But the brew itself cannot be registered. It doesn't fit in any of those little boxes. It doesn't fit in any of those books (Gusmão *apud* Santos, 2018, p. 107).

The IPHAN representative refers to the four intangible heritage domains: knowledge, celebrations, expressions, places. Thus, ICEFLU's request that the registration should begin with the beverage itself did not fit the current legislation, as ayahuasca was not subject to registration, only the practices associated with it. In Gusmão's view, there was a bigger problem to be faced. Until that moment, a specific framework had not been defined that could fit the norms stipulated by the Brazilian legislation. Thus, the challenges in implementing public policies surpassed the difficulties of equating a multiplicity of voices and different demands. The need to consider the claims of actors within a pre-established legal and institutional framework required a prior negotiation process between state actors and the interested parties to define which practices not only should but could integrate the cultural inventory.

In addition to debates on the IPHAN recognition process, the event's organizers held a closed-door meeting to discuss proposals for recognizing ayahuasca as a cultural heritage of humanity by UNESCO. The universalist tone of the proposal was heavily criticized by Indigenous representatives, who opposed the idea of their knowledge being appropriated through international policies. Indigenous leaders also extended their critique to representatives of ayahuasca religions. According to Labate and Goulart (2017), they questioned the "authenticity," "originality," and "traditionality"—or lack thereof—of religious groups. As one Indigenous representative remarked, "While Mestre (Master) Irineu is a hundred years old, we are millenary" (MacRae, n.d.). These tensions revolve around notions of ancestrality and tradition, highlighting the divergences and the critical stance of some Indigenous leaders toward the claims of ayahuasca religions as bearers of knowledge surrounding the ritual use of ayahuasca.[13]

The dissatisfaction of Indigenous peoples was reaffirmed in the Carta Aberta dos Povos Indígenas do Acre / Brasil a II Conferencia Mundial da Ayahuaska (*Open Letter of the Indigenous Peoples of Acre, Brazil, to the II World Ayahuasca Conference*) (Acre, 2016). As stated in the document, despite the considerable number of Indigenous participants, they felt excluded from the event's conception and organization. The letter emphasized the need for active Indigenous participation in the ayahuasca patrimonialization process and recommended holding Indigenous meetings with the presence of government agencies responsible for the process. It also proposed the creation of an ethics council "to discuss the issue of origin and define criteria on the use and patrimonialization of ayahuasca" (Acre, 2016). Undoubtedly, the event marked an important milestone. From that moment on, various Indigenous peoples from Acre adopted a different political strategy, distancing themselves from neo-ayahuasca and religious groups in southeastern Brazil. Furthermore, their questioning of the "authenticity" and "originality" of ayahuasca religions, along with their efforts to develop an independent political agenda, signaled a shift in the Indigenous stance on ayahuasca. From then on, the priority became forging an exclusively Indigenous alliance to discuss the patrimonialization process.

Overall, the debates, disputes, and negotiations observed throughout the conference highlight the complexity of the political processes involved in recognizing cultural expressions as intangible heritage in Brazil. In the case of ayahuasca, this process reflects a redefinition of the debate, along with the emergence of new alliances and demands for recognition. In this shifting landscape, the growing presence and increasing leadership of Indigenous peoples have played a key role in challenging previously established categories and classifications in the public debate on ayahuasca use in Brazil. Indigenous groups have begun to organize themselves as a new

[13] Despite Indigenous criticism of ayahuasca religions, establishing historical connections to these traditions can also serve as a means of authenticating Indigenous practices. This is evident in the claims made by different Indigenous groups that they were the ones who introduced Mestre Irineu to ayahuasca, a narrative used to legitimize their role in the current landscape (Labate & Coutinho, 2014).

political force in the disputes over the patrimonialization of ayahuasca's religious use. Their perspectives and demands not only question the label of "traditional" attributed to ayahuasca religious groups but also challenge the legitimacy and capacity of the Brazilian state to address their concerns.

3.3 Original Rights and Political Protagonism of Indigenous Peoples

Although Indigenous peoples became involved in the public debate on the patrimonialization of ayahuasca in the 2010s, their presence in the urban ayahuasca scene—until then largely dominated by ayahuasca religions and neo-ayahuasca groups—dates back to the 2000s. Their activities included hosting multicultural festivals in Acre villages, leading workshops in major Brazilian cities, and organizing retreats and ceremonies for middle-class participants and foreigners (Labate & Coutinho, 2014). Notably, in the early 2000s, Indigenous leaders from certain Acre villages introduced a new economic model known as "ethnotourism," or "shamanic tourism" (Platero, 2018). While festivals celebrating the use of "forest medicines"—such as ayahuasca (*uni*), *sipá* (a plant used for fumigation), *rapé*[14] (*rumã*), and occasionally *sananga*[15] and *kambô*[16]—had already been taking place since the late 1990s, they initially attracted only a small number of non-Indigenous participants. However, by 2002, the festivals began to draw broader audiences, including municipal and state government representatives, corporate partners, and a growing number of Brazilian and international participants interested in experiencing Yawanawá practices (Platero, 2018, p. 131–132).

In the realm of public policy, Indigenous groups made their first significant entry into the patrimonialization debate approximately 4 months after the *Seminar: Traditional Ayahuasca Communities*. In August 2010, representatives of the Pano peoples met with the executive secretary of the Ministry of Culture, Alfredo Manevy, to emphasize the need for Indigenous participation in the patrimonialization process[17] (Labate & Coutinho, 2014). This initial initiative laid the groundwork for a

---

[14] Rapé is tobacco snuff used by Indigenous Amazonian peoples, made from finely ground tobacco (Nicotiana rustica) and other medicinal plants. It is traditionally blown into the nostrils using a pipe, promoting focus, grounding, and spiritual cleansing.

[15] Sananga is an eye drop made from the roots of the *Tabernaemontana* shrub, used by Indigenous groups in the Amazon for vision enhancement, spiritual purification, and energetic alignment. It is known for its intense burning sensation and is believed to sharpen perception and clear negative energies.

[16] Kambô is the name of the secretion produced by the giant leaf frog (*Phyllomedusa bicolor*), traditionally used as medicine by Indigenous peoples of the Amazon basin. It is applied by burning small points on the skin and placing the secretion directly onto the wounds, allowing it to enter the bloodstream.

[17] Although Indigenous peoples were included later in the public policy process regarding the religious use of ayahuasca, their political activism in Brazil is far from recent. Their engagement in

growing Indigenous presence in the debate, which gained momentum, particularly following the *II World Ayahuasca Conference*. As noted in the previous section, the event sparked strong reactions from Indigenous groups in the Amazon, who challenged the way the patrimonialization process was being conducted and demanded a more central role in shaping its direction.

Many of these criticisms were reiterated at the *I Yubaká Hayrá—Ayahuasca Indigenous Conference*, held from December 14–17, 2017, in the Poyanawa Indigenous Land, Acre. The event was organized by the *Organização dos Povos Indígenas do Rio Juruá* (OPIRJ), the *Organização dos Povos Indígenas de Tarauacá* (OPITAR), the *Organização dos Povos Indígenas do Rio Envira* (OPIRE), and the *Associação dos Seringueiros Kaxinawá do Rio Jordão* (ASKARJ) (Silva, 2018a). It was primarily an Indigenous-led gathering, bringing together leaders from the Juruá River and Alto Purus regions, alongside a few public officials, including representatives from the IPHAN. The event featured artistic exhibitions and ayahuasca ceremonies and was conceived, according to its organizers, as a response to the *II World Ayahuasca Conference*, particularly in reaction to the secondary role assigned to Indigenous peoples in that event.

The conference agenda covered several key topics, including the significance of ayahuasca as a cornerstone of Indigenous cultures in Acre, as well as experiences of sharing and disseminating ayahuasca as an Indigenous medicine within Brazil and internationally. It also addressed traditional practices surrounding its use, sustainability and management of plant species, the implications of National Council on Drug Policy (CONAD) resolutions for Indigenous communities, and the patrimonialization process (Dias, 2018). The conference opened with the reading of a letter written by indigenist Dedê Maia, an excerpt of which is transcribed below:

> I heard on several occasions from the organizers of the event (II World Ayahuasca Conference)—the Spaniards—when responding to our insistence on including Indigenous representatives on certain Western scientist roundtables, that "it was not an Indigenous conference, but a scientific conference." Or, they would arrogantly argue that "the Indigenous people were only special guests." But we understood otherwise. We saw the Indigenous representatives as the true hosts. These organizers were coming to our land—a land from which the scientific knowledge of the forest, known worldwide as ayahuasca, spread like a *samaúma* seed across the world a hundred years ago. We believed that the issues addressed by Western scientists were deeply relevant to Indigenous peoples, the guardians of this knowledge for centuries. However, the arrogance and Western scientific elitism, led by some so-called "doctors," prevented them from breaking away from the rigid academic format of their conferences. [...] Here, you are free to speak, to engage in dialogue, and to explore possible paths forward with the sacred and ancestral knowledge of Indigenous peoples (Maia, 2018).

Maia's letter delivered a pointed critique of the *II World Ayahuasca Conference*, highlighting underlying tensions between a "science of the forest" and "academic

---

the Brazilian public sphere dates back to the 1970s and gained further momentum during the country's redemocratization in the 1980s (Silva, 2018b). However, their activism initially centered on the struggle for land demarcation. Their involvement in the realm of cultural heritage is a more recent development, primarily involving Indigenous groups from the Amazon.

science," as well as the question of who should be considered guests and hosts in this debate. Beyond challenging the academic sphere's legitimacy in speaking about—and on behalf of—ayahuasca, the letter also raised critical concerns regarding the patrimonialization process and the role of the IPHAN. These issues were powerfully articulated in the speech of Benki Pianko, a prominent Indigenous leader from Acre and an Ashaninka representative. Benki directly questioned IPHAN's role in the ayahuasca heritage process, calling into question the agency's legitimacy in formulating policies that truly reflect the interests of Indigenous peoples.

> Who do these council participants think they are to conduct an evaluation process that is supposedly meant to defend the Indigenous right to use ayahuasca? Are we even interested in obtaining this resource? [...] We are the original people, experts on this plant, which is now being shared with others around the world. [...] So that they may understand how we use it as a tradition and also see how people today are choosing to use it, as a church (Benki Pianko *apud* Santos, 2018, 134).

Beyond questioning IPHAN's role, Benki's speech underscored the concept of "original people," emphasizing the fundamental role of Indigenous groups in the expansion of ayahuasca use, particularly among religious organizations. Notably, he drew a clear distinction between "tradition," framed as something inherently Indigenous, and "church." In Benki's speech, the use of ayahuasca by religious groups is not portrayed as a tradition in itself but rather as a new configuration of ayahuasca consumption that originates from Indigenous practices. In contrast, Biraci Júnior Yawanawá, leader of the Nova Esperança village, characterized religious groups as part of the broader traditions of ayahuasca use. Like Benki, however, he criticized IPHAN's role in the patrimonialization process, particularly the absence of Indigenous representation within the institution. He even proposed the possibility of recognizing different traditions of ayahuasca use through distinct patrimonialization processes tailored to each tradition.

> Who analyzes this? Is there a pajé (shaman) present to evaluate it alongside these people? In reality, the request for registration did not come from Indigenous peoples—it came from religious groups. Then, during the process, they remembered: Indigenous peoples use it too. [...] So, there are riverside communities, rubber tappers, Indigenous peoples, and ayahuasca religions. Each has its own way of using it, its own path, its own tradition. [...] What are the possibilities of having different registrations? (Biraci Júnior apud Santos, 2018, p. 132).

Biraci Júnior's speech emphasized the challenges of establishing universal parameters for patrimonialization processes and the difficulties in defining common characteristics that could encompass the various forms of ayahuasca consumption. Furthermore, the unclear potential reach, scope, and impacts of the recognition process raised significant concerns. As Biraci Júnior expressed: "To patrimonialize ayahuasca is to patrimonialize every relative of the one sitting here and those in the villages, because we are them, and they are us. Are we going to become your heritage? Are we going to be the heritage of the big cities, of the museums?" (Biraci Júnior apud Santos, 2018 p. 131). The questioning of the legitimacy of the ayahuasca patrimonialization process in relation to Indigenous peoples, as well as the suggestion to seek independent recognition from other ayahuasca groups, was also evident in other statements. According to Francisco Pianko, an Ashaninka leader:

> The issue of the origin of Kamarãmpi [ayahuasca] should not be a question for anyone—it belongs to Indigenous peoples. Because we know more about it than anyone else. [...] The widespread use they are trying to implement is also not up to Indigenous peoples. This is a matter of regulation, of placing Indigenous peoples within the same framework as other groups, which ultimately weakens our struggle, our achievements, and our rights. [...] We need to have our own way, our own rights (Francisco Pianko *apud* Santos, 2018, p. 133–134).

Once again, the call for an independent recognition process is made explicit. Pianko also argued that indigenous knowledge had been appropriated by other groups, and that incorporating the various expressions of ayahuasca use into a single process would dilute Indigenous demands. Daiara Tukano echoed this sentiment, even suggesting the development of an Indigenous notion of "heritage."

> To what extent do we really need to adapt to this entire system of recognizing cultural heritage? [...] We fought a battle for decades to have Indigenous rights recognized as original rights. This means that original rights precede those of anyone who has set foot on this land, claiming that their science is better, that it comes first, that it precedes ours. [...] Is it worth engaging in this process, or should we create our own process to recognize what our heritage is? What is heritage from the Indigenous perspective? Because those who should define the concept, the idea of heritage, are not white people. We need to have our own science, our own policy, our own definitions (Daiara Tukano *apud* Santos, 2018, p. 132–133).

Despite differences in the speeches, it is evident that questioning the legitimacy of IPHAN and its registration instruments, along with the call for a distinct patrimonialization process for Indigenous peoples, were recurring themes in the criticisms voiced by the speakers at the event. Daiara's inquiry about the limits of a "white" notion of heritage, highlighting the necessity of an Indigenous-defined version, is particularly notable. This criticism can be interpreted as either a radical challenge or even a break from the registration project championed by IPHAN, which allows claimants to participate but retains the authority to define heritage within the confines of its experts and technicians.

An analysis of these speeches reveals no singular stance on ayahuasca religions. However, the repeated emphasis on distinguishing Indigenous and religious uses of ayahuasca signals the emergence of a new Indigenous claim. Through these alliances, a clear agenda is taking shape—one that prioritizes Indigenous interests. This is evident in recurring calls for a patrimonialization process focused exclusively on Indigenous ayahuasca use. Indigenous leaders have led the criticism of IPHAN's legitimacy, denouncing its lack of dialogue with Indigenous Peoples and questioning its ability to address their needs.

A key outcome of the discussions at the I Ayahuasca Indigenous Conference was the drafting of the *Declaration of the 1st Brazilian Indigenous Ayahuasca Conference*, signed by representatives of various Indigenous groups present at the event. The letter criticizes the concept of 'diffuse rights,' arguing that it weakens Indigenous claims by placing Indigenous ayahuasca use on par with religious groups and other non-Indigenous entities (The Representatives of the Indigenous Peoples of the Juruá Valley 2017, p. 2). The document proposes several actions, including the presence of *pajés* in the IPHAN commission overseeing the ayahuasca

INRC. It also recommends that the recognition process align with Indigenous perspectives and calls for the formation of a Working Group to monitor IPHAN's efforts and other research on traditional medicines (The Representatives of the Indigenous Peoples of the Juruá Valley 2017, p. 3). Additionally, the declaration expresses concern over the perceived inappropriate use of ayahuasca by religious groups and others, particularly regarding its commercialization. It further accuses regulatory bodies of disrespecting the circulation of ayahuasca among Indigenous peoples. In response, it proposes that Indigenous associations be registered under the *Cadastro Nacional da Pessoa Jurídica* (CNPJ)[18] to facilitate the legal shipment of ayahuasca within Brazil. This issue is particularly pressing, as CONAD regulations require a CNPJ as a religious institution to receive, send, and transport ayahuasca.

As Indigenous peoples from the Amazon increasingly engage with Brazil's urban ayahuasca scene, they face challenges related to its circulation. Speaking at the I Indigenous Conference, Gusmão noted that registering ayahuasca as intangible cultural heritage would not solve transportation issues. According to the IPHAN representative, the agency had no control over cultural assets once registered. Instead, the responsibility falls to the National Anti-Drug Secretariat and the CONAD, the public agencies authorized to address this matter (Gusmão apud Santos, 2018, p. 108). The question of being registered as religious institutions, as per CONAD's stipulations, is another point of contention among Indigenous peoples. Some argue that the use of ayahuasca is inherently an Indigenous religion. For them, the problem lies in the need to institutionalize what is already seen as a fundamental part of Indigenous spirituality. Biraci Brasil, who has been prevented from traveling with ayahuasca and barred from airports in Acre on multiple occasions, illustrates this concern:

> Authorization? That's outrageous! Just like traditional and ancient knowledge, Christians have their Bibles all over the world (in hotels, on planes, in churches...). Muslims and the Quran are respected everywhere. What about our religion? (Biraci Brasil *apud* Santos, 2018, p. 136).

However, some adopt a more radical stance on the instruments created by the CONAD and the regulatory procedures established by the Federal Police. In fact, certain speeches have even questioned the legitimacy of the legal mechanisms set by public bodies regarding the use and circulation of ayahuasca by Indigenous peoples. This criticism is particularly evident in Francisco Pianko's speech:

> If we are going to use these instruments, creating organizations to be able to use our ayahuasca, we will be giving in, undermining ourselves. I think we need to look at this more closely and use these instances to educate these "bullies" [Federal Police]. [...] This is clearly not something that can be solved just by writing it on paper. This is a deeper process (Francisco Pianko *apud* Santos, 2018, p. 138).

[18] The Cadastro Nacional da Pessoa Jurídica (CNPJ) is a registration number issued by the Brazilian Federal Revenue Service to identify legal entities, such as businesses, non-profit organizations, and religious institutions. It functions similarly to a tax identification number in other countries, and is required for entities that engage in legal, financial, or commercial activities, including the transportation and distribution of ayahuasca.

These statements make it clear that Indigenous representatives' demands regarding the use of ayahuasca extend beyond the scope of heritage policies. Their claims touch on the domains of drug policies and the public bodies responsible for regulating the religious use of ayahuasca in Brazil. What is striking, however, is that the procedures set by regulatory bodies are criticized not only by Indigenous peoples but also by public authorities. In a speech at the conference, Claudia Aguirre—a member of the State Attorney's Office in Acre—addressed the issue of ayahuasca circulation by Indigenous peoples, arguing that "it is not the white man, from the outside, who is going to regulate this. Nor can it be. Do not give us that power. The Convention 169 states that the traditional methods of conflict resolution must be respected" (Santos, 2018, p. 54). Aguirre's speech references the 1989 Convention 169 of the International Labor Organization (ILO) on Indigenous and Tribal Peoples, arguing that this international treaty legitimizes Indigenous peoples' right to establish their own mechanisms for regulating their practices and knowledge. She also cites the convention to question the requirement for Indigenous associations to register in order to circulate with ayahuasca in Brazil.

> Do you need a register to defend rights? Strictly speaking, no. Because, if you consider the Convention 169, there is no need for an association, nor the need for a legal register, to exercise one's rights. That is not necessary, either, according to the Federal Constitution [...]. If CONAD allows the religious use, why doesn't it allow the sacred use within Indigenous traditions, which is guaranteed by the Federal Constitution? I can't guarantee that the Judiciary system will accept this stance, but this is a daily struggle. The Convention 169 did not fall from the sky; it was developed because many people started saying, 'This notion of human rights does not serve us much.' The Convention 169 was very much a rereading of this [notion of human rights]. So, you must bear that idea in mind and make use of it (Santos, 2018, p. 151).

Aguirre's speech reinforces criticism of the Brazilian State's lack of legitimacy in creating public policies that address Indigenous demands. By invoking an international legal framework, she highlights a perspective that extends beyond national boundaries. She also questions the Brazilian State's ability to address and regulate the diverse forms of ayahuasca use, which extend beyond religious expressions.

> [The Indigenous] use is not restricted to religious use; it is part of a whole. A much larger whole than what we, "pale faces," understand as religious. [...] The law will never account for all forms of medicine uses. And the danger lies in the fact that we want to regulate it, defining that x, y, and z can be used. But suddenly, there are uses like a, b, and c, which aren't covered by the law and will remain in limbo (Aguirre apud Santos, 2018, p. 52–53).

The debates consistently highlighted the lack of regulation and its far-reaching effects on Indigenous ayahuasca use. Rather than presenting separate agendas for IPHAN and CONAD, these discussions revealed a web of overlapping claims, reflecting a spectrum of interests that transcend the confines of heritage policies. This convergence is particularly striking in Daiara Tukano's testimony at the conclusion of the I Ayahuasca Indigenous Conference, where the complexities of these entangled demands came into sharp focus:

> There was also a discussion about the patrimonialization of ayahuasca as a cultural heritage of Indigenous peoples. It was a very important conversation because we concluded that this medicine is from our origins. Brazilian and international legislation, along with

> international treaties, already recognize Indigenous rights as original rights. The most important of these rights is their cultural practice, which defines their identity. Therefore, our practice with the medicine, our ceremonies, and our way of life is an original right, and this right is protected by Brazil's entrenched clauses. The original right supersedes other laws because we are the original peoples of this land. This concern led us to discuss how to engage in dialogue with the competent authorities, the Brazilian government, as well as other institutions around the world, such as UNESCO and even other countries, to clarify what Indigenous rights are.[19]

Daiara's speech weaves together two distinct yet interconnected perspectives. On one hand, her reference to UNESCO and international treaties underscores the strategic deployment of global legal frameworks, situating Indigenous claims within a broader, universal discourse on rights—one that transcends the territorial and legal confines of the nation-state. On the other, her invocation of "original rights" asserts the unique legal status of Indigenous peoples within Brazilian law, exposing the inherent inadequacies of state-centered legal systems in addressing their demands. Her appeal to UNESCO further reflects the expanding transnational dimension of policymaking, where international legal norms increasingly shape and, at times, supersede national legislation. This theme of looking beyond the state was echoed in Biraci Brasil's speech, in which he urged Indigenous leaders to move past the constraints of domestic legal structures and, if necessary, bring their struggles before international bodies. Provocatively, he challenged the audience, asking:

"What are we afraid of? [We need] to use our structures, our alliances, to go to the United Nations, wherever necessary […]. I want to challenge my brothers, Indigenous leaders, and the authorities of our country so that we can start a new history in this country" (Biraci Brasil apud Santos, 2018, p. 127). While he emphasized the need for international support, he also expressed concern about the necessity of Indigenous protagonism in the political landscape.

> Our partnership is important, and I defend it, whether national or international. But it must be responsible, respecting each other's differences. Only then can we move forward properly. […] They can contribute a lot to us. Scientists can offer valuable technical and scientific insights. However, when it comes to spirituality and these medicines, ask the owners—and that's us! (Biraci Brasil apud Santos, 2018, p. 129)

The first Indigenous Ayahuasca Conference marked a pivotal moment in the history of Indigenous peoples, serving as both a testament to their resilience and a platform for their voices to be heard. While heritage policies were central to the discussions, the growing external interest in ayahuasca emerged as a primary concern. Indigenous leaders voiced deep fears about the commodification and commercialization of their "sacred medicine" on a global scale. This inaugural gathering, therefore, became a crucial step in safeguarding cultural practices and asserting sovereignty over Indigenous knowledge amid mounting external pressures. Over the years, the Indigenous Ayahuasca Conferences have developed into vital political forums, empowering Indigenous peoples to refine and expand their collective agenda. As we will explore, each successive conference has built upon the foundation laid by the

[19] https://www.youtube.com/watch?v=9QidmaDBEHA

first, incorporating new concerns and responding to shifting political and cultural landscapes. What began as a focus on the protection of cultural practices has gradually expanded into a broader vision—one that links ayahuasca to Indigenous sovereignty, environmental stewardship, and the pursuit of legal protections. This ongoing process is captured in the series of declarations issued from 2018 to 2025, each reflecting the trajectory of Indigenous advocacy. These documents trace how core themes have been steadfastly reinforced, while new priorities have emerged. The following section delves into these declarations, offering a deeper understanding of Indigenous perspectives on ayahuasca and how their agenda has been shaped by both internal deliberations and external challenges.

3.4 The Indigenous Agenda: Ayahuasca as a Political Catalyst

The five declarations resulting from the Brazilian Indigenous Ayahuasca Conferences, spanning from 2018 to 2025, reflect a progressively evolving Indigenous agenda concerning the use, regulation, and cultural significance of ayahuasca. An analysis of these documents reveals recurring themes, shifting priorities, and increasingly urgent demands (The representatives of the Indigenous Peoples of the Juruá Valley 2017, 2018, 2019, 2022, 2025). Within this framework, comparing these declarations allows us to trace how Indigenous perspectives and strategies regarding ayahuasca have transformed over time.

From the first declaration to the most recent, the conferences consistently underscore ayahuasca as a pillar of cultural and spiritual identity. Indigenous peoples reaffirm their role as "the guardians of ayahuasca from time immemorial" (The representatives of the Indigenous Peoples of the Juruá Valley 2022). Over time, this perspective deepens and expands. Earlier conferences primarily focused on the demarcation of Indigenous lands, yet more recent declarations reflect an escalating urgency in response to mounting external pressures. By 2022, concerns about biopiracy and the unregulated commercialization of ayahuasca took center stage, leading to calls for ethnozoning and legal protections. There were also concerns about cultural appropriation, the misuse of Indigenous medicines, and the exploitation of Indigenous knowledge.

> We affirm that the separation of knowledge into areas and the differentiation between molecules, substances, plants, and products does not correspond to Indigenous thinking about the spirit and life of the beings that heal us. We warn of the dangers and serious consequences of the death of our territories, the misuse of our medicines, and cultural appropriation. We emphasize the importance of prior and informed consultation, the violence of the extractivism of our knowledge, and biopiracy, and we take a stand against the threats of exploitation and the exclusion of our peoples (The representatives of the Indigenous Peoples of the Juruá Valley, 2022).

The following declaration reinforces the link between cultural safeguard and environmental stewardship, positioning ayahuasca as an integral part of the broader struggle for Indigenous sovereignty. Moreover, it pushes earlier demands further, advocating for stricter oversight of patents, measures to prevent unauthorized production and sale of traditional medicines, and the enforcement of international agreements. The Indigenous organizations emphasized "*the need for oversight, prohibition, and accountability in cases of patent attempts without proper consultation and approval, as well as the unauthorized production, sale, and use of traditional medicines based on ancestral Indigenous knowledge*" (The representatives of the Indigenous Peoples of the Juruá Valley, 2025, p. 2).

Although these concerns are not new, they have grown increasingly pressing with the rise of ayahuasca tourism and the emergence of global markets that commodify Indigenous practices. Initially, Indigenous leaders sought to establish ethical guidelines for sharing ayahuasca with outsiders. Over time, however, their stance hardened. The most recent declaration unequivocally condemns exploitative commercialization and calls for legal measures to curb unethical practices. Among the most proactive measures introduced is the proposal for an online platform to report ethical violations, holding external actors accountable:

> We agree on the creation of an online platform to receive reports, expose and create institutional pressure, leading to legal action and reputational risks for pharmaceutical companies, public institutions, and research entities that fail to respect ethics in their exploration of Indigenous knowledge (The representatives of the Indigenous Peoples of the Juruá Valley, 2025, p. 3).

Gender issues, once absent from early declarations, have also become central to the Indigenous ayahuasca agenda. By 2019, conference letters explicitly denounced gender-based violence as a form of colonial oppression. Subsequent declarations strengthened protections for women, youth, and elders while emphasizing the leadership and spiritual roles of Indigenous women. The 2025 declaration expands on this, celebrating their contributions and reaffirming *"the value of Indigenous women's leadership and their journeys as spiritual guides and masters of tradition"* (The representatives of the Indigenous Peoples of the Juruá Valley, 2025, p. 3).

As the movement gained momentum, its scope also expanded beyond national borders. Whereas early declarations primarily focused on Indigenous rights within Brazil, by 2019, leaders began calling attention to the criminalization of Indigenous spiritual practices abroad. The 2022 declaration marked a turning point by demanding the release of individuals imprisoned for ayahuasca use in Mexico and Spain. By 2025, this trajectory culminated in an even broader vision—that seeks diplomatic engagement at both national and international levels. Indigenous representatives now advocate for direct dialogue with organizations such as the United Nations, the World Intellectual Property Organization (WIPO), and national governments to ensure protections extend beyond Brazil.

Still, international advocacy is just one component of a broader strategy. To guarantee long-term protections, the 2025 declaration calls for the establishment of an Indigenous Council of Spiritual Leaders—an institution designed to mediate relationships with the non-Indigenous world, establish ethical guidelines, and consolidate Indigenous governance over ayahuasca-related matters. More than a symbolic body, the council is envisioned as both protective and proactive, ensuring that Indigenous voices remain central in shaping policies related to ayahuasca (The representatives of the Indigenous Peoples of the Juruá Valley, 2025, p. 4). This institutional development is reinforced by a broader legal and political strategy. Indigenous organizations call for the creation of a technical and legal advisory team to mediate conflicts with public and private institutions regarding traditional medicines and cultural appropriation. Additionally, they emphasize the need for sustained diplomatic engagement across multiple levels—both nationally and internationally—to advance Indigenous rights and protections. A key demand centers on fostering diplomatic dialogue across institutions and forums in Brazil and worldwide.

Beyond direct advocacy, the 2025 declaration also pushes for legislative action and Indigenous oversight to prevent the exploitation of "sacred knowledge." Indigenous representatives call for engagement with key governmental bodies to create and strengthen public policies safeguarding Indigenous medicine. In this context, the document reaffirms the need to *"articulate, represent, and oversee national and international institutions to build, expand, and strengthen legal frameworks, public policies, and administrative procedures that safeguard Indigenous rights over ayahuasca"* (The representatives of the Indigenous Peoples of the Juruá Valley, 2025, p. 5). At the same time, Indigenous leaders denounce the risks posed by external research and institutional partnerships. While earlier conferences expressed cautious optimism about collaboration with non-Indigenous researchers, the 2025 declaration adopts a more critical stance. It stresses the need for consultation and Indigenous oversight in research projects, particularly those conducted in Indigenous territories. The declaration emphasizes the necessity of working alongside the Ministry of Health and university ethics committees to ensure research on ayahuasca and other traditional medicines respects Indigenous sovereignty. Furthermore, any research involving Indigenous traditional knowledge must receive explicit approval from the Indigenous communities that hold this ancestral wisdom, in accordance with their customs, practices, and legal protections (The representatives of the Indigenous Peoples of the Juruá Valley, 2025, p. 5).

The development of the Indigenous ayahuasca agenda across five conferences is notable. It also reveals a decisive shift from internal discussions on identity and cultural preservation to assertive engagement in political and legal battles. The 2025 declaration weaves together legal advocacy, diplomatic engagement, and transnational alliances to ensure that Indigenous knowledge is safeguarded on a global scale. More than just reacting to external threats, Indigenous leaders are actively shaping policy and institutional frameworks. Their push for ethical guidelines, international legal protections, and strategic alliances signals an increasing capacity to navigate complex global dynamics. As the Indigenous ayahuasca movement continues to grow, future conferences will likely build on these strategies, ensuring that Indigenous perspectives remain central in discussions surrounding the use of ayahuasca. No longer merely subjects of policy, Indigenous leaders are asserting their place as key architects of the legal and ethical frameworks that will govern the future of ayahuasca in Brazil and abroad, on their own terms.

3.5 The Shifting Terrain of Heritage

The recognition of ayahuasca as intangible heritage has not only redefined public policy in Brazil but has also unsettled the roles of those traditionally involved in heritage-making. While anthropologists once played a central role in formulating heritage policies, their influence has waned in recent debates on the patrimonialization of ayahuasca. Although anthropology remains indispensable to these processes—not only in their conception but also in their implementation—its practitioners no longer dictate the terms of the debate. Instead, they have been repositioned as secondary figures within a broader, more decentralized political landscape where Indigenous leaders, policymakers, and NGOs now set the agenda. However, this shift is not merely a redistribution of authority; it also exposes tensions regarding the legitimacy of traditional populations versus the role of expertise, as well as the right to define what constitutes heritage and how it should be protected.

One of the paradoxes emerging from this process is that while anthropologists have lost their once-dominant role, they have also become objects of suspicion. As ethnographic studies intersect with political struggles, research itself is no longer perceived as a purely intellectual pursuit. Instead, it is entangled in power dynamics where knowledge production is viewed as a potential site of appropriation, exploitation, or distortion. This creates a dilemma: while anthropology has been foundational to the very policies that now enable heritage claims, it is increasingly questioned as an external practice that risks imposing its frameworks and notions. The contested nature of knowledge production has, in turn, complicated collaborative efforts, raising the stakes for those who seek to document and analyze these disputes.

Despite these broader shifts in the patrimonialization process, it should be noted that the initial impetus for the recognition of ayahuasca as intangible heritage came from religious groups in Acre. However, their request was initially rejected, and the scope of the registration process was subsequently broadened to encompass a wider range of expressions, including the Indigenous use of ayahuasca. This expansion has introduced further complexities into the landscape, as it brought into focus not only the religious dimension of ayahuasca but also its Indigenous roots. The inclusion of diverse practices under the umbrella of heritage has resulted in new tensions and disputes over legitimacy and the politics of representation, complicating the very idea of what it means to safeguard ayahuasca as a cultural expression.

Another critical tension stems from the shifting meaning of heritage itself. The recognition of ayahuasca as intangible heritage was initially conceived as a means of cultural preservation, an effort to protect and legitimize traditional knowledge within a national framework. However, rather than stabilizing ayahuasca's status, the patrimonialization process has generated new disputes, making the boundaries between cultural heritage and political rights increasingly porous. The categories that once structured institutional efforts—such as religious versus Indigenous use, spiritual versus therapeutic applications, or local versus global concerns—have become unstable, forcing both the state and civil society to confront dilemmas they had not anticipated, such as who has the authority to speak for ayahuasca?

One of the predicaments of the patrimonialization of ayahuasca is the role of the state in defining what constitutes culture and religion. While heritage policies ostensibly aim to protect traditional practices, they also institutionalize them, subjecting different expressions to fixed definitions and external criteria of authenticity. This raises a fundamental question: To what extent does state recognition transform the very practices it seeks to safeguard? These issues have been further exacerbated by the transnationalization of Indigenous advocacy. What began as a negotiation over cultural heritage has evolved into a new political agenda—one that transcends heritage policies and national borders, seeking international protections and institutional reforms at the highest levels. While ayahuasca remains central to this mobilization, it now serves as a vehicle for broader struggles over sovereignty, environmental protection, and legal recognition. This creates a paradox: whereas early institutional efforts attempted to contain ayahuasca within a national heritage framework, the Indigenous agenda has pushed it outward, transforming it into a form of activism with international political significance.

As Meyer and van de Port (2018, 11) observe, while consensus on what constitutes heritage remains elusive, actors are becoming increasingly skilled in navigating its complex vocabularies. Extending this insight, I argue that beyond heritage, these actors are also becoming fluent in the language and frameworks of rights. Moreover, they have been increasingly employing legal terminology and judicial avenues to challenge, uphold, or reinterpret the law (Montero et al., 2023). These developments were largely unforeseen by legislators and policymakers. The initial frameworks designed to accommodate cultural diversity within Brazil's heritage system have thus given rise to new arenas of negotiation and dispute that exceed the original scope of patrimonialization efforts. Today, it is increasingly difficult to speak about or on behalf of the many actors involved. The politics of recognition have outgrown the institutions meant to contain them, producing unexpected tensions, paradoxes, and dilemmas that continue to reshape the landscape of ayahuasca regulation. As this process unfolds, the question remains: How can heritage policies, which are based on fixed definitions and stable categories, adapt to the fluidity and constant reconfiguration of the social practices and groups they seek to safeguard?

References

Acre. (2010). *Carta das Comunidades Tradicionais da Ayahuasca, Rio Branco - Acre*. Seminário "Comunidades Tradicionais de Ayahuasca - Construindo Políticas Públicas". https://www.bialabate.net/wp-content/uploads/2008/08/Carta_Comunidades_Tradicionais_Ayahausca_Rio_Branco_2010.pdf

Acre. (2012). *1° Fórum setorial de culturas ayahuasqueiras de Rio Branco. 2ª Carta das comunidades ayahuasqueiras de Rio Branco*.

Acre. (2016). *Carta Aberta dos Povos Indígenas do Acre / Brasil a II Conferencia Mundial da Ayahuaska (Nixi Pae, Huni Pae, Uni Pae, Kamarãbi, Kamalanbi, Shuri, Yajé, Kaapi...).* https://www.bialabate.net/wp-content/uploads/2018/07/Carta_Aberta_Povos_Indigena_II_AYA_-Rio_Branco_2016.pdf

Antunes, H. F. (2023). "It is not solved just by writing it down on paper:" Patrimonialization policies and the religious use of ayahuasca as a Brazilian intangible cultural heritage. In P. Montero, C. Nicácio, & H. Antunes (Eds.), *Religious pluralism and law in contemporary Brazil* (pp. 111–140). Springer.

Arantes, A. A. (2009). Ayahuasca - From dangerous drug to national heritage: An interview with Antonio A. Arantes. *International Journal of Transpersonal Studies, 28*, 53–64.

Assis, G. L., & Rodrigues, J. A. (2017). De quem é a ayahuasca? Notas sobre a patrimonialização de uma "bebida sagrada" amazônica. *Religião e Sociedade, 37*(3), 46–70.

Barros, G. C. (2016). *Tradição e modernidade no campo ayahuasqueiro: uma análise dos processos de regulamentação e patrimonialização da ayahuasca no Brasil no período de 1985/2016.* Dissertation, Social Sciences, Federal University of Campina Grande.

Alverga, A. P. de. (2011). Comunicado da Igreja do Santo Daime (ICEFLU - Igreja do Culto Eclético da Fluente Luz Universal. Patrono: Padrinho Sebastião Mota). Letter sent to the Meeting of the Ayahuasca Diversity, 2011.

Dias, L. C. A. (2024). *Ministério Público Federal, procuradoria da república no acre 5° ofício PR-AC-00005822/2024.*

Dias, M. (2018). *1ª Conferência indígena da ayahuasca yubaka-hayra no Acre a sabedoria dos antigos.* https://www.bialabate.net/news/1a-conferencia-indigena-da-ayahuasca-yubaka-hayra-no-acre-a-sabedoria-dos-antigos

Instituto do Patrimônio Histórico e Artístico Nacional (Iphan). (2000). *Inventário nacional de referências culturais: Manual de aplicação*. Iphan.

Instituto do Patrimônio Histórico e Artístico Nacional (Iphan). (2000). *Inventário nacional de referências culturais: Manual de aplicação*. Brasília.

Labate, B. C. (2010d). As religiões ayahuasqueiras, patrimônio cultural, Acre e fronteiras geográficas. *Ponto Urbe, 7*, 1–9. https://doi.org/10.4000/pontourbe.1640

Labate, B. C., & Assis, G. L. (2018). Genealogia do processo de patrimonialização da ayahuasca no Brasil. In B. C. Labate & F. Policarpo (Eds.), *Drogas: Perspectivas em Ciências Humanas* (pp. 207–230). Gramma/Terceiro Nome/NEIP.

Labate, B. C., & Coutinho, F. (2014). "O meu avô deu a ayahuasca para o Mestre Irineu": Reflexões sobre a entrada dos índios no circuito urbano de consumo de ayahuasca no Brasil. *Revista de Antropologia USP, 57*(2), 215–250.

Labate, B. C., & Goulart, S. L. (2016). Religião, política e cultura: O uso da ayahuasca como patrimônio cultural. *30ª Reunião Brasileira de Antropologia*, João Pessoa.

Labate, B. C., & Goulart, S. L. (2017). Da Amazônia ao Norte Global e de volta: As várias ayahuascas da II Conferência Mundial da Ayahuasca. *V Congreso de la Asociación Latinoamericana de Antropología - XVI Congreso de Antropología en Colombia*, Bogotá.

MacRae, E. (n.d.). *Eu brilho na floresta*. Editora Yagé.

Maia, D. (2018). Conferência Indígena da Ayahuasca: Longe é um lugar que não existe. *Xapuri Socioambiental*. https://www.xapuri.info/sagrado-indigena/conferencia-indigena-ayahuasca/

Meyer, B., & van de Port, M. (2018). Introduction – Heritage dynamics: Politics of authentication, aesthetics of persuasion, and the cultural production of the real. In B. Meyer & M. van de Port (Eds.), *Sense and essence: Heritage and the cultural production of the real* (pp. 1–39). Berghahn Books.

Montero, P. (2018). *Syncretism and pluralism in the configuration of religious diversity in Brazil.* Mecila Working Paper Series, 4, São Paulo.

Montero, P., Nicácio, C., & Antunes, H. F. (2023). Introduction: Religious pluralism and law in contemporary Brazil. In P. Montero, C. Nicácio, & H. F. Antunes (Eds.), *Religious pluralism and law in contemporary Brazil. Law and religion in a global context* (Vol. 4). Springer. https://doi.org/10.1007/978-3-031-41981-2_1

Neves, A. C. (2017). *Reflexões sobre a patrimonialização da ayahuasca: conquistas, disputas e tensões*. Master's Thesis, Social Sciences, Federal University of Bahia.

Neves, M. V. (2011). *Sign of the times – A new policy for ayahuasca in Brazil*. https://www.bialabate.net/wp-content/uploads/2008/08/Marcos_Vinicius_Neves_Sign-of-the-Times_English.pdf

Platero, L. D. (2018). *Reinvenções daimistas: Uma etnografia sobre a aliança entre uma igreja do Santo Daime e o povo indígena Yawanawá (Pano)*. Doctoral Dissertation, Sociology and Anthropology, Federal University of Rio de Janeiro.

Reinhardt, B. (2018). Intangible heritage, tangible controversies: The Baiana and the Acarajé as boundary objects in contemporary Brazil. In B. Meyer & M. van de Port (Eds.), *Sense and essence: Heritage and the cultural production of the real* (pp. 75–111). Berghahn Books.

Rio de Janeiro. (2011). *Manifesto da Diversidade Cultural Ayahuasqueira*. https://www.bialabate.net/wp-content/uploads/2009/07/Manifesto_Diversidade_Cultural_Ayahuasqueira_RJ_2011.pdf

Santos, F. L. (2018). *"Índio não usa droga, ele usa medicina": A criminalização da ayahuasca indígena*. Master's Thesis, Safeguard of Cultural Heritage, Instituto do Patrimônio Histórico e Artístico Nacional, Iphan.

Silva, D. B. (2018a). Yubaka Hayrá: Notas sobre a Conferência Indígena da Ayahuasca. *Campos, 19*(1), 183–194.

Silva, E. C. A. (2018b). Povos indígenas e o direito à terra na realidade brasileira. *Serviço Social e Sociedade, 133*, 480–500.

Chapter 4
On Rights and Risks: The Legal Victories of the União do Vegetal and Santo Daime in the United States

The intersection of religious rights and drug policies in the United States is a legally fraught and ever-changing terrain. As interest in the religious use of psychedelics grows, the question of legal protections or the possible criminalization of these practices becomes a subject of increasing interest. In the U.S., people can legally use a controlled substance in religious ceremonies if a court decides their beliefs are truly sincere and religious, and their practices do not seriously harm important government interests (Hoots, 2025, p. 99). Consequently, legal exemptions are not easily granted. Courts, along with the Drug Enforcement Agency (DEA), have developed forms of assessing religious beliefs and practices to determine whether individualized exemptions should be allowed, reinforcing the state's role in defining the boundaries of legitimate religious exercise. These legal precedents, which have historically privileged Judeo-Christian frameworks, further complicate the issue of the recognition of the religious use of psychedelics (Hoots, 2025, p. 99–100). This chapter examines the role of state agencies and courts acting as arbiters of religious legitimacy, determining which beliefs and practices are deemed acceptable and which remain outside the bounds of legal recognition. It also explores how these institutions invoke notions of risk and public health to justify restrictions on ayahuasca.

The use of ayahuasca in the United States began in the 1980s with the international expansion of Santo Daime and União do Vegetal (UDV). For over a decade, its presence remained largely unnoticed, with only a few groups operating underground. However, the late 1990s marked a turning point. During this period, ayahuasca attracted the attention of U.S. authorities, leading to the first legal cases that reignited debates about the limits of religious freedom when it involves psychoactive substances.

Despite these tensions, ayahuasca use has expanded in the U.S. at an unprecedented rate since the early 2000s. Today, the landscape is even more complex, as states and cities such as Oregon, Colorado, Santa Cruz, Oakland, and others have begun reforming their drug policies regarding psychedelics. However, these changes

H. Fernandes Antunes, *Religion, Drug, or Cult?*, Law and Religion in a Global Context 5, https://doi.org/10.1007/978-3-032-04368-9_4

are restricted to certain states and cities, and the question of how to regulate psychedelics at a national level remains unresolved, generating intense debate. This chapter takes a step back to examine the first legal disputes between the U.S. government and two ayahuasca groups: a UDV church in New Mexico and a Santo Daime branch in Oregon. These cases ultimately led to the establishment of a legal framework for the religious use of ayahuasca in the country. Given the similarities between them, I will emphasize the UDV's legal battle, as it was the first to reach the highest level of the U.S. judiciary—the Supreme Court—before the Santo Daime church filed its lawsuit. The analysis of these key legal cases will help us understand how ayahuasca groups navigate this contested and complex terrain.

This chapter is based on a comprehensive review of legal documents, including injunction requests, complaints against the federal government, expert witness testimonies and reports, court rulings, and legal agreements between ayahuasca institutions and the U.S. government. Additionally, I draw on academic literature to fill temporal gaps and provide context beyond what is available in legal records. I also resort to interviews with ayahuasca leaders, members, and other key actors involved in these legal disputes.

The goal is to explore the tensions, negotiations, and disputes, with a focus on the categories and arguments employed throughout these legal cases. I examine how different actors navigate a complex web of laws, statutes, and judicial decisions, ultimately shaping the regulatory framework for ayahuasca's religious use. These cases can provide a better understanding of the ways in which the U.S. government and courts regulate the religious use of ayahuasca and to a broader extent, frame the possibilities and limits for the religious use of psychoactive substances in the country. Before delving into these cases, however, it is important to address a few pivotal legal precedents that influenced the trajectory of ayahuasca-related disputes.

4.1 Employment Division v. Smith and the Religious Freedom Restoration Act

The legal definition of religion in the United States has evolved through a complex and often contradictory series of court decisions. While the Constitution prohibits favoring one religion over another, courts have historically applied criteria rooted in Judeo-Christian traditions when assessing minority religious practices (Hoots, 2025). Early legal interpretations tied religion to belief in a "Supreme Being," as seen in an 1890 Supreme Court ruling that defined religion in terms of one's relationship with a Creator and moral obligations. However, later cases such as *United States v. Ballard* (1944) and *United States v. Seeger* (1965) expanded protections by recognizing sincere, nontraditional beliefs as religious, so long as they played a role in believers' lives comparable to that of conventional faiths (Hoots, 2025, p. 100).

Despite this broadening definition, subsequent rulings reintroduced restrictive standards. In *Wisconsin v. Yoder* (1972), the Court ruled that religious exemptions required not just personal belief but deep conviction shared by an organized group, closely tied to daily life. Similarly, *Africa v. Pennsylvania* (1981) established a three-part test for religion, emphasizing comprehensiveness, formalized structures, and alignment with familiar religious models. By favoring established frameworks of faith, courts have often sidelined non-orthodox practices, particularly those involving psychoactive substances, which often do not fit neatly into standard definitions of organized religion. Despite the issue of psychoactive substances, the judicial discrepancy when it comes to defining religion reveals an ongoing tension between new demands for expanding the notion of religious freedom and conventional notions based on Protestant frameworks (Hoots, 2025, p. 101).

This tension became particularly evident in Employment Division v. Smith (1990), a case that significantly reshaped the legal landscape for religious exemptions. It was undoubtedly a landmark case in the discussion of religious freedom in the United States, especially in relation to the application of laws that in any way burdened religious practices. The case involved Alfred Smith and Galen Black, two Native Americans who worked as counselors at a drug rehabilitation clinic in the state of Oregon. They were fired for using peyote in Native American Church[1] (NAC) ceremonies. Specifically, the dismissal occurred because the use of peyote was a violation of the company's policies on drug use, which made no exceptions for religious practices. After their dismissal, they applied for unemployment benefits, but the Employment Division of Oregon denied their request, arguing that their dismissal was for cause, since their use of controlled substances was a violation of state law.

Smith and Black challenged the decision, arguing that the rehabilitation clinic's position and the denial of benefits violated their religious freedom, enshrined in the First Amendment of the U.S. Constitution. The case was brought before the Supreme Court, which had to decide whether a law can be enforced even if it violates the principle of religious freedom. The court, in a 6-3 decision, ruled that general laws banning the use of controlled substances do not need to make exceptions for religious practices. They argued that allowing such an exception could lead to a complex legal framework where religious groups would seek exemptions from laws they considered oppressive or unjust. Justice Anthony Kennedy, who wrote the court's opinion, stated that the government had the power to regulate behavior, even if those regulations affect religious practices, as long as the laws are neutral and generally applicable (Employment Division v. Smith, 1990).

This decision was significant because it reduced the protection of religious freedom by establishing a standard that made it difficult to obtain legal exemptions for religious practices. From Smith onwards, the government could apply laws prohibiting certain actions, even if those actions were part of a religious practice, as long as they met the requirements set by the court. In doing so, the court changed the

---

[1] The Native American Church is a religious organization that blends Indigenous practices with Christian elements. The NAC is primarily present in the United States and Canada. Founded in the early twentieth century, it centers on ceremonies involving peyote, a cactus with psychoactive effects, which is used as a sacrament. The NAC has a legal exemption for peyote use in the United States, allowing it for sacramental purposes despite federal restrictions on the substance.

language of the jurisprudence on the free exercise of religion. Prior to this decision, the government could not pass or enforce a law that burdened the exercise of religion, unless the law was the least restrictive means of achieving a compelling social interest. The case led to heated debates about the need for a balance between the protection of religious freedom and law enforcement, mobilizing sectors of the media, scholars, members of Congress and religious interest groups, who expressed clear unease and concern about the consequences of the decision for the free exercise of religion in the country (Ryan, 1992, p. 1408–1409).

Three years after the Smith case, in 1993, the U.S. Congress passed the Religious Freedom Restoration Act (RFRA), seeking to strengthen the protection of religious freedom. The statute can be interpreted as a direct reaction to the outrage that followed the Smith decision, expressed by many of the congressmen present at the hearing on RFRA, who showed dismay at the Supreme Court's ruling (Ryan, 1992, p. 1439). Consequently, the legislation was designed to restore the strongest standard of protection for religious freedom. The RFRA reestablished the "strict scrutiny test",[2] which is referred to as the "compelling interest test",[3] to evaluate whether the government met its legal burden to justify an infringement on a person's religious freedom. It allows providing a claim or defense to persons whose religious exercise is substantially burdened by government (Chacruna Institute for Psychedelic Plant Medicines, & Hoots, 2021, p. 16). The RFRA provides that the government may restrict the practice of a religious belief only if it can demonstrate that the restriction is necessary to serve a compelling governmental interest. In addition, the government must prove that the initiative is the least restrictive way to achieve that interest. In contrast, to bring a claim under RFRA, a plaintiff must prove that there has been a substantial burden imposed by the government on the sincere exercise of his or her religion. However, when assessing an RFRA case, courts must first evaluate whether the religious beliefs involved are recognizable as a religion and, secondly, determine if there is evidence of sincerity (Hoots, 2025, p. 104).

---

[2]As Hoots (2025) stresses, despite the constitutional precept that "Congress shall make no law respecting an establishment of religion, or prohibiting the free exercise thereof," the protection of this fundamental right depends on judicial interpretations of religion, and the appropriate balance between rights and government interests. Courts apply different levels of scrutiny to evaluate government actions that may burden constitutional rights. The "rational basis" test, the least stringent, applies when a law is rationally related to a legitimate government interest, often in cases involving economic regulation or age-based classifications. The "intermediate scrutiny" test, used in cases of gender discrimination and quasi-suspect classifications, requires that the law serve an important government interest. The "strict scrutiny" test, the most rigorous standard, applies when a law affects fundamental rights such as race, national origin, or religion. Under strict scrutiny, the government must demonstrate that the law is narrowly tailored to achieve a compelling interest (Hoots, 2025, p. 102).

[3]"A compelling interest is usually identified by the government and must be evaluated by the courts. While there is little guidance from the U.S. Supreme Court, compelling interests have been described as 'only those interests of the highest order' and can be justified when 'only the gravest abuses, endangering paramount interest, give occasion for permissible limitation' of rights under the law" (Chacruna Institute for Psychedelic Plant Medicines & Hoots, 2021, p. 28).

In 1997, the Supreme Court ruled in *City of Boerne v. Flores* (1997) that the application of the RFRA was limited to federal agents and institutions, rather than state. The case began when a Catholic church in Boerne, Texas, was denied a permit to expand due to a local historic preservation ordinance. Arguing that this denial violated its rights under RFRA, the church took its claim to the Supreme Court. However, when the case reached the highest court, the focus shifted from the church's expansion to the broader issue of RFRA's constitutionality and, specifically, its application to state governments.

In a 6-3 decision, the Supreme Court held that Congress had exceeded its constitutional limits by applying RFRA to state and local governments. Justice Anthony Kennedy, writing for the majority, argued that Congress did not possess unrestricted power to enforce the Fourteenth Amendment,[4] which was the basis used to justify RFRA's application to the states. The Court found that RFRA placed requirements on state governments that were excessively broad and disproportionate to the intended protection of religious freedom, thereby exceeding Congress's authority. This decision had a significant impact on the scope of the RFRA, limiting its application solely to federal government actions and releasing state and local governments from its mandates. In response, many states passed their own versions of the RFRA to protect religious freedom at the state level.[5]

Due to its impact on the legal system, the RFRA has been invoked in several cases since its enactment, challenging laws that, according to the petitioners, would violate their religious freedom. Cases such as *Burwell v. Hobby Lobby Stores* (2014) and *Zubik v. Burwell* (2016) are just a few examples in which the RFRA was used to argue against the enforcement of certain laws in contexts of health and workers' rights. In *Burwell v. Hobby Lobby Stores* (2014), the Supreme Court ruled that family-owned businesses had the right, based on the RFRA, to refuse to provide contraceptive coverage on religious grounds. The case had important implications for the RFRA interpretation, given the fact that the ruling stated that it was not for the courts to say that one's religious beliefs are mistaken or insubstantial, but to determine whether there is an honest conviction. The *Zubik v. Burwell* (2016) case, in turn, involved several religious institutions challenging the requirement to provide contraceptive coverage to their employees as mandated by the Affordable Care Act (ACA). The institutions argued that this requirement violated their religious beliefs. The Supreme Court decided not to resolve the issue definitively but remanded the case for the parties to reach a settlement.

As one can see, the scope and limits of the RFRA have sparked an intense debate over the balance between religious freedom and other civil rights, such as

---

[4] According to the Fourteenth Amendment, no state shall make or enforce any law which shall abridge the privileges or immunities of citizens of the United States; nor shall any state deprive any person of the right to life, liberty or property without due process of law, or deny to any person within its jurisdiction the equal protection of the laws.

[5] Thirty-two states have passed laws equivalent to the RFRA or have state Supreme Court decisions adopting RFRA standards for the protection of religious freedom. Seven states have chosen not to adopt RFRA-like protections, and the law is unclear in a number of states (Hoots & Labate, 2024).

reproductive health rights and LGBTQ+ rights, raising questions about the extent of religious exemptions and their limits in relation to other laws. Interestingly, legislation passed in response to a legal decision regarding the religious use of psychoactive substances not only became a landmark for religious rights in the country but, as we will see next, was crucial for the victories of the UDV and Santo Daime (CHLQ).

4.2 What Legally Constitutes a Religion? The United States v. Meyers Case

Legal debates over religious freedom often hinge on a fundamental question: What constitutes a religion? In United States v. Meyers (1996), the focus was on the intersection of federal drug laws and the right to freedom of religion. David Meyers, a member of a group that used cannabis as part of its ceremonies, faced charges related to the possession and distribution of marijuana. Meyers argued that his use of cannabis was a religious practice protected by the First Amendment, which guarantees the free exercise of religion. The case raised important questions about what constitutes a legitimate religious belief and practice, which had significant implications for later decisions, such as those involving the religious use of ayahuasca.

The court had to consider whether the government's interest in enforcing drug laws outweighed Meyers' right to practice his alleged religion. This involved assessing whether marijuana use was fundamental to his faith and whether the government's restrictions were justified. The court examined the sincerity of Meyers' beliefs, which is typically a determining factor in cases involving religious freedoms in the United States. The very definition of religion was examined to determine whether Meyers' beliefs met the criteria established by previous case law.

Meyers testified that he was the founder and reverend of the Church of Marijuana and that he held the sincere belief that his religion compelled him to use, possess, cultivate, and distribute marijuana for the good of humanity and the planet Earth. The court considered whether Meyers' convictions were "religious beliefs" or whether they constituted a "philosophy or way of life." The Supreme Court concluded that, in light of the secular nature of Meyers' views on the medical, therapeutic, and social benefits of cannabis, his beliefs aligned more closely with a philosophy or way of life than a religion.

> There is no dispute that Meyers' beliefs are sincerely held and that they are substantially burdened by 21 U.S.C. §§ 841 and 846 and 18 U.S.C. § 2. The issue is whether his sincerely held beliefs are "religious beliefs," rather than a philosophy or way of life. In analyzing this issue, the district court examined the cases that have delved into the question of "what is religion" and cataloged the many factors used to determine whether a set of beliefs is religious in nature. […] Under the district court's thorough analysis of the indicators of religion, which we adopt, we hold that Meyers' beliefs more accurately reflect a philosophy and/or way of life rather than a "religion" (United States v. Meyers, 1996, p. 5–7).

In the trial, the pressing issue was not the sincerity of Meyers' beliefs, but rather whether these beliefs were, in fact, religious. Given the lack of clear criteria for determining whether a belief is religious, the court sought to establish, through previous cases, a set of elements to clarify the religious nature of a group. These included: Do they raise questions about life and death? Do they involve metaphysical beliefs? Are they endowed with ethical and moral values? Do they have religious symbols and paraphernalia? Do they have founders, prophets, or teachers? Do they have important writings, meeting places, rituals, structure, or organization? Based on this set of elements, the court decided that Meyers' beliefs were not religious (United States v. Meyers, 1996, p. 5–6).

Ultimately, the court had to weigh Meyers' rights against the government's interests. The ruling hinged on whether the court recognized his practices as a legitimate religious exercise. The court's decision emphasized that, although Meyers' beliefs could be sincere, they did not fit the legal parameters set to define a religion. This added a layer of complexity, as the court not only had to address Meyers' sincerity, but also had to assess what beliefs could be characterized as religious. Despite Meyers' loss, the case underscored the importance of evaluating the sincerity of an individual's religious beliefs, highlighting possible paths for the legal recognition of groups and practices that may not fit traditional legal definitions of religion but might still warrant protection under the First Amendment and the RFRA. However, one of the most significant points was the court's attempt to establish a series of criteria to differentiate religious practices from philosophical and scientific worldviews, creating a normative framework to define the basic characteristics of a religion.

4.3 The UDV and the Tensions with the U.S. Government

The UDV arrived in the United States in 1987 at the request of an American who met the group on a visit to Brazil and asked the institution to send two masters to the U.S. Despite this first initiative, an effort to solidify the UDV's presence in the country only intensified in the following decade. In 1990, Jeffrey Bronfman[6] made his first trip to Brazil and began to organize the visit of a larger number of masters in order to start UDV ceremonies in the U.S. Three years later, the UDV became an official church in the state of New Mexico. According to Bronfman, the UDV held meetings and sessions for 6 years, during which time it expanded to different cities. However, the end of the 1990s represented the beginning of tensions between the

[6] Jeffrey Bronfman is an educator and environmentalist. He got to know ayahuasca and the UDV on a trip he took to the Amazon to create an environmental protection reserve. He became a member of the UDV in 1992 and, in 1994, became the institution's first master outside Brazil (Bronfman, 2015, p. 3). He served as the institution's vice-president in the USA and a member of the board of directors, as well as participating directly in the disputes surrounding the regulation of UDV in New Mexico and publishing a series of articles on the subject (Bronfman, 2006 [2004], 2011a, 2011b, 2013, 2015). He was, for years, the main person responsible for coordinating all of the UDV's institutional relations in the country.

institution and the U.S. government. In May 1999, agents from the U.S. Customs Service and the Federal Bureau of Investigation (FBI) went to Bronfman's office to carry out a "controlled delivery." After accepting delivery of a shipment of hoasca sent from Brazil, a SWAT team entered his office. The agents stayed there for around 8 hours, confiscating computers, personal records and a series of documents. The incident led to an investigation into the UDV's activities in the country, when federal agents were sent to five different states in order to find information that could be used against the institution in a criminal case (Bronfman, 2006 [2004], p. 12).

Although no members of the UDV were arrested, the institution was informed that the government was considering prosecuting it for violating the Controlled Substances Act (CSA)[7] with regard to the import, distribution and consumption of DMT, a controlled substance under the country's drug law. In addition, threats to destroy the seized hoasca were also directed at the institution, a fact later pointed out by the UDV as a "sacrilege" and a "blasphemy." According to UDV representatives, the seizure of the hoasca and the threat of legal proceedings caused them to suspend their activities, imposing a burden on their religious practices and putting the presence of the institution in the country at risk (O Centro Espírita Beneficente União do Vegetal v. Reno, 2000, p. 9–10). After the interruption of their activities, Bronfman and other members of the UDV met with representatives of the Department of Justice to try to reach an agreement that could placate both parties. In a 2004 article, the UDV representative briefly describes UDV's predicament:

> Plants have been used as tools to gain awareness of the spiritual dimension of life for tens of thousands of years. They have played a fundamental role in the religious history of humanity. I am a member of a contemporary church called União do Vegetal, which emerged in Brazil and continues this noble tradition of using sacred plants in a religious context. A few years ago, the US government took legal action against the religion I practice, initiating legal proceedings against me. I was threatened with years in prison if I continued to practice my religious faith. Some church members and I met with representatives of the Department of Justice to try to help them understand the meaning of the sacred tea we use in our religious practice. We brought in a group of experts to make presentations. Among them were scientists, doctors, anthropologists and members of the UDV (Bronfman, 2006 [2004], p. 2).

After 18 months of unsuccessful attempts to negotiate an agreement with representatives of the Department of Justice in which, according to Bronfman (2006 [2004], p. 12–13), the government agency showed no sign of working towards a consensual decision, the UDV took the initiative to file a lawsuit in the 10th Circuit Court—which has jurisdiction over the state of New Mexico—against the U.S. Customs Service, the Department of Justice and the Drug Enforcement Agency (DEA) seeking a legal exemption for the use of hoasca.

[7] The Controlled Substances Act (CSA) is the federal statute regarding the control of psychoactive substances in the USA.

4.4 The UDV's Complaint

> We have taken a stand for the right to be able to receive the gifts of nature and use them in a disciplined, safe and structured, reverent and sacred way. For more than forty years, this has been the case in modern Brazil, and it has also been the case in the Amazon region throughout the centuries. The people I have met in Brazil who have been drinking this Hoasca tea for twenty, thirty, forty years are lucid, open-hearted, humble and kind. They had wisdom to share and healthy families with children whose eyes shone with happiness and peace. Our government has taken a position of banning the use of a substance that really seems to offer great social benefits to those who use it ceremonially (Bronfman, 2006 [2004], p. 8–9).

Following the U.S. government's intervention, UDV representatives filed a lawsuit against a series of government agencies on December 22, 2000, arguing that there had been an arbitrary application of the country's drug law, infringing on the religious freedom of its members. The UDV presented itself as a Brazilian Christian religious organization and requested an injunction against the government, stating that the classification of ayahuasca as a controlled substance was illegal and unconstitutional, causing a burden on the religious use of the brew. The institution also claimed that the federal government had acted beyond its legal authority by carrying out searches and seizures on the properties of its members. The UDV requested a declaration that hoasca should not be classified as a controlled substance and that the CSA should not be applied to its sacramental use. Finally, there is a request for the court to order the return and protection of the property seized by the government (O Centro Espírita Beneficente União do Vegetal v. Reno, 2000).

In response, the Justice Department assembled a team of lawyers from the fields of criminal, civil, constitutional, and public health law, as well as international law, to handle the UDV's case. The team also included members of the Food and Drug Administration (FDA) and the DEA. The federal government later responded to the UDV's complaint by arguing that "certainly neither the Controlled Substances Act nor the Religious Freedom Restoration Act required the government to wait until it was faced with a 'large scale drug epidemic' before it attempted to stem the tide of use" (Bronfman, 2006 [2004], p. 14). The government asserted its responsibility to protect public health, claiming that there were insufficient studies on the subject and that potential risks associated with ayahuasca use had not yet been fully considered. Its defense rested on three central arguments: adherence to international treaties and conventions, the alleged health risks of ayahuasca, and the dangers of diversion for recreational use.

On the other side of the dispute, the UDV claimed that all its members in the U.S. were sincere adherents of the institution's teachings, asserting that communion through the consumption of the tea was a necessary and essential aspect of its religious practices and ceremonies. The UDV also emphasized that the use of ayahuasca was legally recognized and protected under Brazilian law. Regarding the tea specifically, the document stated that hoasca was a sacrament produced exclusively in a ritual context under the supervision of trained religious leaders called *mestres*. UDV representatives argued that adherents received the "Divine Holy

Spirit" upon ingesting the sacrament and that the spirit of hoasca was a divine manifestation contained within the tea. The institution claimed that its ceremonies constituted the core of its religion and that many essential teachings were imparted only during rituals in which the tea was consumed. Therefore, the UDV contended that banning hoasca would prevent its members from freely exercising their religion[8] (O Centro Espírita Beneficente União do Vegetal v. Reno, 2000, p. 6–7).

The document further highlighted that most UDV members in the U.S. were American citizens, while others held Brazilian nationality. Many had been born into the religion or had practiced it for decades. The UDV argued that these individuals had migrated to the U.S. with the expectation that the country's tradition of religious tolerance would allow them to continue worshiping freely. The institution also asserted that it maintained strict oversight of *hoasca's* receipt and distribution to ensure its use remained strictly within ritual settings. Additionally, it referenced scientific studies on the religious consumption of *hoasca* within UDV ceremonies, which concluded that the tea posed no risk of abuse, caused no harm to human health, and lacked the dangers typically associated with controlled substances. Lastly, the complaint underscored that, according to anthropological research, the tea had been safely consumed in religious contexts for over 1500 years (O Centro Espírita Beneficente União do Vegetal v. Reno, 2000, p. 7–8).

Regarding the accusations directed at the government, the UDV stressed the significance of the RFRA violation. The complaint highlighted that the RFRA was enacted by the U.S. Congress to prevent undue government interference in the free exercise of religion. From the UDV's standpoint, classifying hoasca as a controlled substance imposed an unjustified burden on its members' religious practice. The institution contended that criminalizing the sacrament served no compelling government interest and, even if it did, a total ban was not the least restrictive means of addressing the issue (O Centro Espírita Beneficente União do Vegetal v. Reno, 2000, p. 10–11).

The UDV accused the government of misapplying drug laws, challenging the claim that the presence of DMT in one of hoasca's constituent plants was sufficient to classify the tea as a Schedule I controlled substance. Building on this argument, UDV representatives asserted that hoasca was not subject to U.S. drug regulations, emphasizing that Congress had explicitly included certain plants in the controlled substances list only when deemed necessary, as in the case of peyote and its active compound, mescaline. The UDV further contended that the mere presence of a chemical compound did not automatically warrant a plant's inclusion on the controlled substances list. Since none of the plants used to prepare hoasca appeared in the CSA schedule, the institution argued that the seizure of the tea and the threat of prosecution for its importation, possession, and distribution were based on an erroneous and unlawful determination that hoasca was a controlled substance under

[8] It is worth highlighting that the UDV has suspended the consumption of hoasca until the final decision issued by the Supreme Court, opting to drink water instead of hoasca during its ceremonies.

U.S. drug laws (*O Centro Espírita Beneficente União do Vegetal v. Reno*, 2000, pp. 14–15).

Regarding First Amendment violations, the UDV referenced the Supreme Court's ruling in *Employment Division v. Smith* (1990), which held that a law imposing a burden on religious practice does not require justification if it is neutral and generally applicable. However, the UDV argued that U.S. drug laws failed to meet these criteria, as they granted the Native American Church (NAC) an exemption for the ceremonial use of peyote while denying similar protections to other religious groups. The UDV also pointed to additional exceptions within the Controlled Substances Act (CSA), such as allowances for medical and scientific use, further undermining the law's neutrality and general applicability (*O Centro Espírita Beneficente União do Vegetal v. Reno*, 2000, pp. 12–13). According to Bronfman (2006 [2004], p. 13), the UDV also invoked the Fourteenth Amendment, citing the preferential treatment granted to the NAC as evidence of unequal protection under the law.[9]

The UDV argued that importing and receiving the tea was not illegal, as hoasca was not classified as a controlled substance. Therefore, the institution accused the government of unlawfully seizing its sacrament without probable cause. It also contended that by confiscating the shipment without prior notice or a hearing, the government deprived its members of their property rights, violating the Fifth Amendment. Additionally, the UDV claimed the government's actions breached the Administrative Procedure Act, describing them as "arbitrary and capricious, an abuse of discretion contrary to law; contrary to plaintiffs' constitutional and statutory rights; an excess of statutory jurisdiction and authority; and a failure to follow procedures required by law" (O Centro Espírita Beneficente União do Vegetal v. Reno, 2000, pp. 16–17).

Beyond domestic law, the UDV accused the U.S. government of disregarding international legal commitments. It invoked the doctrine of comity, which encourages states and nations to respect one another's judicial, executive, and legislative acts. The institution emphasized that U.S. federal agencies themselves recognize this principle when handling international matters. Based on this precedent, the UDV maintained that Brazil's regulation of hoasca for religious use should be acknowledged in accordance with U.S. foreign policy. Furthermore, the UDV appealed to global protections of religious freedom, citing the Universal Declaration of Human Rights, the United Nations International Covenant on Civil and Political Rights, and the International Religious Freedom Act, which supports multilateral

[9] Shortly before the court ruling, the NAC submitted an amicus curiae brief opposing the UDV's request for an injunction. In the document in question, the NAC indicated that it was not trying to present new evidence, but to advise the court on the case at hand, preserving its greater interest in protecting the exception made to the religious use of peyote. According to the institution, the aim was to help the court with issues related to indigenous religious and constitutional rights. More specifically, the NAC criticized both parties involved in the case for failing to consider the sui generis relationship between Indian tribes and the US government (Native American Church, 2002, p. 1–3).

efforts to uphold religious liberty (O Centro Espírita Beneficente União do Vegetal v. Reno, 2000, pp. 17–18).

4.5 O Centro Espírita Beneficente União do Vegetal v. Ashcroft

Between October 22 and November 2, 2001, the 10th Circuit Court held hearings featuring experts from various fields, including religion, health, psychiatry, public safety, and drug policy. On August 12, 2002, Judge Parker of the Federal District of New Mexico issued his ruling. He recognized the UDV as a religion, describing it as a church that blended Christian theology with traditional Indigenous beliefs. He also acknowledged that consuming hoasca was central to the group's religious ceremonies. However, this recognition marked only the beginning of the legal battle between the UDV and the federal government.

The decision centered on the UDV's claim that the selective enforcement of drug laws violated its members' right to freely practice their religion under the First Amendment. The court emphasized that any case involving religious freedom must first establish that a government action imposes a burden on a specific religious practice. While the court did not challenge the UDV's argument that classifying hoasca as a controlled substance restricted its religious exercise, it was still necessary—following Supreme Court precedent—to determine whether the Controlled Substances Act was truly neutral and generally applicable.

The UDV argued that the drug law did not satisfy the requirements of neutrality and general applicability because, in addition to the exemption for the NAC, it allowed numerous exceptions and licenses for the use of controlled substances in non-religious contexts, such as research or medicinal use. In response, the court drew upon the Supreme Court's rulings in Employment Division v. Smith (1990)[10] and United States v. Meyers (1996).

As previously discussed, in United States v. Meyers, the Supreme Court rejected the defendant's claim that cannabis distribution prohibition violated his religious freedoms. The prevailing argument in both Meyers and the UDV case was that the Controlled Substances Act (CSA) was a neutral law of general applicability because it did not specifically target religious practices and applied to various other uses (O Centro Espírita Beneficente União do Vegetal v. Ashcroft, 2002, p. 9). Nevertheless, the UDV contended that the exceptions for scientific research and other non-religious uses undermined the law's neutrality and general applicability.

To assess the neutrality and generality of the CSA, the court referenced Church of the Lukumi Babalu Aye, Inc. v. Hialeah (1993), in which a Santeria church

[10] Judge Parker noted that Congress enacted the RFRA in response to the Supreme Court's ruling in the *Smith* case, aiming to reinstate the compelling interest test for government actions (O Centro Espírita Beneficente União do Vegetal v. Ashcroft, 2002, pp. 26–27).

challenged a series of ordinances passed by the city of Hialeah, Florida. These ordinances banned ritual animal sacrifice after the establishment of a Santeria house of worship. The Supreme Court ruled that the city's ordinances were neither neutral nor generally applicable, as the city prohibited ritual sacrifice while permitting various non-religious forms of animal slaughter. In the court's view, the Hialeah regulations were arbitrary, as they pursued a governmental interest that targeted only conduct motivated by religious beliefs (O Centro Espírita Beneficente União do Vegetal v. Ashcroft, 2002, pp. 10–11).

The Lukumi case established that, to demonstrate a law's partiality, it must be shown that the law specifically targets religious practices. Following this reasoning, the court determined that the CSA was neutral because it did not aim to suppress or discriminate against the religious use of controlled substances. The court concluded that the drug statute did not differentiate between religious and secular uses, as it allowed exceptions for secular purposes, including scientific, medical, and industrial uses. However, the court emphasized that the CSA was contrary to one particular secular use: recreational consumption. Judge Parker highlighted that a significant portion of the population who sought to use controlled substances recreationally had their freedom curtailed by the CSA, which did not distinguish between religious and secular users. The judge further concluded that the UDV failed to demonstrate that the federal government's application of the drug law was intended to prohibit religious use specifically (O Centro Espírita Beneficente União do Vegetal v. Ashcroft, 2002, pp. 11–12).

Despite this, Judge Parker acknowledged that the government could not impose a burden on conduct merely because it was motivated by religious beliefs. Therefore, a law could not be considered generally applicable if its purpose only targeted religious conduct without addressing non-religious practices. In Lukumi, the city of Hialeah argued that one of the purposes of the law was to prevent cruelty to animals. However, the Supreme Court found that many non-religious forms of animal killing, such as fishing, hunting, rodent extermination, and euthanasia in shelters, were neither prohibited nor specifically allowed. The Court ruled that, although the city sought to address animal cruelty, the law's restrictions were aimed only at a limited set of deaths linked to religious sacrifices (O Centro Espírita Beneficente União do Vegetal v. Ashcroft, 2002, pp. 12–13).

Following the reasoning outlined in the Lukumi case, the court assessed the general applicability of the CSA to hoasca by asking whether the law effectively curbs non-religious conduct that jeopardizes state interests in the same way it prohibits the ceremonial use of controlled substances. The court concluded that the primary focus of the law was secular, particularly aimed at curbing recreational use. It determined that some uses of controlled substances in scientific research or medical treatment did not conflict with the government's interest in promoting public health. In contrast, unregulated religious use of controlled substances could pose health risks. Based on this reasoning, the court found that the CSA met the requirement of general applicability, as it applied to both secular and religious uses of controlled substances that endangered public health (O Centro Espírita Beneficente União do Vegetal v. Ashcroft, 2002, pp. 12–13).

In addition to evaluating the neutrality and general applicability of the drug law, the court also addressed the specific issue of how hoasca fit into the legislation. The UDV argued that hoasca should not be classified as a controlled substance. While the UDV acknowledged that one of the plants used to make ayahuasca, *Psychotria viridis*, contains small amounts of DMT, the institution contended that only synthetic DMT is banned by the CSA, not plants that naturally contain the substance. To resolve the issue, the court referred to the CSA itself. According to the statute, DMT is classified as a hallucinogenic substance under Schedule I of controlled substances, the category with the greatest restrictions.[11] The court's decision was based on the CSA principle, which states that "any material, compound, mixture or preparation, which contains any quantity of the following hallucinogenic substances" is considered a Schedule I substance (Controlled Substances Act, 1970). This definition formed the basis for the court's ruling that hoasca should be classified as a controlled substance (O Centro Espírita Beneficente União do Vegetal v. Ashcroft, 2002, pp. 19–20).

In response, the UDV turned to international law, arguing that the CSA's interpretation, which banned hoasca, conflicted with Brazilian law and violated the general principles of freedom of belief and religious practice found in international treaties to which the United States was a party, such as the International Covenant on Civil and Political Rights. The UDV presented testimony from Dr. Glacus de Souza Brito, a physician involved in the Hoasca Project,[12] who testified that religious use of ayahuasca is legal in Brazil and that ayahuasca entities are recognized as legitimate religions. The UDV also referenced the International Religious Freedom Act, passed to promote religious freedom as a U.S. foreign policy, to support the rights of individuals persecuted for their religious practices in other countries. While acknowledging the arguments presented by international law, the court considered that U.S. drug law, which took precedence over international treaties, left no room for such interpretations. Judge Parker ruled that hoasca's inclusion in the CSA as a Schedule I controlled substance did not violate the constitutional right to freely exercise religion under the First Amendment to the U.S. Constitution (O Centro Espírita Beneficente União do Vegetal v. Ashcroft, 2002, pp. 24–25).

---

[11] A Schedule I substance is considered a psychoactive with a high potential for abuse and there are no accepted medical treatment for such substances in the United States (Controlled Substances Act 1970).

[12] As noted in Chap. 2, the *Hoasca Project* was the first biomedical study on ayahuasca, conducted in the early 1990s through a collaboration between the União do Vegetal (UDV) and a team of biomedical researchers from the United States, Finland, and Brazil (Grob et al., 2002).

4.6 The Court's Stance on the Applicability of the RFRA

After addressing the issue of hoasca's status under the country's drug law and the potential violation of the First Amendment, the court proceeded to analyze the UDV's claim, which was based on the argument that the federal government's stance violated the requirements of the RFRA. However, before delving into the merits of the UDV's claim, the court emphasized a critical distinction between this case and others in which individuals or institutions had challenged the country's drug laws based on the principle of religious freedom.[13]

Judge Parker acknowledged that the UDV was a legitimate religion, with its members sincerely holding its principles, and that the application of the CSA to the ceremonial use of hoasca created a substantial burden on their religious practice. The U.S. government did not dispute the judge's view and conceded that the CSA imposed a substantial burden on the sincere exercise of religion by UDV members. Nevertheless, the government asserted that it had a legitimate interest in applying drug law to hoasca. It was therefore the government's responsibility to demonstrate that the ban on ayahuasca was necessary to achieve a governmental interest and that it was the least restrictive means of addressing the ceremonial use of the substance (O Centro Espírita Beneficente União do Vegetal v. Ashcroft, 2002, p. 26–27). As previously noted, the government argued there were at least three key interests in banning the importation of hoasca: preventing health and public safety risks associated with its consumption, preventing its diversion to recreational use, and fulfilling the U.S. obligations under the 1971 UN Convention on Psychotropic Substances.

The ruling recognized that the lack of research on ayahuasca had turned the substance into a contentious issue, with experts on both sides offering differing interpretations, particularly regarding its potential health risks. The court noted that, despite the central role of the tea in religious ceremonies and devotional practices of UDV members, there had been insufficient research into the physical and psychological effects of its ceremonial use. The UDV acknowledged this research gap but argued that the studies conducted thus far suggested that the religious use of ayahuasca posed no proven health risks (O Centro Espírita Beneficente União do Vegetal v. Ashcroft, 2002, p. 33–34).

To support this stance, the UDV presented testimony from Dr. Charles Grob, a professor of psychiatry at the University of California, Los Angeles, who led the

[13] On this matter, Parker referred to several other cases in which the RFRA was used to challenge the application of drug laws, where the applicants' beliefs were either not recognized as religious or were deemed insincere, particularly the case of United States v. Meyers (1996). Despite its significance, other rulings have ventured into defining what constitutes a religion in legal terms. Labate and Feeney (2012) cite a 1968 case in which a U.S. federal court ruled that a group called the "Neo-American Church," which considered psychedelics its sacraments, could not be classified as a religion, as it lacked "evidence of belief in a supreme being, religious discipline, ritual, or principles to guide the daily existence of individuals" (United States v. Kuch, 1968, p. 444 apud Labate & Feeney, 2012, p. 158).

Hoasca Project research team.[14] According to Grob, while the study had limitations, it found no harmful effects associated with ayahuasca use among a group of men who had consumed the substance for many years in a religious context. In contrast, Grob emphasized that the research highlighted the consistency of the data showing the high functional status of participants who had used ayahuasca over an extended period. Finally, Grob noted that many of the participants reported having exhibited self-destructive behavior before joining the UDV, and that their experiences with hoasca helped them lead responsible and fulfilling lives (O Centro Espírita Beneficente União do Vegetal v. Ashcroft, 2002, p. 34).

In contrast, the government contended that it had evidence indicating that hoasca use posed serious health risks. Initially, the government questioned the reliability of the Hoasca Project in demonstrating the safety of the drink. Government experts pointed out several limitations in the research, especially from a methodological perspective. One of the alleged limitations was the small sample size. Additionally, the study was criticized for lacking baseline data that could have been used to compare participants' conditions before and after engaging in UDV rituals.

Dr. Alexander Walker, a Professor of Epidemiology at the Harvard School of Public Health, argued that selection bias weakened the study's findings. He claimed that by selecting long-term UDV members, the research team inevitably included individuals capable of adhering to the church's teachings for extended periods, ensuring the group had a favorable psychological profile. Dr. Lorne Dawson, an expert in religious studies presented by the government, concurred with this view, noting that limiting the sample to long-term users raised methodological issues. He argued that it would have been preferable to include a larger sample, comprising individuals who had recently joined the church or left it for various reasons (O Centro Espírita Beneficente União do Vegetal v. Ashcroft, 2002, p. 35–36). In addition to concerns about the Hoasca Project's findings, the government raised broader issues related to the religious consumption of ayahuasca by the UDV. Dr. Sander Genser, a member of the National Institute on Drug Abuse, presented a series of studies on the potential risks of DMT. However, Genser emphasized that his concerns about hoasca use were not limited to what was known about other forms of DMT consumption, but also included data on other hallucinogenic substances. The government's expert cited a broad range of adverse neuropsychological effects linked to other hallucinogens, such as lysergic acid diethylamide (LSD). Genser

[14] During an interview, Dr. Grob (personal communication, 2024) recalled: "In June of '93, we gathered in Manaus—Dennis [McKenna], Jace Calloway, Glaucus, and several Brazilian medical and psychological researchers. We conducted a study with 15 long-term UDV members, focusing on their physiological and psychological responses to ayahuasca. We observed no neuropsychological or cognitive impairments; in fact, on some measures, the participants outperformed control groups. Many had histories of severe depression, anxiety, or substance abuse prior to joining the UDV, but their symptoms improved significantly after their first ayahuasca experience and remained stable. Their struggles with alcoholism appeared to resolve completely, and they showed improved social responsibility, job performance, and emotional regulation. However, since the group was self-selected, we couldn't assess those who left the tradition without experiencing similar benefits."

underscored the risk of LSD triggering prolonged psychotic reactions in individuals with preexisting mental health conditions. The expert also emphasized that LSD users may develop a persistent condition known as "flashbacks," in which they unexpectedly relive the drug's effects even when not under its influence (O Centro Espírita Beneficente União do Vegetal v. Ashcroft, 2002, pp. 36–37).

The UDV countered the government expert's claim that the institution's ceremonial use of hoasca posed significant risks to its users. Regarding the studies cited by Genser, which involved intravenous DMT administration, the UDV's experts highlighted that the method of administration greatly influenced the substance's effects. Dr. David Nichols, a professor of Medicinal Chemistry and Molecular Pharmacology at Purdue University, argued that oral consumption of hoasca induced a less intense and more manageable altered state of consciousness, which was psychologically safer. Regarding the government's evidence on the risks of other hallucinogens, like LSD, Nichols pointed out the absence of any evidence linking hoasca to flashbacks (O Centro Espírita Beneficente União do Vegetal v. Ashcroft, 2002, p. 36–37). Additionally, Nichols stressed that the "set" and "setting"[15] surrounding the consumption of a hallucinogenic substance were crucial in shaping the individual's experience. Reinforcing this view, one of Dr. Grob's primary points about the Hoasca Project was that research had shown the UDV had established a structured ritual environment that prioritized safety and minimized the potential for adverse outcomes.[16] To further support Grob's claims, the UDV emphasized its rigorous safety protocols, including psychological screenings for new members and close monitoring of any issues during church ceremonies (O Centro Espírita Beneficente União do Vegetal v. Ashcroft, 2002, p. 38).

Nevertheless, government representatives maintained that there were additional concerns about the safety of hoasca use in the UDV. They presented data from the DEMEC, the UDV's Medical-Scientific Department in Brazil, showing instances of psychotic outbreaks among UDV members. According to DEMEC, from 1996 onwards, 24 cases of psychosis were reported during religious ceremonies in the country's three most populated regions (O Centro Espírita Beneficente União do Vegetal v. Ashcroft, 2002, p. 41). The UDV's experts, on their part, contested the likelihood of hoasca use causing significant psychotic events. Grob, addressing the

[15] The "set" refers to the psychological and social conditions of the user, while the "setting" refers to the social environment in which the substance is consumed (Zinberg, 1984).

[16] Grob (personal communication, 2024) recalled, "I remember the first ceremony I attended, I was sitting next to Annelise, my interpreter, and my Portuguese was very limited, and there was a very active dialogue going back and forth between the master and some people in the audience. It really struck me that whatever it was they were talking about seemed important. Annelise dozed off. I nudged her and asked: 'What are they saying?' She said: 'They are saying how important it is that if you say you are going to be someplace at a certain time, you be there.' That is good. They are teaching them responsibility in a hyper-suggestible state. And some of the other facets addressed during the sermon were about being more responsible out in the world, being more responsible at work, treating your employees better, treating your employer better, being more responsible towards family, being a better spouse, being a better parent, being a better child to your parents. And it was all about taking responsibility in a very pro-social manner."

DEMEC documents, noted that many of the psychiatric problems reported were transient and resolved over time. In the rare cases of more severe mental illness, he pointed out that those individuals had pre-existing conditions, making it imprudent to directly attribute the incidents to hoasca. Furthermore, he reinforced his position by asserting that, considering the large number of participants in the ceremonies and the considerable time the UDV had dedicated to studying such episodes, the reported cases were statistically insignificant (O Centro Espírita Beneficente União do Vegetal v. Ashcroft, 2002, pp. 42–43).

When weighing the arguments from both sides, the court acknowledged that, in other scenarios, the risks identified by the government might have been enough to prevent the use of hoasca until further research could be conducted. Judge Parker noted that even the UDV's scientific experts admitted the need for more research on the health implications of ayahuasca. Still, he ruled that, based on the balance of evidence provided by both parties, the federal government failed to demonstrate that ayahuasca posed health risks to UDV members (O Centro Espírita Beneficente União do Vegetal v. Ashcroft, 2002, p. 44–45).

Despite losing on the health risk issue, the government maintained its concern for the safety of individuals consuming hoasca outside of a religious context. The government argued that if the UDV were permitted to use hoasca in its religious ceremonies, the tea could be misused in non-religious, potentially harmful environments without proper supervision. To support this claim, they presented the testimony of Dr. Donald Jasinski, a professor at the Johns Hopkins School of Medicine, who approached the issue from a pharmacological standpoint. Jasinski expressed the view that the risk of hoasca abuse was substantial, given the effects typically associated with DMT, such as transient changes in mood, thoughts, feelings, and perceptions. He suggested that the euphoria induced by hoasca could be a significant factor leading people to experiment with the substance and possibly develop an abuse pattern (O Centro Espírita Beneficente União do Vegetal v. Ashcroft, 2002, p. 45–46).

In addition to Jasinski's testimony, the government turned to the testimony of Terrance Woodworth, deputy director of the Drug Enforcement Administration's Office of Diversion Control. Woodworth identified several key factors in assessing the potential for recreational use of a controlled substance, including the form of the substance, the existence of an illegal market for it, its cost, its circulation methods, the levels of control attached to it, and the possibility of commercialization and publicity about its consumption. He highlighted that, according to drug consumption patterns in the United States, ayahuasca held significant potential for abuse. During the evidentiary hearing, Woodworth referred to the results of the Household Survey on Drug Abuse, which showed a substantial increase in the use of hallucinogens in the country. He suggested that the growing interest and demand for hallucinogens would substantially increase the potential for abuse of any substance with hallucinogenic properties. Woodworth also attributed the relatively low level of ayahuasca abuse in the United States to its limited availability, asserting that allowing its importation would increase its physical presence in the U.S., heightening the likelihood of misuse.

In response, the UDV contested the idea that hoasca would be diverted for non-religious uses, reaffirming its minimal potential for abuse. To support this claim, the UDV presented the testimony of Dr. Kleiman, a professor of Policy Studies at the University of California, Los Angeles, who argued that demand for the drink would remain relatively low due to its negative side effects and the availability of alternative substances. Kleiman emphasized that users of hallucinogens would likely be less tolerant of nausea compared to users of other drugs. He also pointed out that, according to specialized literature, hallucinogenic substances like DMT have a significantly lower tendency to create dependence compared to other substances, such as opiates. Furthermore, Kleiman argued that the wide availability of pharmacologically equivalent substitutes for DMT—some with fewer undesirable side effects and legal risks—would substantially reduce any incentive for diversion for abuse.

Additionally, Kleiman noted that the UDV had a strong interest in preventing the misuse of the drink, as hoasca was considered a sacrament, and its use outside the religious context would be viewed as sacrilege. He explained that, according to church doctrine, the UDV had a vested interest in preventing misuse and would likely cooperate with authorities to track any diverted shipments. The court, after considering the evidence from both sides, found that the government had failed to demonstrate a compelling interest regarding the diversion of ayahuasca. As a result, the government's claims on this matter were rejected, and both of their first two arguments were dismissed. The third point remained for further analysis (O Centro Espírita Beneficente União do Vegetal v. Ashcroft, 2002, p. 50–52).

The government's final argument in support of the ayahuasca ban was rooted in the country's commitment to a specific international treaty, the 1971 United Nations Convention on Psychotropic Substances (CSP). The government argued that adhering to the terms of the CSP was a compelling interest, emphasizing the need for nations to honor international law and treaty obligations. It also highlighted the country's central role in the war on drugs and its interest in securing cooperation from other nations in the global fight against drug trafficking. Ultimately, the government asserted that failing to uphold the CSP obligations would undermine U.S. efforts to encourage other countries to comply with the treaty, potentially damaging future international relationships and agreements (O Centro Espírita Beneficente União do Vegetal v. Ashcroft, 2002, p. 54).

From Bronfman's perspective (2013, p. 16), the federal government's argument about honoring international treaties posed challenges for the UDV. After an extensive search for commentaries on the treaty, UDV representatives found a fully annotated version of the CSP in an international agreements library in Austria. This version indicated that the treaty was not intended to target the historical use of psychoactive plants in religious rituals. To reinforce this point, Bronfman cites an excerpt from the annotated treaty:

> List I of the treaty does not list any of the material natural hallucinogens in question, but only the chemical substances constituting the active principles contained in them. Neither the crown, fruit or bud of the peyote cactus [...] nor the psilocybin mushrooms themselves are included in Schedule I, but only their respective active ingredients—mescaline, DMT and psilocybin. (United Nations 1971 apud Bronfman, 2013, p. 16)

The court acknowledged the UDV's argument that the CSP contained a provision allowing nations to create exceptions for traditional religious uses of psychoactive plants. Judge Parker emphasized that the possibility of a future ban on peyote, psilocybin mushrooms, or other hallucinogenic plants used in traditional spiritual practices would depend on the ability of the parties involved to request an exception to continue their religious practices. In light of this, the court determined that ayahuasca was not covered by the CSP. The judge concluded that the government's declared interest in adhering to the treaty's rules did not justify extending the DMT ban to the ceremonial use of ayahuasca.

From the court's perspective, the government failed to meet the first requirement set by the Religious Freedom Restoration Act (RFRA), namely, proving that there was a compelling interest in banning ayahuasca. Additionally, the court found that the government's actions regarding the religious practices of UDV members did not meet the second requirement of RFRA, as they were not considered the least restrictive means of addressing the religious use of ayahuasca (O Centro Espírita Beneficente União do Vegetal v. Ashcroft, 2002, p. 58).

In his conclusion, Judge Parker ruled in favor of the UDV, recognizing that irreparable harm would occur if the injunction were denied and that the burden on the UDV outweighed any potential harm to the U.S. government. The judge determined that granting the injunction did not go against the public interest, as the violation of religious freedoms protected by RFRA would cause irreparable harm to the institution and its members. To support this reasoning, the court referenced the Kikumura case, which asserted that "the denial of plaintiff's right to the free exercise of his religious beliefs is an evil that cannot be adequately compensated for monetarily" (Kikumura v. Hurley 2001 apud O Centro Espírita Beneficente União do Vegetal v. Ashcroft, 2002, p. 59).

4.7 The Court of Appeals and the Supreme Court's Final Decision

> A religious sect with origins in the Amazon receives communion by drinking a sacramental tea brewed from unique plants in the region that contains a hallucinogen regulated by the federal government under the Controlled Substances Act. The government recognizes that this practice is a sincere exercise of religion, yet seeks to prohibit the sect's small American branch from engaging in the practice because the Controlled Substances Act bars all uses of the hallucinogen (Gonzales v. O Centro Espírita Beneficente União do Vegetal, 2006, p. 1).

In 2002, the 10th Circuit Court issued an injunction prohibiting the government and its agents from interfering with the UDV's importation, distribution, and religious use of hoasca. The ruling required the UDV to import hoasca in compliance with federal regulations, ensuring that control over the tea remained with authorized church officials and that members were informed of its potential risks. The court also mandated that the government coordinate with UDV representatives to oversee the importation and distribution of the brew (*Petition for a Writ of Certiorari,*

Gonzales v. O Centro Espírita Beneficente União do Vegetal, 2006, pp. 7–8). Additionally, the injunction allowed the government to seek revocation of the religious use authorization if new evidence emerged indicating that hoasca posed a health risk to UDV members or if a shipment contained dangerously high levels of DMT (Gonzales v. O Centro Espírita Beneficente União do Vegetal, 2006, p. 6).

The government appealed the case to the Court of Appeals, which, despite some disagreements with the 10th Circuit Court's reasoning, upheld the original decision. Judge Seymour emphasized that the primary consideration in the injunction analysis should be the balance of harm. In her view, the tangible and ongoing harm to the UDV outweighed the potential risks cited by the government, including concerns over diversion, health hazards, and national security threats. She also downplayed the harm caused by violating the Convention on Psychotropic Substances (CSP), noting that when the United States joined the treaty, it retained the right to establish exceptions for the religious or ritual use of native plants, as permitted by the convention. In a separate opinion, Judge McConnell concurred with the majority, agreeing that the UDV's request for an injunction was justified. He pointed out that the government had failed to prove that an outright ban was the least restrictive means of ensuring compliance with the CSP. Furthermore, he underscored that the federal government was legally obligated to accommodate the religious use of hoasca (Petition for a Writ of Certiorari, Gonzales v. O Centro Espírita Beneficente União do Vegetal, 2006, pp. 10–11).

Justice Murphy dissented, arguing that preventing the government from enforcing its drug laws would result in irreparable harm. He contended that Congress had determined that the importation and consumption of controlled substances were contrary to the public interest. Moreover, he warned that an injunction requiring the U.S. to violate an international treaty would undermine its ability to collaborate with other nations in controlling the global flow of illegal substances. Murphy further asserted that Congress had already established a compelling interest in regulating drug laws through the least restrictive means and that RFRA could not be used to circumvent the government's authority over controlled substances (Petition for a Writ of Certiorari, Gonzales v. O Centro Espírita Beneficente União do Vegetal, 2006, pp. 9–12).

Despite divided opinions, the Court of Appeals upheld the 10th Circuit Court's original decision. The majority ruled that, based on the evidence presented, the government had failed to demonstrate significant health risks or the potential for diversion associated with recreational use. The claim that DMT posed an unacceptable public health threat was deemed insufficient to satisfy RFRA's strict requirements. Regarding the government's assertion that the CSP prohibited the importation of ayahuasca, the court concluded that the government had not proven that treaty compliance was the least restrictive means of advancing its interest in upholding international agreements (Petition for a Writ of Certiorari, Gonzales v. O Centro Espírita Beneficente União do Vegetal, 2006, pp. 8–9). Like the 10th Circuit Court, the Court of Appeals found that the federal government had failed to meet RFRA's necessary legal standard.

Following its defeat in the Court of Appeals, the government appealed to the Supreme Court, arguing that the ruling conflicted with prior decisions on religious exemptions to national drug laws. It sought a uniform national application of drug regulations to resolve inconsistencies among district courts. From the government's perspective, the Court of Appeals' decision hindered the enforcement of criminal drug laws and disregarded Congress's determination that Schedule I substances under the CSA should never be deemed safe for use. The government further contended that courts' refusal to reassess administrative decisions based on religious freedom considerations highlighted the dangers of controlled substance consumption, whether for secular or religious purposes. It insisted that all evidence presented by both parties should be weighed in assessing the risks associated with hoasca use (Petition for a Writ of Certiorari, Gonzales v. O Centro Espírita Beneficente União do Vegetal, 2006, pp. 13–19).

The government further argued that allowing the importation and distribution of hoasca would violate the CSP, weakening the country's commitment to international cooperation in combating transnational drug trafficking and potentially harming its credibility as a leader in anti-drug policy. This, in turn, could lead to diplomatic complications. Government representatives maintained that the CSA and CSP should take precedence, emphasizing the broader goal of preventing and controlling drug use among the general population—whether for widely available substances like marijuana or emerging ones like ayahuasca. The federal government asserted that banning ayahuasca was essential not only to protect public health but also to uphold international drug control agreements, preserve diplomatic relations, and maintain leverage over other nations to ensure compliance with U.S. anti-drug policies (Petition for a Writ of Certiorari, Gonzales v. O Centro Espírita Beneficente União do Vegetal, 2006, pp. 19–29).

On November 1, 2005, the United States Supreme Court heard arguments from both the federal government and the UDV. Attorneys Edwin Kneedler and Nancy Hollander represented the government and the UDV, respectively, presenting their cases and responding to the justices' questions. According to the UDV's legal team, numerous civil and religious organizations had either produced or endorsed documents in support of the UDV's petition, which were submitted to the Supreme Court. Among the endorsing organizations were the Catholic Bishops of North America, the Joint Baptist Committee, the National Council of Evangelical Christians, the Presbyterian Church of the United States, the American Civil Liberties Union, and the American Jewish Congress (Bronfman, 2006 [2004], p. 18).

The Supreme Court document outlined discussions regarding the potential health risks associated with hoasca and concerns about its misuse for non-religious purposes. Notably, the government did not challenge the findings of the 10th Circuit Court or dispute its conclusion that the evidence on these issues was evenly balanced (Gonzales v. O Centro Espírita Beneficente União do Vegetal, 2006, pp. 1–6). The Supreme Court determined that the UDV had convincingly demonstrated that its sincere religious practices were significantly burdened and that the government had failed to prove that this burden served a compelling interest or was the least restrictive means of regulating the religious use of ayahuasca (Argument Transcripts, Gonzales v. O Centro Espírita Beneficente União do Vegetal, 2006).

The Court emphasized that its ruling was based on a careful balance between a government action that caused real and irreparable harm and a potential risk that lacked sufficient supporting evidence. It rejected the notion that the UDV bore the responsibility of disproving the government's claims, reaffirming that the burden of proof lay with the government. The government could have prevailed only by demonstrating that the alternatives proposed by the Court were less effective than an outright ban—a claim the Supreme Court found unsubstantiated (Gonzales v. O Centro Espírita Beneficente União do Vegetal, 2006, pp. 7–8).

The government had argued that the classification of DMT, the active ingredient in ayahuasca, as a Schedule I substance under the Controlled Substances Act (CSA) categorically precluded any exceptions. It contended that the regulatory framework of the CSA required strict and comprehensive enforcement, which would be compromised by judicial exemptions. Moreover, the government maintained that recognizing a religious exception could lead to misinterpretations, potentially undermining the perceived dangers of the substance. Thus, it insisted that the CSA served a compelling interest and did not allow for exemptions (Gonzales v. O Centro Espírita Beneficente União do Vegetal, 2006, p. 9).

In response, the Supreme Court underscored the importance of the RFRA in the case. The Court stressed that RFRA required the government to demonstrate that any law burdening an individual's sincere religious practice met the compelling interest test. This necessitated a thorough evaluation of the potential harm caused by denying religious exemptions, going beyond the general justifications for the law's applicability. In the UDV case, the government was obliged to provide a justification that went beyond merely invoking drug laws.

While acknowledging the government's argument that Schedule I substances, such as DMT, were particularly hazardous, the Supreme Court held that there was no evidence indicating that the Schedule I classification of DMT accounted for the specific religious use of ayahuasca by the UDV. Despite Congress's stance on drug laws, the Court ruled that the case at hand did not absolve the government of its duty to prove a compelling interest, as required by the RFRA (Gonzales v. O Centro Espírita Beneficente União do Vegetal, 2006, p. 11).

The Court emphasized that, more than three decades earlier, an exception had been made for the religious use of peyote by the NAC. Given the widespread acceptance of peyote use among hundreds of thousands of Native Americans, the Court concluded that it would be difficult to justify denying a similar exception for the approximately 100 UDV members who sought to practice their faith (Gonzales v. O Centro Espírita Beneficente União do Vegetal, 2006, pp. 12–13). Additionally, the Court noted that the exception granted for peyote use directly contradicted the government's claim that the CSA established a closed regulatory system that did not accommodate exceptions under the RFRA.

The Supreme Court contended that the government's argument relied on a simplistic assumption that one exception would inevitably lead to more exceptions. In contrast, the Court held that the RFRA required consideration of exceptions to rules of general applicability, mandating a test to assess the balance between religious freedom and competing government interests. The Court acknowledged that there could be cases where the need for uniformity in drug enforcement might argue against religious exceptions. However, this was not such a case, given the CSA's longstanding exemption for the religious use of peyote and the fact that Congress enacted the RFRA specifically to address the denial of religious use of a controlled substance. In this context, the Court pointed out that the government had failed to present evidence demonstrating that granting an exemption to the UDV would cause the type of administrative harm that could be considered a compelling interest (Gonzales v. O Centro Espírita Beneficente União do Vegetal, 2006, pp. 15–16).

The Court claimed that the fact that hoasca was covered by the CSA did not automatically imply that the government had shown a compelling interest in applying the law. The Court pointed out that the government had not provided any evidence addressing the international consequences of granting an exemption to the UDV, offering only two statements from State Department officials asserting the general importance of honoring international obligations and maintaining the U.S. leadership position in the international war on drugs. Although the Court did not question the validity of the interests presented by the government, it stated that the mere assertion of such interests was not sufficient to win the case for the federal government, given the requirements of the RFRA (Gonzales v. O Centro Espírita Beneficente União do Vegetal, 2006, p. 17).

Finally, the Court highlighted that the government had repeatedly invoked the results and objectives underlying the CSA but emphasized that Congress also had a strong interest in enacting the RFRA. The Court held that the RFRA clearly contemplated the possibility of courts recognizing exceptions and that an individual whose religious exercise had been burdened could bring a claim or lawsuit and obtain adequate redress from the government. Additionally, the Court reaffirmed in its conclusion that Congress had recognized the potential for neutral laws to create a burden on religious exercise and thus instituted the compelling interest test as a tool for courts to strike a balance between religious freedom and government interests. Applying this test, the Supreme Court concluded that the 10th Circuit Court had not erred in determining that the government had failed to demonstrate a compelling interest in prohibiting the religious use of hoasca (Gonzales v. O Centro Espírita Beneficente União do Vegetal, 2006, pp. 18–19).

The significance of Gonzales v. O Centro Espírita Beneficente União do Vegetal lies in its landmark ruling that reinforced the protection of religious freedom in the United States, particularly in the context of the use of psychoactive substances. By recognizing the UDV's right to use ayahuasca as part of its religious practice, the Supreme Court set a precedent for religious groups seeking exemptions from controlled substances regulations under the RFRA. This case not only affirmed the importance of balancing government interests with the protection of religious practices but also demonstrated a critical shift in jurisprudence regarding the intersection of religious freedom and drug laws. It paved the way for other ayahuasca groups to seek legal recognition for the religious use of psychoactive substances, establishing a broader framework for how the law should accommodate religious practices involving these substances. The decision has had profound implications for future legal challenges, highlighting the potential for religious exemptions in the context of public health and drug regulation and setting an important precedent for the evolving relationship between religious freedom, the law, and psychoactive substances in the United States.

4.8 The UDV DEA Agreement

After the Supreme Court ruled in favor of the UDV, the question of how to regulate or administer the religious use of ayahuasca remained unresolved. As a result, the case was sent back to the 10th Circuit Court, which had initially ruled that the UDV and the DEA should negotiate a settlement. Bronfman explained that this need arose from ayahuasca's classification as a controlled substance, meaning its import, distribution, and use would be subject to DEA regulations. According to Bronfman (2013, p. 4), the UDV chose not to contest the court's decision, instead opting for a cooperative relationship with federal agencies responsible for enforcing the nation's drug laws.[17]

A resolution was soon reached, culminating in a 21-page document that outlined which controlled substance regulations would apply to the UDV. Before examining the document's specifics, it's important to note that the agreement did not indicate a mutual concession on the core issues of the dispute. The UDV consistently maintained that its religious practices should not be subject to government regulation. However, it agreed to adapt many of its activities to align with DEA protocols. Conversely, while the DEA was open to resolving the issue amicably, it made clear that it would not abandon its stance that controlled substances were generally not exempt from regulation. As a result, the agreement stipulated that no government agency would be prevented from enforcing the country's laws on the UDV and its members, except in the case of the religious use of hoasca (O Centro Espírita Beneficente União do Vegetal v. Holder, 2010, p. 3–4).

Under the terms of the agreement, the UDV agreed to comply with certain practices required of pharmacies and researchers when importing, distributing, and storing controlled substances. In turn, the DEA agreed not to impose or expect the UDV to follow regulations that apply to non-religious entities. One example Bronfman (2013, p. 5) cites involves the Code of Federal Regulations, which mandates that importers and distributors of controlled substances record the "dosage strength" of each drug batch, based on the active compounds. This requirement, however, would not apply to the UDV's religious use of ayahuasca.

Another key point raised by the UDV concerns the DEA's authority to issue licenses for distributing controlled substances within narcotics treatment centers.

[17] According to information provided by Bronfman, by 2013, 12 religious communities linked to the UDV in the United States were currently registered with the DEA as licensed importers, manufacturers, and distributors of a product belonging to Schedule 1 of Controlled Substances.

According to Bronfman, extending this authority to the UDV would be unacceptable, as it would allow the DEA to determine who could or could not be a UDV master—the religious leader who administers the sacrament during ceremonies. As a result, the negotiation ensured that the DEA's licensing authority would not extend to the UDV's religious activities.

A careful review of the document reveals a discrepancy between the agreed-upon measures and the DEA's standard procedures for regulating controlled substances. The Supreme Court's recognition of an exemption to the CSA for religious use of ayahuasca forced the DEA to strike a balance between its enforcement priorities and the UDV's religious freedoms. While the DEA sought to retain its established control and inspection mechanisms, it had to yield on certain points, such as the selection of those authorized to administer the sacrament and even the terminology used in regulations—where terms like "potency" and "concentration" lost their conventional meaning.

This outcome is not merely a technical inconsistency; it underscores the complexity of creating a regulatory framework when two parties hold fundamentally different views—both in how the law should be applied and in their understanding of specific legal categories. This stands in stark contrast to the Brazilian case, where the recognition of ayahuasca as a cultural and religious tradition gradually diminished its classification as a drug (Antunes, 2012, 2015). By the 2000s, the notion of hallucinogenic had been removed from the deliberations of Brazil's National Anti-Drug Secretariat (CONAD). In Brazil, the legal status of ayahuasca as a sacrament—an essential part of a religious and cultural practice—led to its exclusion from drug-related classifications. In contrast, the UDV's case in New Mexico reflects an effort to carve out a legal exception within the existing drug control framework, rather than reframe ayahuasca outside it altogether.

4.9 The Legal Dispute Between a Santo Daime Church and the Federal Government

The first Santo Daime church in the United States, Céu do Beija-Flor, was founded in Massachusetts in 1988. Just 2 years after its establishment, the church faced a major setback when its leader, Rex Beynon, was arrested following the interception of a daime shipment from Brazil. Beynon spent 4 months in custody, though the case never proceeded to trial, as prosecutors ultimately chose to drop the charges. Despite this legal reprieve, the consequences were severe: Beynon was permanently deported to Wales, leading to a 3-year hiatus in Santo Daime activities across the country.

According to Jonathan Goldman (personal communication, 2016), a member of the church, this suspension was a mutual decision between Santo Daime practitioners in the United States and Brazil. At the time, the supply of daime was extremely limited, and both groups agreed to abstain from any attempts to send or receive new shipments. This self-imposed pause lasted until 1993 when Goldman sought approval from padrinho Alfredo Gregório de Melo, the head of ICEFLU, to establish a new Santo Daime center in Oregon, known as CHLQ. Over the next 6 years, Goldman led the center and continued receiving shipments of daime from Brazil without encountering any interference from U.S. authorities.

That changed in 1999 when a shipment of Santo Daime was seized, triggering a legal confrontation between the federal government and CHLQ members. According to the complaint filed by the institution, on May 20, federal agents intercepted a shipment addressed to Goldman. Backed by the Treasury and Justice Departments, the DEA swiftly obtained a search and seizure warrant for his residence. Armed agents raided his home, confiscating the shipment along with several personal items. Goldman was arrested and detained for 12 hours before being released on bail (The Church of the Holy Light of the Queen v. Mukasey, 2009, p. 8).

Shortly after the incident, the CHLQ reached out to the Oregon Board of Pharmacy (OBP), the state agency responsible for overseeing controlled substances, to request permission to conduct their ceremonies within a religious framework (Haber, 2011, p. 307). In November 2000, the OBP held a hearing where he CHLQ presented the same arguments that would later appear in their 2008 lawsuit against the government. The agency ultimately ruled that the state of Oregon "does not consider the sacramental use of Santo Daime tea in church ceremonies to constitute abuse of a controlled substance," further stating that it "does not possess or intend to exercise regulatory authority with respect to the religious practices of the Santo Daime church in Oregon" (Oregon Board of Pharmacy 2008 apud The Church of the Holy Light of the Queen v. Mukasey, 2009, p. 9).

Despite this decision, CHLQ representatives reported that the federal government remained unswayed, asserting that the tea was not only unsafe but also posed a public health risk to the country (The Church of the Holy Light of the Queen v. Mukasey, 2009, p. 10). Although neither Goldman nor the institution faced formal prosecution, a former Oregon state attorney informed the church in October 2001 that "the decision to prosecute them for their conduct remains an open question pending the U.S. Department of Justice's decision on their request for a controlled substance exemption" (The Church of the Holy Light of the Queen v. Mukasey, 2009, p. 8).

Just 8 days later, the U.S. Department of Justice issued a response, stating that it "believes that prohibiting the importation, distribution, and possession of ayahuasca tea is the least restrictive means of furthering a compelling government interest." However, according to the CHLQ, the government failed to clarify exactly what that interest entailed (The Church of the Holy Light of the Queen v. Mukasey, 2009, p. 9). Goldman emphasized that the church members interpreted the government's refusal to reach an agreement as an ongoing threat to their religious practice. In response, CHLQ members chose to continue their ceremonies in secrecy, ceasing documentation of Santo Daime shipments and church activities. Unlike the UDV, which halted hoasca imports and began conducting its ceremonies with water, the CHLQ opted to maintain its practices despite the risk of arrest and prosecution (The Church of the Holy Light of the Queen v. Mukasey, 2009, p. 8).

Attempts to reach an agreement seemingly came to an end by mid-2001. In 2008, 6 years after the UDV's initial complaint and 2 years after the Supreme Court's final ruling in favor of the UDV, the CHLQ decided to sue the federal government, presenting the same legal arguments that the UDV had put forth in 2000. According to Goldman (personal communication, 2016), the delay in formalizing the lawsuit stemmed from internal disagreements—both among Santo Daime churches in the U.S. and with ICEFLU, the Brazilian institution overseeing the church, which opposed taking legal action against the government. Faced with this impasse, the CHLQ chose to sever its ties with ICEFLU, declaring itself an independent church. Following its separation, the CHLQ formally filed a lawsuit against the U.S. government, identifying itself as a Christian religious organization. In the complaint, Jonathan Goldman, members of the CHLQ Council, and other church members accused the federal government of violating multiple legal protections, depriving them of the rights, privileges, and immunities guaranteed by law. Like the UDV, the CHLQ argued that the government had infringed upon the RFRA and violated their rights under the First, Fifth, and Fourteenth Amendments of the U.S. Constitution.

Specifically, the plaintiffs sought a court order declaring that the government's threats to arrest and prosecute Santo Daime practitioners for importing and consuming their sacrament in religious ceremonies were unconstitutional and unlawful, as they placed an undue burden on religious practices. Additionally, the CHLQ requested an injunction prohibiting the federal government from blocking the importation or use of Santo Daime in religious ceremonies, as well as from arresting or prosecuting members for ritual consumption of the tea (The Church of the Holy Light of the Queen v. Mukasey, 2009, pp. 1–2).

Following the legal strategy established by the UDV, the CHLQ also described itself as part of a Brazilian religious tradition with ancestral roots in centuries-old Amerindian practices. The complaint emphasized how these Indigenous traditions had been absorbed into Christian beliefs through the influence of missionaries in the region, resulting in syncretic religions emerging deep within the Amazon. After outlining this historical context, the document underscored the central role of Daime in the CHLQ's religious beliefs and rituals, as well as its connection to Christianity. According to the CHLQ, the sacrament of daime was essential to church ceremonies, as it was believed that only by drinking the tea could a church member experience a direct connection with Jesus Christ, whom they venerated as their savior.

The institution asserted that Santo Daime was not merely a means of direct communion with God but the very embodiment of the Holy Spirit, as conveyed through the church's hymns. According to the CHLQ, the doctrine, which equates the presence of daime with the presence of Christ, was transmitted through hymns received by religious leaders over the past century during ceremonies where the tea was consumed. Without the tea, the church argued, its religion could not exist, as daime is an indispensable component of its ritual. The act of drinking daime was described as a form of communion, a fundamental expression of faith for the CHLQ members (The Church of the Holy Light of the Queen v. Mukasey, 2009, p. 4–5).

The CHLQ also addressed the botanical and chemical composition of ayahuasca. It emphasized that Banisteriopsis caapi, one of the plants used to prepare the brew, contains three alkaloids, none of which are classified under the CSA, while Psychotria viridis contains only trace amounts of DMT. In addition to discussing these legal and scientific aspects, the CHLQ pointed to Brazil's regulatory framework for ayahuasca as an exemplary public policy model. The institution highlighted that in the late 1980s, CONFEN conducted a comprehensive 2-year study on the religious use of ayahuasca before officially sanctioning it.

The complaint then presented key arguments from the UDV's case against the U.S. government. It underscored that in all legal proceedings, the government had failed to demonstrate a compelling interest in prohibiting the importation, distribution, or consumption of ayahuasca in religious ceremonies. The document noted that the government had been unable to prove that the tea posed any significant health risks to UDV members or the public or that it was susceptible to diversion for recreational use. Given these legal precedents, the CHLQ contended that the government lacked a compelling reason to prevent the importation of Santo Daime as well.

The church argued that the federal government should be barred from revisiting concerns related to public health and safety, especially since, in November 2007, it had conceded that it had no evidence to support its position. Furthermore, the CHLQ asserted that there was no proof that Santo Daime was being diverted to illicit markets. As with the UDV case, the CHLQ maintained that ongoing threats of persecution and confiscation of the tea infringed upon its members' rights to religious practice. It also highlighted that some of its members held dual Brazilian-American citizenship, enabling them to legally practice their religion in Brazil while facing the threat of arrest in the United States (The Church of the Holy Light of the Queen v. Mukasey, 2009, p. 17–18).

The institution further contended that the government's actions were not only unconstitutional but amounted to an overreach of authority. The CHLQ representatives accused the government of engaging in unlawful acts by harassing, intimidating, and obstructing their religious practices without legal justification. To reinforce this position, the CHLQ cited the U.S. Commission on International Religious Freedom's "Year 2000" report, which commended Brazil's tolerance of "syncretic religions"—including Santo Daime—recognized by both the Brazilian government and civil and religious institutions such as the Brazilian Catholic Church. Based on this recognition, the CHLQ argued that the U.S. government's actions violated the doctrine of comity, which calls for mutual respect of legal systems between nations (The Church of the Holy Light of the Queen v. Mukasey, 2009, p. 19).

Finally, the CHLQ claimed that granting the UDV permission to use ayahuasca for religious purposes while denying the same right to Santo Daime members constituted a violation of the Fourteenth Amendment's equal protection clause. The institution contended that the balance of harms weighed in its favor, as the government had no adequate legal justification for its actions. Without judicial intervention, CHLQ members would continue to suffer irreparable harm, making it imperative for the courts to prevent further government interference in their religious practices.

4.10 The District Court's Ruling

The district court issued its decision 1 year after the CHLQ filed its complaint. Judge Panner opened his argument by emphasizing the credibility of Jonathan Goldman's testimony, recognizing him as the spiritual leader, or "*padrinho*" (godfather) of the CHLQ. He underscored Goldman's deep commitment to Santo Daime, highlighting his decades-long dedication. Goldman had traveled to Brazil more than 20 years earlier to study the religion, making frequent return visits. He had learned Portuguese to understand the Santo Daime hymns—central to the church's doctrine—and had been formally initiated into the tradition. Nearly two decades before the case, in 1993, Goldman had founded the CHLQ with authorization from Santo Daime's mother church in Brazil (ICEFLU). Panner concluded that Goldman's leadership and long-standing dedication demonstrated his sincerity and commitment to the faith (The Church of the Holy Light of the Queen v. Mukasey, 2009, p. 1–2). This question of sincerity was central to the case, as the government contended that Goldman's decision to hold ceremonies in secrecy indicated a lack of genuine religious conviction. Unlike in the UDV case, where the government conceded that the plaintiffs had a legitimate claim under the RFRA, they challenged whether Goldman was sincerely practicing his religion. The court, however, disagreed with the government's argument.

> In the UDV litigation, at least at the preliminary injunction hearing, the government conceded that the UDV plaintiffs had made a prima facie claim under RFRA. Here, however, defendants challenge plaintiffs' sincerity, citing plaintiffs' decision to conduct ceremonies in secret until the Supreme Court ruling in favor of the UDV plaintiffs. Plaintiffs' secrecy does not show a lack of sincerity. Instead, it shows that plaintiffs remained committed to practicing their religion despite the threat of criminal prosecution and loss of professional status. (Church of Holy Light of Queen v. Mukasey, 2009, p.19)

The court found Goldman's sincerity evident in his lifelong dedication: traveling to Brazil, learning Portuguese to deepen his understanding of the doctrine, and securing authorization to establish a church in the United States. Beyond the question of sincerity, the court also delved into the origins of Santo Daime in Brazil. Panner characterized Santo Daime as a syncretic religion, blending Catholicism with indigenous Amazonian and African spiritual traditions. He highlighted that Santo Daime practitioners regard ayahuasca as the blood of Christ, analogous to wine in Catholic communion, and view the drink as a sacred entity, integral to their ceremonies. Without ayahuasca, a Santo Daime church like the CHLQ could not function (The Church of the Holy Light of the Queen v. Mukasey, 2009, p. 3–4).

Panner concluded his discussion of Santo Daime by outlining the history of ayahuasca regulation in Brazil. He emphasized that after extensive study of Santo Daime's practices and the effects of the tea, the Brazilian government had recognized it as a legitimate religion, allowing its ritual use of ayahuasca. Panner also noted that the UDV had undergone a similar process in Brazil. Though differing from Santo Daime in doctrine and ritual, the UDV was likewise acknowledged as a syncretic faith and permitted to use ayahuasca as a sacrament in its ceremonies (The Church of the Holy Light of the Queen v. Mukasey, 2009, p. 5).

The court also devoted significant attention to the health implications of ayahuasca consumption, dedicating an entire section of the ruling to the issue. Panner noted that both the prosecution and defense addressed the potential risks associated with the tea's use in Santo Daime ceremonies. He acknowledged that, if misused, the drink could pose dangers. Nonetheless, he also pointed out that a series of experts presented by the CHLQ suggested ayahuasca might offer physical and mental health benefits, even as they recognized the need for further rigorous scientific studies to substantiate these claims (The Church of the Holy Light of the Queen v. Mukasey, 2009, p. 8).

Ultimately, the court determined that the government failed to present evidence that Santo Daime tea could lead to addiction or long-term health problems. The government's experts, Frankenheim[18] and Tella,[19] had based their arguments on studies involving pure LSD, DMT, and other hallucinogens. However, Judge Panner found these studies only marginally relevant in assessing the risks associated with the religious use of Santo Daime. He noted that intravenous or inhaled DMT produces much stronger but shorter-lasting effects compared to the DMT consumed in daime tea (The Church of the Holy Light of the Queen v. Mukasey, 2009, p. 9–10).

Regarding health risks, the court referenced a study by psychiatrist John H. Halpern, which had the support of CHLQ members. Panner emphasized Halpern's extensive research on the use and abuse of hallucinogenic substances, including a study on the health of NAC members (Halpern et al., 2005). He also cited Halpern's 2008 report on the CHLQ, which was the only study conducted among Santo Daime practitioners in the United States (Halpern et al., 2008). Although Halpern himself acknowledged the study's limitations, Panner considered the research valuable for evaluating the health effects of Santo Daime among CHLQ members.

Judge Panner noted that Halpern's findings aligned with those of the Hoasca Project, which observed that UDV participants often lost interest in consuming alcohol, cocaine, and other addictive substances (Callaway et al., 1999). Panner highlighted Halpern's conclusion that religious consumption of the tea did not result in physical or social harm, even for individuals predisposed to mental health issues.

---

[18] Jerry Frankenheim is a neuroscientist and neuropharmacologist who serves as director of the Functional Neuroscience Research Branch, and the Division of Neuroscience & Behavioral Research at the National Institute on Drug Abuse (NIDA), National Institutes of Health (NIH) and the U.S. Department of Health and Human Services (DHHS) (Frankenheim, 2008, p. 1).

[19] Srihari Tella is a pharmacologist who teaches in the pharmacology department at Georgetown University School of Medicine. In 2002, she joined the DEA in the area of pharmacology (Tella, 2008).

On the contrary, many participants experienced improvements in anxiety and panic disorders (The Church of the Holy Light of the Queen v. Mukasey, 2009, p. 10–11).

Addressing the federal government's claim that Santo Daime consumption could be fatal, Panner stated that no evidence had been presented linking daime or hoasca to any deaths. Experts for the CHLQ countered that the risk of a toxic overdose was mitigated by the tea's natural emetic effect. Panner further noted that thousands of individuals in Brazil consume the tea regularly, and the Brazilian government would not have permitted the operation of the UDV and Santo Daime churches if the tea posed a lethal risk to members.

Another significant issue Panner discussed was the Santo Daime church's prohibition of proselytizing. He referenced the church's structured screening process for new members, based on information provided by the CHLQ. Panner noted that most new members learned about Santo Daime through personal connections—typically friends or relatives—and were required to have a current member serve as their guardian. If the candidate's responses during the screening process were deemed acceptable, they would receive reading materials and an orientation about the church's practices. Panner underscored Goldman's assertion that Santo Daime is a demanding spiritual path unsuitable for most people. The CHLQ, he explained, seeks to admit only those with a serious and respectful attitude toward the religion. Given the institution's rigorous spiritual commitment, the screening process was specifically designed to exclude individuals seeking a recreational drug experience (The Church of the Holy Light of the Queen v. Mukasey, 2009, p. 12–13).

The court determined that Santo Daime consumption was strictly confined to religious rituals and that CHLQ members ingested the tea only within the framework of a controlled ceremony. It was emphasized that access to the tea was restricted to three or four church leaders, with the spiritual leader overseeing the ritual and personally administering the sacrament to each participant. Any consumption outside the church setting, the court noted, would be considered sacrilegious (The Church of the Holy Light of the Queen v. Mukasey, 2009, p. 14–15).

Addressing concerns about potential diversion, the government argued that the CHLQ might permit non-members, including individuals seeking the tea for recreational use, to access it. To support this claim, the government relied on the testimony of DEA Deputy Director Denise Curry, who stated that the quantity of tea confiscated from Goldman's residence suggested the CHLQ had more than necessary for its members. However, the court pointed out that no evidence had been presented to show that the CHLQ had ever authorized the tea's use outside its religious framework. Judge Panner underscored that, for CHLQ members, Santo Daime was a sacrament, and any use beyond the church's authority would directly violate their religious tenets. He further emphasized that the government had failed to demonstrate the existence of a viable illicit market for the tea. Additionally, the court noted that, apart from the years when the CHLQ was forced to conduct its ceremonies in secrecy (1999–2006), the church had maintained detailed records tracking the tea's circulation, with only a select few leaders granted access to the supply (The Church of the Holy Light of the Queen v. Mukasey, 2009, p. 16–17).

After thoroughly examining the health risks and the possibility of diversion for recreational purposes, the court ruled that the government had not provided sufficient evidence to justify its concerns. The CHLQ, on the other hand, successfully demonstrated the sincerity of its religious beliefs and the fundamental role of Daime tea in its practice. Hence, Judge Panner concluded that banning the consumption of Santo Daime would impose a substantial burden on the CHLQ's religious exercise. The court paraphrased the California Supreme Court's stance on the role of peyote in the NAC, affirming that daime tea was a sine qua non of CHLQ's faith—the essential and exclusive means through which its members practiced their religion (The Church of the Holy Light of the Queen v. Mukasey, 2009, p. 18–19).

Finally, Panner issued an opinion intended to guide the parties in reaching an agreement on the procedures for importing, storing, distributing, and using Santo Daime in CHLQ ceremonies. Still, according to Jonathan Goldman (personal communication, 2016), no formal agreement has yet been established between the DEA and the CHLQ regarding the regulation of Santo Daime's religious use. As a result, the church continues to operate without any official contract or document governing its practices.

4.11 A Balance of Rights and Burdens: The Regulation of Religion by State Agencies and Courts

The similarity between the cases of the UDV and the CHLQ is not random; on the contrary, it helps us to understand the ways in which the problem of the religious use of ayahuasca has taken shape in the United States. The legal disputes and their developments are the result of the particular way in which the legal framework for ayahuasca was established, that is, as a controlled substance, but one that can enjoy an exemption for religious use from the application of the country's drug law under specific circumstances. This framing was at odds both with the position of the ayahuasca groups, for whom the categorization of ayahuasca as a drug was problematic, and with the federal government, which argued that the establishment of exceptions to the country's drug law was legally unjustified.

Thus, at all stages of these legal cases, it was possible to highlight an effort on the part of federal government agencies to classify ayahuasca as a controlled substance and curtail the practices of ayahuasca groups. In both cases, the government underscored the possible health risks posed by ayahuasca, the potential for diversion to recreational use, as well as claiming that possible exceptions would call into question the capacity of its institutions to implement public policies and would jeopardize its leadership role in the war on drugs compared to other nations. Furthermore, throughout the legal disputes, representatives of the federal government and its experts insisted on defending the dangers of ayahuasca, arguing that both groups had no right to request an exemption for religious use.

In contrast, the UDV and the CHLQ maintained at all times that ayahuasca should not be included in the country's drug law and that the government had neither the legitimacy nor the appropriate legal mechanisms to regulate their free exercise of religion. Both institutions made a strong effort to emphasize that the drink was a sacrament, whose health risks were negligible as long as it was consumed in a controlled manner, in a religious context. Thus, at no point was a consensus established on the arguments and positions of the federal government and ayahuasca churches.

The decisions of the courts, on the other hand, were different from both positions. Even though ayahuasca was considered a controlled substance, all the courts in which the issue was analyzed decided that the ayahuasca groups had a legitimate claim under the RFRA. Hence, even though they classified ayahuasca as a "drug," the courts ruled that the government had to prove that it had a legitimate interest in denying the exemption requests, demonstrating that the religious use of ayahuasca posed a real risk, and justifying the need for its prohibition not only as necessary but as the least restrictive way possible to deal with the problem in question. Ultimately, the final outcome of the disputes can best be described using the metaphor of a scale on which weighed, on the one hand, the burden imposed on the religious freedom of members of ayahuasca groups and, on the other, a potential risk that ayahuasca would present to its users and to the government. In the opinion of all the courts, the balance tipped in favor of the UDV and Santo Daime churches.

A crucial factor in these legal disputes was the Christian identity of the groups involved. Since both UDV and Santo Daime explicitly identify as Christian and had a legal history of recognition, particularly in Brazil, it was difficult for the U.S. government to challenge the religious nature of their practices outright. In fact, from the outset, both the courts and government agencies acknowledged the religious legitimacy of the UDV and Santo Daime churches, recognizing them as bona fide religious institutions. As such, the legal disputes did not revolve around whether these groups qualified as religions under U.S. law, but rather whether their use of ayahuasca posed a sufficiently compelling threat to justify government intervention. In the case of the CHLQ, for example, expert testimony provided by anthropologist Michael Winkelman (personal communication, 2024) focused not on attesting the group's religious status, but rather on assessing the potential risks of diversion of ayahuasca to non-religious or recreational use. The emphasis on risk rather than outright denial of religious status aligns with the broader legal tradition in the United States, which historically grants significant weight to religious freedom but allows for government intervention if compelling state interests, such as public health and safety, are at stake.

The Christian identity of these groups also aligns with the broader legal framework of religion in the U.S., which has been shaped by Protestant traditions. Within this framework, belief often takes precedence over practice, and sincerity is prioritized over institutional structure. This emphasis on sincerity—deeply rooted in Protestant thought—is a key factor in the legal debates, shaping how religious legitimacy is assessed and defining the boundaries of religious exemptions. While religious freedom holds a central place in U.S. law, it has also been a persistent source of tension in state-religion relations. It should be noted, however, that the controversy surrounding the limits of religious freedom is part of a broader debate on the balance between state intervention and individual liberties. Scholars such as Brandwein (1999), Cristi (2001), DeLombard (2007), Parker (2011), and Hovenkamp (2015) have examined how these tensions stem from a longstanding ideological landscape shaped by anti-statist ethics and a deep-seated suspicion of centralized authority. Engaging with these perspectives, one can see that religious rights are not merely legal constructs but also expressions of broader American anxieties about government overreach and personal freedom.

The cases in question also touch on the paradox pointed out by Sullivan (2005), which highlights the inherent contradiction in laws that guarantee religious freedom while simultaneously requiring courts, legislatures, or administrative bodies to define what constitutes a "religion" in order to determine whether a practice is legally protected. This paradox was evident in the UDV and the CHLQ cases, as legal authorities had to navigate the complexities of categorizing ayahuasca practices as religious while balancing governmental concerns over public health and drug control. The necessity for legal recognition ultimately placed the courts in the position of arbiters of religious legitimacy, reinforcing the ongoing tensions between religious rights and state authority.

Despite the resolution in favor of ayahuasca churches, this did not mark the end of government scrutiny. As the next chapter will explore, new groups seeking religious exemptions, particularly those without Christian foundations, have faced renewed challenges. In these cases, questions about what constitutes a legitimate religion and whether a practice can be considered a sincere religious exercise have taken center stage. Additionally, government agencies have continued to refine their strategies, developing new initiatives to contest the legitimacy and safety of ayahuasca use. These ongoing disputes illustrate how the legal battles over ayahuasca are far from settled and continue to evolve in response to shifting legal, political, and religious landscapes.

References

Africa v. Pennsylvania, 662 F.2d 1025, 1031 (3rd Cir. 1981).

Antunes, H. F. (2012). *Droga, religião e cultura: um mapeamento da controvérsia pública sobre o uso da ayahuasca no Brasil.* Master's Thesis, Anthropology, University of São Paulo.

Antunes, H. F. (2015). Políticas públicas, religião e patrimônio cultural: mapeando a controvérsia pública sobre o uso da ayahuasca no Brasil. In P. Montero (Ed.), *Religiões e controvérsias públicas: Experiências, práticas sociais e discursos* (pp. 125–148). Editora Terceiro Nome/ Editora da Unicamp.

Argument transcripts, Gonzales v. O Centro Espírita Beneficente União do Vegetal, 126 S. Ct. 1211 (2006).

Brandwein, P. (1999). *Reconstructing reconstruction: The Supreme Court and the production of historical truth.* Duke University Press.

Bronfman, J. (2006). The extraordinary case of the United States versus the União do Vegetal Church. *Bioneers Conference.*

Bronfman, J. (2011a). The legal case of the União do Vegetal vs. the government of the United States. In B. Labate & H. Jungaberle (Eds.), *The internationalization of Ayahuasca* (pp. 287–300). Lit Verlag.

Bronfman, J. (2011b). A luta pela liberdade religiosa da União do Vegetal nos Estados Unidos: Um caso histórico. In J. Bernardino-Costa (Ed.), *Hoasca: Ciência, sociedade e meio ambiente* (pp. 205–210). Mercado de Letras.

Bronfman, J. (2013). Federal government licensing of ayahuasca use and related issues of personal and religious freedom. *MAPS Psychedelic Science Conference*.

Bronfman, J. (2015). The globalization of ayahuasca: Public policy considerations. *MAPS Bulletin Special Edition: Psychedelics and Policy, 25*(1).

Burwell v. Hobby Lobby Stores, Inc., 573 U.S. 682 (2014).

Callaway, J. C., McKenna, D. J., Grob, C. S., Brito, G. S., Raymon, L. P., Poland, R. E., Andrade, E. N., Andrade, E. O., & Mash, D. C. (1999). Pharmacokinetics of Hoasca alkaloids in healthy humans. *Journal of Ethnopharmacology, 65*(3), 243–256. https://doi.org/10.1016/S0378-8741(98)00180-6

Chacruna Institute for Psychedelic Plant Medicines, & Hoots, A. (2021). *Guide to RFRA and best practices for psychedelic plant medicine churches*. Chacruna Institute for Psychedelic Plant Medicines.

Church of the Lukumi Babalu Aye, Inc. v. Hialeah, 508 U.S. 520, (1993).

City of Boerne v. Flores, 521 U.S. 507 (1997).

Controlled Substances Act 21 U.S.C. §§ 801–971 (1970).

Cristi, M. (2001). *From civil to political religion: The intersection of culture, religion and politics*. Wilfrid Laurier University Press.

DeLombard, J. M. (2007). *Slavery on trial: Law, abolitionism, and print culture*. The University of North Carolina Press.

Employment Division v. Smith, 494 U.S. 872 (1990).

Frankenheim, J. (2008). Mended expert witness statement in *The Church of the Holy Light of the Queen v. Mukasey*, No. 08-364-PK (D. Or. 2008).

Gonzales v. O Centro Espírita Beneficente União do Vegetal, 546 U.S. 418 (2006).

Grob, C. S., McKenna, D. J., Callaway, J. C., Brito, E. O., Andrade, G., Oberlaender, G., Saide, O. I., Labigani, E., Jr., Tacla, C., Miranda, C. T., Strassman, R. J., Boone, K. S., & Neves, E. S. (2002). Farmacologia humana da Hoasca: efeitos psicológicos. In B. C. Labate & W. S. Araújo (Eds.), *O uso ritual da ayahuasca* (pp. 651–670). FAPESP/Mercado das Letras.

Haber, R. (2011). The Santo Daime road to seeking religious freedom in the USA. In B. Labate & H. Jungaberle (Eds.), *The internationalization of ayahuasca* (pp. 301–318). Lit.

Halpern, J. H., Sherwood, A. R., Hudson, J. I., Yurgelun, T. D., & Pope, H. G. Jr. (2005). Psychological and cognitive effects of long-term peyote use among Native Americans. *Biological Psychiatry, 58*(8), 624–631.

Halpern, J. H., Sherwood, A. R., Passie, T., Blackwell, K. C., & Ruttenber, A. J. (2008). Evidence of health and safety in American members of a religion who use a hallucinogenic sacrament. *Medical Science Monitor, 14*(8), 15–22.

Hoots, A. (2025). The legal definition of religion in the context of modern religious exercise with psychedelics: Protection, double standards, and potential expansion under RFRA. In J. Breau & P. Gillis-Smith (Eds.), *Psychedelic intersections: 2024 conference anthology*. Center for the Study of World Religions, Harvard Divinity School. https://doi.org/10.70423/0001.15

Hoots, A., & Labate, B. C. (2024). *How can you protect your psychedelic plant medicine church, community, and clients?* [Workshop]. Chacruna Institute for Psychedelic Plant Medicines. https://chacruna.net/protect-psychedelic-plant-medicine-church/

Hovenkamp, H. (2015). *The opening of American law: Neoclassical legal thought, 1870–1970*. Oxford University Press.

Labate, B. C., & Feeney, K. (2012). Ayahuasca and the process of regulation in Brazil and internationally: Implications and challenges. *International Journal of Drug Policy, 23*, 154–161.

Native American Church. (2002). *Motion amicus curiae in O Centro Espírita Beneficente União do Vegetal v. Ashcroft*. U.S. District Court, District of New Mexico.

O Centro Espírita Beneficente União do Vegetal v. Ashcroft, 2002.

O Centro Espírita Beneficente União do Vegetal v. Holder, 2010.

O Centro Espírita Beneficente União do Vegetal v. Reno, No. [1647] (D.N.M. 2000).

Parker, K. M. (2011). *Common law, history, and democracy in America, 1790–1900*. Cambridge University Press.

Petition for a writ of certiorari, *Gonzales v. O Centro Espírita Beneficente União do Vegetal*, 126 S. Ct. 1211 (2006).

Ryan, J. E. (1992). Smith and the Religious Freedom Restoration Act: An iconoclastic assessment. *Virginia Law Review, 78*(6), 1407–1462.

Sullivan, W. F. (2005). *The impossibility of religious freedom* (New ed.). Princeton University Press.

Tella, S. (2008). Mended expert witness statement in *The Church of the Holy Light of the Queen v. Mukasey*, No. 08-364-PK (D. Or. 2008).

The Church of the Holy Light of the Queen v. Mukasey, (2009).

United States v. Ballard, 322 U.S. 78, 86-87 (1944).

United States v. Kuch, 288 F. Supp. 439 (D.D.C. 1968).

United States v. Meyers, 95 F.3d 1475 (10th Cir. 1996).

United States v. Seeger, 380 U.S. 163, 156-166, 85 S. Ct. 850, 854, 13 L. Ed. 2d 733 (1965).

Wisconsin v. Yoder, 406 U.S. 205, 216, 92 S. Ct. 1526, 1533, 32 L. Ed. 2d 15 (1972).

Zinberg, N. E. (1984). *Drug, set, and setting: The basis for controlled intoxicant use*. Yale University Press.

Zubik v. Burwell, 578 U.S. 403 (2016).

Chapter 5
Ayahuasca's Path in the United States: The RFRA and the Sincere Exercise of Religion

The legal victories of the UDV and Santo Daime churches in securing religious exemptions for the ceremonial use of ayahuasca under the RFRA marked a significant development in the legal landscape for ayahuasca groups in the United States. These cases set important precedents, acknowledging the legitimacy of ayahuasca's use in religious ceremonies, while also opening the door for future claims seeking similar exemptions. Simultaneously, the underground use of ayahuasca grew, indicating an increased interest among Americans in the Amazonian brew.

In the years following these legal victories, ayahuasca increasingly became a subject of public interest. The 2016 article in *The New Yorker*, titled "The Drug of Choice in the Age of Kale" (Levy, 2016), offered a detailed exploration of ayahuasca's emergence as a part of contemporary wellness culture, particularly in urban areas such as Brooklyn and Silicon Valley. Tracing the brew's journey from the Amazon to some of the major American cities, the article highlighted the increasing mainstream interest in ayahuasca, including public endorsements from figures like actress Susan Sarandon and self-help guru Tim Ferriss. The narrative portrayed ayahuasca's rise as a landmark of a broader cultural trend prioritizing mindfulness, detoxification, and holistic health, positioning it as the antithesis to the materialism associated with substances like cocaine in previous decades.

Despite its professed growing cultural acceptance, ayahuasca is still considered a controlled substance by the DEA. This designation underscores the ongoing tensions between its recognition as a legitimate religious sacrament and its legal status as a drug deemed to have no accepted medical use and a high potential for abuse. As a result, federal agencies and courts still face the issue of defining the boundaries of religious freedom concerning ayahuasca use. For religious groups advocating for its ceremonial consumption, the main concern often becomes the determination of the sincerity of their beliefs, which plays a critical role in legal outcomes. This chapter aims to explore this complex intersection of legal and regulatory dynamics. A close examination of legal disputes, shifts in DEA policy, and the perspectives of scholars and advocacy organizations makes

H. Fernandes Antunes, *Religion, Drug, or Cult?*, Law and Religion in a Global Context 5, https://doi.org/10.1007/978-3-032-04368-9_5

it possible to trace how evolving interpretations of concepts like "religion" and "sincerity" are shaping the legal and cultural landscape of ayahuasca use, potentially setting precedents for future cases.

5.1 The DEA Exemption Process: A Drug Agency Regulating Religious Practices

In 2009, in response to challenges posed by the UDV and the CHLQ cases, the DEA introduced its "Guidance Regarding Petitions for Religious Exemption from the Controlled Substances Act,"[1] outlining the requirements for individuals or organizations seeking exemptions under the RFRA. The guidance requires petitioners to provide a comprehensive written statement accompanied by supporting documentation to establish that the enforcement of the CSA would impose a substantial burden on their sincere religious exercise. The content of the petition should also include other essential components such as detailed descriptions of the religion's history, beliefs, practices, and structure; specifics about religious activities involving controlled substances; the type and amount of the substance in question; and the logistics of its anticipated use or distribution. The DEA encourages petitioners to submit exhaustive information to substantiate their claims, although they are not confined to the outlined topics.

Moreover, the guidance states that the DEA may require additional documents or written statements on topics that the agency deems necessary. The document also determines that petitioners cannot engage in any activity prohibited under the CSA unless the petition has been granted. Even if a petition is granted, it is subject to revocation in view of the regulations of the CSA and the RFRA. This initiative points to a possible openness of the DEA to accommodate institutions that engage in the religious use of psychoactive substances, given that the process is not restricted to ayahuasca, but has a broader target audience that can include other psychoactive substances.

Yet, since its implementation in 2009, only one exemption has been granted. The DEA's delays in reviewing exemption requests and also the agency's approach were highly scrutinized. In a 2019 article, attorney Brad Bartlett criticized the measure saying that the DEA has established a lengthy and often costly process and that "the provisions in the guidance requiring petitioning and DEA registration do not have the force and effect of law" (Bartlett, 2019). In the following year, Bartlett published another article on the topic, in collaboration with Martha Hartney, member of the legal team of the Church of the Eagle and the Condor (CEC), the first non-Christian church to obtain a religious exemption for the religious use of ayahuasca. The article's title alluded to the metaphor of "a fox guarding the henhouse" (Hartney

[1] The guide was updated in 2020, without substantial changes (Drug Enforcement Administration, 2020a).

& Bartlett, 2020). At the time, the authors stressed that, unsurprisingly, after more than 15 years, the DEA's RFRA Guidance had failed to grant a single religious exemption to CSA prohibitions.[2] Not only was the agency's willingness to grant exemptions questioned but also its authority on the matter:

> While seemingly straightforward on its face, the DEA's RFRA Guidance fails to articulate a legal standard governing law enforcement's review of petitions, to impose a time frame for agency decision-making, or delineate judicial remedies. It also leaves petitioners vulnerable to criminal sanctions by exposing themselves to law enforcement scrutiny and potentially forfeiting Fifth Amendment rights. Further, the guidance fails to identify legal authority articulating law enforcement's ability to register religious activity, which is especially critical where, as here, the enforceability of DEA's RFRA Guidance has been called into question. (Hartney & Bartlett, 2020)

The article contends that the DEA does not have the legal authority to mandate that religious groups petition and register with the agency to obtain exemptions from the CSA under the RFRA. The authors underscore that, historically, the United States Congress had been cautious in granting federal agencies authority to evaluate religious claims, limiting such powers to rare circumstances. Moreover, Hartney and Bartlett argue that the RFRA does not empower agencies like the DEA to process claims administratively, but dictates that claims regarding burdens on religious exercise be addressed through federal courts. They also stress that DEA's actions under the CSA only permit the agency to register activities related to medical, scientific, or industrial purposes, with no provision for religious exemptions. In sum, the attorneys claim that Congress did not delegate the DEA the authority to regulate or evaluate religious practices involving controlled substances, nor to require religious adherents to petition for administrative relief before seeking judicial remedies under RFRA. Hartney reiterated this at the Sacred Plants in the Americas II, a Virtual Psychedelic Summit on the Globalization of Plant Medicines and Indigenous Reciprocity that took place in 2021:

> First let me say that I actually don't believe that the DEA should be the organization making that decision, because it's like the fox guarding the henhouse, which I wrote about on Chacruna. I don't think the DEA is rightly tooled to make a decision between what is religion, what is not, and what is sincere and what is not, nor is there any statutory authority given to the DEA to make those decisions. It's not in the Controlled Substances Act. There's no authority for them to regulate for religious purposes in the Controlled Substances Act, nor is it in the RFRA. So try as we might, we can't find any actual real legal authority for them to make a decision like that.[3]

The same point was made by Jack Silver, co-counsel in the case of the CHLQ, contesting the DEA's authority to establish if one's religious belief is genuine or not. In his view, this constitutes an overreach by the agency that could set a bad precedent for the groups, and he encourages them not to apply for the exemption process.

[2] In May 2025, the DEA granted its first exemption for the religious use of ayahuasca to the Church of Gaia (see last section).

[3] Available at https://www.youtube.com/watch?v=P767lozYlhk

> In my opinion, filing a petition with the DEA for religious exemption from the CSA is counterproductive to the goals that most of us have for the religious use of entheogens. I'll tell you why. Also, when I use the word religion or religious, that includes any spiritual or shamanic practices. Within the concept of the separation of church and state, neither the DEA, nor any agency of the U.S. government, has a legal authority to determine if a person has a genuine religious belief or practice. Yet this is exactly what the DEA is proposing, and for those that apply for an exemption, they may be waiving certain constitutional rights that are guaranteed to them and also setting a bad precedent.[4]

The DEA's procedure was also heavily criticized by Litman (2023) for exposing and putting at risk practitioners and groups. In her article "Psychedelics, the DEA, and Regulating Religion," she highlights the constitutional flaws and practical shortcomings of the guidance. Litman argues that the process is inherently punitive, requiring applicants to disclose illegal activities without protection from prosecution, to cease religious practices while awaiting a response, and facing near-certain denial, as the DEA has never voluntarily granted an exemption (up to the time of her article's publication). Litman (2023, p. 9) suggests that these requirements not only place religious communities at greater risk of criminal enforcement but also deter many from applying altogether.

Litman's article underscores the broader tension between religious freedom—described as a core American value enshrined in the First Amendment and the RFRA—and the DEA's role in regulating religious practices. While courts and legislatures have historically avoided probing religious sincerity to prevent entanglement with the Establishment Clause, the DEA, she argues, asserts this prerogative despite being particularly ill-equipped to assess the sincerity of religious beliefs or practices. While acknowledging the government's legitimate interest in public health, Litman argues that burdening religious practitioners drives their practices underground, undermining both religious liberty and public safety. Her critique frames the DEA's exemption process as both constitutionally suspect and impractical for religious practitioners (Litman, 2023, p. 9).

These critiques give further insight on how the DEA's actions are perceived and dealt with. They also make it clear that groups that consume psychedelics and the legal experts that support their decriminalization are making a clear effort to navigate the hurdles put forward by government agencies. In this scenario, two issues are vital: What constitutes a church and how to prove sincerity? Hartney suggests that:

> Something I think that we need to be very cautious about is the government's going to be looking for all of the indicia of deceit, anything that looks like people are making it up on the fly. If it's not really religious, if it's more spiritual. They are splitting that hair. So you'll need to understand what actually constitutes a religion. And what's the difference between religion and spirituality? [...]There's a notion of religion as being more communal, more of a group doing things and also providing structure. [...] This is how we live, this is how we do life, this is how we treat each other, and this is how we treat our world. That's what a

[4] Available at https://www.youtube.com/watch?v=lUnRvmBkHm8

> religion would entail versus my connection to the divine alone as the expression of my religion. They're actually looking for structure, connection and repetitive patterns of behavior.[5]

Given the stance of congress and courts of avoiding defining what a "religion" is, it is up to the practitioners to look for clues to features, practices, and behaviors that can portray the notion of sincere exercise of religion. Hartney, for instance, argues that it must be collective and must encompass not only one's connection with the divine but also the ways in which one interacts with the world. In the case of ayahuasca churches, there is also a complicating factor, as Hartney notes, the necessity of establishing some sort of lineage or connection to a South American religious or Indigenous group.

> There's an article recently on Rolling Stone Magazine that talked about some of the major religions now creating sub denominations of medicine churches in Judaism or Islam or Buddhism and all these other churches, because they're experiencing their own form of psychedelic renaissance inside those churches. So there's a clearer line to a lineage there. Similarly, like the UDV and Santo Daime, they have these connections to a longer, slightly older lineage. It was 40 years old. It wasn't that old. But I think things that are just popping out of nowhere and looking like it is being made up on the fly are going to be a harder sell. It's really a good idea to just maintain the connection with the origination point of that medicine, specifically ayahuasca. It is not a good idea to make things up on the fly or make up dogma.[6]

Hartney's argument reflects on the difficult issue of the legal recognition of new groups and practices as "religious." These difficulties have led to claims for broader interpretations when it comes to the legal definitions of religion. On the same summit, Sean McAllister—lawyer specialized in the regulation of the religious use of psychedelics—spoke on the necessity of a legal change in the approaches to defining religion:

> I think there definitely needs to be changes. I've been reading about Mesoamerican worldview philosophy, or ontology, and the way that native Indigenous people have looked at the world and the big differences with Christianity and major religions. [The latter] look for answers to questions about life. What is the meaning of life? What is God's purpose? Indigenous worldview and philosophy tends to look at what is the way of living. Not an answer so much, but a process in a way. And that's not what the law is designed to acknowledge. It is designed to acknowledge religions that give us answers. And so I think we need a broadening of the concept of religion to include Indigenous concepts that many of us deeply identify with. [...] And I think for other psychedelics in particular, it would be helpful to have that broadening. But ayahuasca has the strongest protections right now in the US of any entheogen. So this is ground zero for this work.[7]

The interesting part of McAllister's statement is not the claim for a broadening of the notion of religion, but his diagnose that the courts have historically operated with certain notions of religion and that the law is ill-equipped to address practices and expressions that fall outside of their frameworks. On the executive level, this

[5] Available at https://www.youtube.com/watch?v=P767lozYlhk

[6] Available at https://www.youtube.com/watch?v=P767lozYlhk

[7] Available at https://www.youtube.com/watch?v=P767lozYlhk

issue could be extended to question what types of training and expertise the DEA applies to consider the sincerity of belief and the religious grounds of one's practices. This is particularly important if we consider Talal Asad's (1993) argument that defining religion was, at first, a theological task, that was later taken up by anthropology and also the legal arena. As Asad states, there can be no universal definition of religion, not only because its constituent elements and relationships are historically specific, but because this definition is itself the historical product of discursive processes. Following Asad's insight, the task at hand thus is to understand the ways in which these legal disputes and regulations develop a specific historical framework to circumscribe what is, and what is not, a religion. In this context, the case of Soul Quest Church of Mother Earth illustrates how the DEA and courts have been applying the notion of "religion" and "sincerity" in relation to groups that use psychedelics.

5.2 The Soul Quest Church of the Mother Earth Case

Chris and Verena Young decided to establish Soul Quest Church of Mother Earth after their personal experiences with ayahuasca in the mountains of Spain. After returning home to Germany, Chris Young said he felt called to bring this revelation to others. They relocated to the United States with the goal of starting a church. Chris stated in a 2018 interview[8] that he started a formal apprenticeship under the guidance of a traditional Brazilian medicine woman who taught him how to perform sacred ceremonies in the Amazonian tradition. Inspired by his personal experiences, he decided to start "Soul Quest Ayahuasca Retreat Center" (Janik, 2023, p. 26). However, given the legal status of ayahuasca in the country, Chris Young decided to create a church. Soul Quest was founded in 2013 but was only formally established 2 years later. On their website, the institution presented itself as a neo-shamanic church and a Christian syncretic religion with connections with Amazonian shamans. According to Chris Young:

> My mission is to exemplify a harmonious blend of traditional indigenous practices and modern therapeutic approaches. By incorporating the sacred traditions of the Yawanawa and Huni Kuin tribes, I provided a respectful and enriching context for thousands of our Church members seeking transformation and healing.[9]

In his attempt to become a legal church, Chris met with the leaders of the Oklevueha Native American Church (ONAC) in order to establish an independent branch of their church that would be protected under their legal organizational umbrella and the RFRA. Upon discovering that the ONAC could not provide that umbrella of legal protection that he sought, Young distanced himself from the institution. In 2015, Soul Quest became a nonprofit corporation and held their first retreat in

[8] Available at https://inspirery.com/soul-quest-ayahuasca/

[9] https://www.ayahuascachurches.org/

Florida, becoming one of the many underground psychedelic churches that have emerged in the U.S. over the last decades (Janik, 2023, p. 26).

Years later, Soul Quest started the Soul Quest Natural Healing Center (SQNHC), a for-profit branch that was connected to the non-profit entity, offering post-ayahuasca ceremony coaching and diet preparation guide for members to follow prior to ayahuasca ceremonies. It should be noted that, besides serving ayahuasca, the center also offered for a period of time other psychoactive substances such as *rapé*[10] and *kambô*.[11] In an attempt to situate Soul Quest within the legal framework of a legalized church, the institution has changed its name several times. Initially, they referred to themselves as a "Native American Church," but eventually changed their institutional description to a "neo-shamanic and Christian syncretic church" and also an "Ayahuasca Retreat Center." The institution established an online presence through the creation of a website and on Facebook, where it advertised its retreats (Janik, 2023, p. 28–29).

Soul Quest claims *The Ayahuasca Manifesto: The Spirit of Ayahuasca and its Planetary Mission* as its main theological source. The manifesto was originally published online in 2011 by an anonymous author. The narrator of the book presents herself as the spirit of ayahuasca, "I am a spirit of spirits. I operate from a vibration superior to the spirits who compose me. I am of a hierarchy superior to that of the spirit of Ayahuasca ('Banisteriopsis Caapi') and of the underestimated Chacruna ('Psychotria Viridis')," whose goal is to "send this correspondence at this historical moment to contribute to the expansion of the Human consciousness in a definitive and significant way" (Anonymous, 2011, p. 1–2).

The document employs a mix of perspectives, alternating between religious/spiritual discourse and a scientific viewpoint, using medical categories and therapeutic language. It also delves into political and legal domains, advocating for regulation and criticizing persecution, as well as environmental concerns, emphasizing preservation and sustainability. The manifesto describes ayahuasca as a spiritual catalyst while also discussing its antidepressant effects and its role as a tool for behavioral modification. At times, the text blends these perspectives, using both metaphysical and scientific terminology to discuss these properties. This interesting combination can be seen, for example, when addressing drug addiction:

> The healing from addictions occurs at the spiritual level, which is metaphysical in nature and blueprints the causality of subatomic particles. The metaphysical healing harmonizes and reorganizes the chemical correspondence, which will finally reflect as a behavioral change (Anonymous, 2011, p. 19).

This 46-page document also explores practical guidance on conducting ceremonies, selecting qualified facilitators, and preparing both physically and mentally for sessions. Additionally, it discusses the social implications of ayahuasca in urban

[10] Rapé is a ceremonial snuff made from powdered tobacco mixed with ashes and other medicinal herbs. It is used by various Indigenous groups in the Amazon basin.

[11] Kambô is a traditional Amazonian healing practice involving the application of secretions from the giant monkey frog (*Phyllomedusa bicolor*) to small burns on the skin.

contexts and underscores the importance of preservation initiatives to protect its cultural and ecological roots. The Manifesto concludes with a reflection on ayahuasca's mission to foster a deeper connection between humanity and the planet. The Manifesto, however, was less significant for its content than for its absence in the DEA interviews with Soul Quest members.

In August of 2016 the DEA contacted Soul Quest asking them to apply for religious exemption under the Controlled Substances Act. One year later, fearing a legal action from the DEA, Soul Quest sent their exemption application. After a period of almost 4 years without any response, in which Soul Quest's legal counsel tried to contact the DEA multiple times about the state of the exemption application, the group decided to file a complaint in the Florida Middle District Court[12] based on the DEA's lack of response. The complaint was filed in April of 2020 and it was based on four specific counts against the DEA. They claimed that the DEA violated Soul Quest's First Amendment rights to freedom of religion and their rights under the RFRA. They also accused the DEA of violation of Soul Quest's right to substantive due process and their right to freedom of speech. Soul Quest sought a declaratory and injunctive relief against the DEA pursuant to the RFRA and the First Amendment allowing them to import, possess, manufacture, and use ayahuasca in their religious ceremonies (Soul Quest Church of Mother Earth, Inc. v. U.S. Drug Enforcement Agency, 2022, p. 2). They argued that the DEA denied their request under RFRA and, therefore, the exclusive jurisdiction provision of the CSA did not apply.

Before the court's ruling, however, the DEA issued a letter in 2021 denying Soul Quest's request for an exemption. The DEA questioned Soul Quest's sincerity of belief in multiple fronts. According to the letter, Soul Quest compared the "Ayahuasca Manifesto" to the Bible or the Koran, arguing that it played a central role in the group. However, the DEA stated that in the multiple interviews with Soul Quest leaders and members over the course of 6 months, the Ayahuasca Manifesto was mentioned only once. The DEA also took issue with the fact that Soul Quest did not require their members to profess belief in the Manifesto or any other religion before participating in a Soul Quest ayahuasca retreat and that they did not tell their members what to believe. They argued that Soul Quest did not require or expect participants to have any continuing involvement with the institution, highlighting that individuals frequently participate only once in Soul Quest's ayahuasca retreats. In the DEA's view, "membership in Soul Quest appears to be a purely pro forma matter to obtain access to ayahuasca, rather than an expression of sincere religious devotion" (Drug Enforcement Agency, 2021, p. 2). The agency also contrasted Soul Quest to the CHLQ which, in contrast, demanded a serious commitment and a regular attendance from its members.

The DEA claimed that, Dr. Scott L. Irwin, Ph.D., the "Senior Minister" and a corporate officer of Soul Quest, did not describe Soul Quest's use of ayahuasca in

[12] Florida is one of the states that has a state version of the RFRA. In Janik's view (2023, p. 135), Florida's RFRA has drawn a number of underground churches to the state given the fact that the prosecution of the religious use of psychedelics is a low priority for the DEA.

religious terms but as a form of integrative medicine or therapy intended to help people deal with trauma or psychological issues. To validate its argument, the agency stated that Dr. Irwin failed to mention the Ayahuasca Manifesto in his interview, highlighting that he "described ayahuasca use as 5, 15, or 20 years of 'psychotherapy in a weekend'" (Drug Enforcement Agency, 2021, p. 3). Moreover, the DEA stated that the church's website and public advertisements did not "support the claim that Soul Quest offers ayahuasca solely for religious purposes and only to members who are exercising religion pursuant to a sincerely held religious belief." The agency noted that the church conducted business as the Soul Quest Ayahuasca Retreat and Wellness Center, offering a broad range of alternative medicinal and wellness services such as yoga, acupuncture, and marital counseling. The DEA also questioned the fact that ayahuasca retreats were "open to any individual who is willing to sign various forms and pay a fee ranging from $350 to $900 for the retreat." The letter concluded that Soul Quest "sells ayahuasca as part of its for-profit secular offerings to the general public" (Drug Enforcement Agency, 2021, p. 3).

The DEA reiterated that the language from the website reinforced the agency's findings that Soul Quest understood and advertised the use of ayahuasca to the public as essentially medicinal. To back its claim, the letter stated that on its website Soul Quest described ayahuasca as plant medicine, a tool for physical health and spiritual growth, highlighting that internet reviews and public comments left by participants in Soul Quest retreats consistently spoke of "the psycho-social, medicinal, and therapeutic properties of the ayahuasca experience, rather than of a religious experience" (Drug Enforcement Agency, 2021, p. 3). According to the letter:

> In practice, Soul Quest thus promotes ayahuasca to the public for self-help and therapeutic reasons, rather than solely to fellow believers for the religious ritual purposes described in the Ayahuasca Manifesto. DEA therefore concludes that Soul Quest's promotion of ayahuasca to the public in this manner does not constitute a sincere exercise of religion under RFRA. Moreover, even if the organizers, officers, and leadership of Soul Quest could establish the sincerity of their own individual religious belief in the use of ayahuasca (which they have not established), they cannot establish that the participants in their ceremonies are using ayahuasca as part of a sincere religious exercise given the ease with which those participants can gain access to controlled substances in Soul Quest events, without meaningful commitment to a coherently religious practice (Drug Enforcement Agency, 2021, p. 4).

The DEA claimed that Soul Quest's historical associations also called into question its sincerity claims, stressing the fact that initially the organization operated under the name "Oklevueha Native American Church Somaveda of Soul Quest, Inc." The agency emphasized that The Oklevueha Native American Church (ONAC) did not consider the Ayahuasca Manifesto to be its foundational text, but operated under a code of ethics. Another crucial point was Chris Young's recognition that "Soul Quest had affiliated with ONAC to obtain legal coverage for Soul Quest's use of ayahuasca and other substances" (Drug Enforcement Agency, 2021, p. 4). The DEA also found problematic the fact that Soul Quest did not import ayahuasca directly from co-religionists in South America but from a business in the Netherlands named "Waking Herbs."

Despite the details shared about the screening procedures for participants and the monitoring of ayahuasca consumption by trained health care professionals, the DEA argued that Soul Quest failed to follow its own procedures. The letter mentioned the death, in 2018, of a participant named Joseph Begley, who died after ingesting both ayahuasca and kambô. Afterwards, the church was sued for wrongful death. Begley's father accused Soul Quest's founders of a 3-hour delay in calling medical aid, which contributed to his son's death.[13]

Consequently, the DEA argued that Soul Quest did not demonstrate the existence of a sincere religious exercise, failing to show that the application of the CSA to the institution's use of ayahuasca would substantially burden a sincere religious exercise. Since the DEA considered that Soul Quest did not prove the sincerity of its religious beliefs, the agency claimed to be exempt from assessing if the application of the CSA's prohibitions on ayahuasca would impose a substantial burden on Soul Quest under the RFRA.

On the following year, the court ruled in favor of the DEA, dismissing the case due to the court's view of Soul Quest's lack of religious sincerity and given the fact that the case was heard in the wrong court (Janik, 2023, p. 137–138). The court stressed that the DEA had a separate and independent basis to deny their request under the CSA given Soul Quest's failure to pass the DEA's standards for the importation, storage, and use of ayahuasca. The court emphasized that, in the DEA's determination letter, the agency stated that even if Soul Quest practices constituted a religious exercise, it could not be "accommodated in a manner that would allow DEA to preserve its compelling interests in public health and safety and in preventing illegal diversion of ayahuasca" (Drug Enforcement Agency, 2021 apud Soul Quest Church of Mother Earth, Inc. v. U.S. Drug Enforcement Agency, 2022, p. 4–5).

Soul Quest appealed based on the argument that the DEA lacked any authority to decide on petitions for religious exemptions. According to Soul Quest, the District Court failed to acknowledge that the DEA disregarded the requirements set forth by the Administrative Procedure Act (APA) and overlooked Congress's clear delegation of jurisdiction to the courts under the RFRA. Moreover, Soul Quest contended that the Major Rules Doctrine prevented the DEA from asserting such authority (Appeal, *Soul Quest Church of Mother Earth, Inc. v. U.S. Drug Enforcement Administration*, 2022). They implied that the DEA's framework for evaluating religious exemptions, as referenced in the agency's denial letter, did not legally exist (Janik, 2023, pp. 147–148).

Soul Quest lost the appeal regarding the use of ayahuasca in religious ceremonies. The court upheld the DEA's decision, citing that Soul Quest failed to prove the sincerity of its religious beliefs. As a result, the DEA was not required to assess whether prohibiting ayahuasca placed a substantial burden on Soul Quest's religious practices. This decision meant that the DEA also did not have to prove that the prohibition served a compelling governmental interest by the least restrictive means, solidifying its stance regarding Soul Quest.

[13] The aftermath of this case will be discussed later in this section.

In addition to these losses, Soul Quest had to face a civil lawsuit on wrongful death. On May 15, 2024, a jury in the Ninth Judicial Circuit Court in Orange County, Florida, determined that the negligence of both Soul Quest and Young contributed as "a legal cause" to Begley's death. The court ordered Soul Quest and Young to pay a combined total of $15 million to Begley's family, assigning 40% of the responsibility to Soul Quest and the remaining 60% to Chris Young.[14] Recently, Soul Quest and Young asserted that they could not provide compensation to the Begleys and subsequently filed for bankruptcy. However, on July 30, a Florida court dismissed Soul Quest's bankruptcy motion, citing the organization's continued provision of ayahuasca to its members.[15] In August 2024, Soul Quest announced its closure "after a decade of serving and healing over 30,000 members" (Young, 2024, p. 1). According to Chris Young, this decision was due to the substantial debt stemming from the Begley lawsuit, along with legal expenses and other struggles.

It is undeniable that the negative press and backlash from the lawsuit contributed significantly to the demise of Soul Quest. Still, it should be noted that the DEA and the Florida court did not rely on this incident to deny Soul Quest's request for a religious exemption. The Soul Quest case offers a compelling lens through which to examine how government agencies and courts define and assess religious sincerity, particularly in cases involving psychoactive substances. It highlights the complex and often paradoxical role of these institutions in deciding what constitutes a religion and its sincere exercise. By denying Soul Quest's claims, the DEA and courts not only dismissed their assertion of religious exemption under the RFRA but also engaged in the delicate task of distinguishing religious practices from therapy, and commerce. This process often involves identifying what is *not* religious or sincere—such as practices deemed overly commercialized or lacking clear theological foundations—to establish legal standards. The question from ayahuasca groups and activists remains: Can a government agency or court legitimately determine the boundaries of religious authenticity without overstepping its competencies and prerogatives? This paradox illustrates the challenges in regulating the use of psychedelics for religious purposes. They have also spurred initiatives from lawyers and NGOs aiming to navigate this intricate legal landscape and address the grey areas it creates. By establishing guidelines and standards, these efforts seek to better equip psychedelic churches to align their practices with legal frameworks and protect their claims to religious freedom.

5.3 The Chacruna Institute's Guide to RFRA

Following the increasing significance of the RFRA in legal disputes over the religious use of psychoactive substances, the Chacruna Institute for Psychedelic Plant Medicines—an American NGO founded by Brazilian anthropologist Beatriz

[14] https://filtermag.org/brandon-begley-soul-quest-wrongful-death/

[15] https://www.vice.com/en/article/the-bankrupt-ayahuasca-church-where-negligence-led-to-death/

Labate—launched a new initiative in 2021: the *Guide to RFRA and Best Practices for Psychedelic Plant Medicine Churches* (Chacruna Institute for Psychedelic Plant Medicines and Hoots, 2021). According to the authors, the guide emerged in response to the complex legal and practical challenges faced by groups that seek a religious exemption from the CSA, offering a structured framework to help these organizations better understand their rights and responsibilities under the RFRA. By addressing the ambiguities at the intersection of religious freedom and controlled substance regulations, it sought to equip these groups with tools to navigate legal hurdles and safeguard their practices (Chacruna Institute for Psychedelic Plant Medicines and Hoots, 2021).

The document explores the legal and practical challenges faced by churches and religious practitioners who incorporate psychedelics into their ceremonies, presenting the text as both an informational and an operational resource. The authors begin by grounding their discussion in the principle of religious freedom enshrined in the First Amendment to the U.S. Constitution, emphasizing the importance of the "Free Exercise Clause" in protecting religious practices from government interference. They highlight ongoing tensions between the legal framework and the exercise of sincerely held religious beliefs, particularly in cases involving controlled substances used in religious ceremonies.

Despite the legal protections established under the RFRA, the authors point out that substantial ambiguities persist, leaving many "plant medicine churches" vulnerable to prosecution under the CSA. As described in the introduction, the Guide aims to address this uncertainty by offering a dual-purpose resource. The first part provides legal background to plant medicine churches. The second part focuses on practical guidance, including policies and operational procedures that such churches can adopt to navigate legal challenges and protect their congregants. The authors emphasize, however, that the Guide does not constitute legal advice but rather serves as a framework for understanding the legal landscape.

> [...] this Guide hopes to set out information that a plant medicine church with sincerely held religious beliefs can use to learn the framework through which their use of controlled substances will be analyzed, how to operate in a manner that may protect the spiritual purpose and the congregants of their church, and to be prepared to defend their freedom of religious exercise (Chacruna Institute for Psychedelic Plant Medicines and Hoots, 2021, p. 11).

The Guide has a section dedicated to the notions of "religion" and "church," exploring the difficulties of defining these concepts within legal and governmental frameworks. While emphasizing the courts' ambiguities when it comes to defining religions, it underlines that laws such as the RFRA deliberately avoid rigid definitions, leaving courts and agencies to assess whether beliefs are religious and sincerely held on a case-by-case basis.

In this regard, the authors highlight that the courts have developed criteria to evaluate religion, such as the Meyers Test (*United States v. Meyers,* 1996, *see chapter 3*), which evaluates five factors: ultimate ideas (addressing existential and moral questions), metaphysical beliefs (recognition of transcendent realities), moral or ethical systems, comprehensiveness of beliefs, and external markers like rituals, places of worship, sacred writings, prophets, holy days, dietary rules or fasting practices, clergy or spiritual leaders, among other features. The test clarifies that in order to be considered a religion, the practices and beliefs must transcend secular philosophies or personal ideologies. Despite these criteria, the Guide stresses that courts usually avoid establishing the validity or substance of religious beliefs as long as they reflect honest conviction rather than an attempt to evade the law (Chacruna Institute for Psychedelic Plant Medicines and Hoots, 2021, p. 13).

The Guide also explores the characteristics utilized by the Internal Revenue Service (IRS) to determine whether an organization qualifies as a church for tax purposes, including having a recognized creed, formal doctrine, ordained ministers, and regular congregations. According to the document, while these criteria are grounded in mainstream religious structures, there is room for flexibility and plant medicine churches, despite differing from traditional religious organizations, could in theory demonstrate compliance by aligning their practices and beliefs with these frameworks. The authors underscore the importance of articulating beliefs and practices within these established parameters when interacting with courts or governmental agencies. In this regard, the section concludes that while the language and expectations of mainstream religion may feel restrictive or frustrating to plant medicine churches, these frameworks provide the tools to establish legal recognition and tax-exempt status.

As expected, the Guide has a section dedicated to examining the role of the RFRA in safeguarding religious exercise, particularly for practices involving controlled substances. One of the main points is the ways in which an individual or organization can invoke the RFRA. The guide posits that:

There are three methods to protect the right of religious exercise pursuant to RFRA:

1. Filing a claim under RFRA in a judicial proceeding alleging that religious exercise has been burdened by the government;
2. Raising a defense under RFRA in a judicial proceeding that religious exercise justifies any act committed that allegedly violates and is burdened by the government's laws; or
3. Filing an application for religious exemption from the CSA through the Drug Enforcement Agency (DEA). (Chacruna Institute for Psychedelic Plant Medicines and Hoots, 2021, p. 13)

The authors highlight, however, that only court proceedings guarantee strict scrutiny analysis, provided a substantial burden on religious exercise is demonstrated. Regarding plant medicine churches, the Guide states that the RFRA requires proving that the CSA's prohibition on their use of a controlled substance constitutes a substantial burden on sincerely held religious beliefs. This involves showing that the plant medicine is central to their religious exercise and that no feasible alternatives exist.[16] As stated in the Guide, a substantial burden occurs when government actions

[16] In contrast, the Guide states that churches that utilize multiple substances face a unique challenge since they need to prove their centrality for their religious beliefs and practices (Chacruna Institute for Psychedelic Plant Medicines and Hoots, 2021, p. 20).

compel individuals to act against their faith under threat, such as criminal prosecution or confiscation of sacred substances.

Another important section is dedicated to analyzing the concept of "religious exercise" as defined under the RFRA and the criteria used by courts and agencies to determine what constitutes religion and religious practice. While the RFRA broadly defines religious exercise as "any exercise of religion," regardless of its centrality to a belief system, leaving courts and agencies to refine the concept through various tests, the authors highlight some prominent legal approaches. The Guide states that the Ninth Circuit offers a more inclusive test, focusing on whether beliefs are held with the conviction of traditional religious faiths, allowing for broader recognition of unconventional belief systems, which could accommodate plant medicine churches. The guide also highlights *Burwell v. Hobby Lobby* (2014), which limits the government's ability to judge the validity of religious beliefs, focusing instead on sincerity. This case is particularly important because it provides some protection for nonconventional practices. However, it leaves significant discretion to courts and agencies in defining what sincerity is (Chacruna Institute for Psychedelic Plant Medicines and Hoots, 2021, p. 23).

Similarly to the notion of religion, courts assess sincerity on a case-by-case basis, relying on credibility and evidence of genuine conviction, often avoiding establishing rigid tests for sincerity and focusing instead on identifying insincerity. Since the courts have the difficult task of assessing one's sincerity, the authors highlight several factors that can undermine sincerity. On this matter, the guide cites the case *United States v. Quaintance*[17] (2010), in which a federal district court in New Mexico identified five factors that could undermine the sincerity of an individual's religious beliefs for a RFRA claim: 1) beliefs created ad hoc to justify political or social views, 2) the absence of ceremony or ritual associated with the belief system, 3) large quantities of a controlled substance suggesting commercial use, 4) the use or possession of other illegal substances, and 5) pursuit of financial gain, which may indicate insincere religious intent.

The authors underline that, in addition to the sincerity of the institution, courts and agencies like the DEA also scrutinize the commitment of members. To illustrate this point, the guide explores the motives for the DEA's denial of Soul Quest's request for a CSA exemption. As presented in the last section, one of the DEA's critiques focused on the fact that Soul Quest allowed one-time participants with no lasting involvement to partake in ceremonies. The authors argue that this lack of commitment led the DEA to view the church as a retreat center rather than a religious organization. To address these challenges, the guide suggests that plant medicine churches clarify their religious frameworks, establish membership requirements,

[17] According to the Guide: "In *Quaintance*, the court stated that the presence of another illegal substance—which was cocaine and not claimed as sacrament—undermined the sincerity of religious exercise because it was purchased from the same person selling the marijuana that was claimed to be a sacrament" (Chacruna Institute for Psychedelic Plant Medicines and Hoots, 2021, p. 27).

and document members' commitment to their beliefs.[18] This would allow the church to demonstrate that participation in ceremonies serves a genuine religious purpose rather than recreational or therapeutic goals. The Guide suggests that payments for ceremonies must also align with religious practices to avoid resembling commercial activity. Another interesting consideration when it comes to religious sincerity has to do with the name selection. As stated in the Guide:

> A plant medicine church may want to select a name composed of words that are primarily spiritual in nature and do not insinuate the church provides services that are solely secular, such as philosophical, medical, therapeutic, or social terms. A church may want to avoid terms like "healing," "therapies," "recovery," or even "medicine," because these words have secular connotations, which may be problematic for establishing the religious beliefs of a psychedelic plant medicine church. (Chacruna Institute for Psychedelic Plant Medicines and Hoots, 2021, p. 49)

It is noteworthy that, ultimately, sincerity under the RFRA depends on demonstrating both the authenticity of the organization and the devotion of its members. Moreover, a successful RFRA claim also involves circumventing the association of religious practices as therapeutic or commercial and avoiding the intersection between religious and philosophical principles. Considering the legal difficulties in establishing one's sincerity of belief, the courts and agencies have searched for practices and beliefs that not only did not appear sincere, but that conveyed principles usually associated with secular arenas such as medicine, philosophy and commerce.

Setting aside the issue of sincerity, the guide also examines RFRA's requirement that the government justify restrictions on religious practices by demonstrating a "compelling interest" pursued through the "least restrictive means." A compelling government interest is defined as one of the highest order. In the case of ayahuasca churches, as seen in Chap. 4, the government typically cites the protection of public health and safety and the prevention of controlled substance diversion as its primary compelling interests in RFRA cases involving the CSA. According to the authors, this would require churches to implement best practices to safeguard their congregants' health and prevent substance diversion, such as thorough health screenings, informed consent, emergency protocols, secure storage, and limiting access to sacramental substances. The Guide emphasizes that demonstrating these measures can help mitigate the government's concerns and support the church's claims of sincere religious practice.

The section dedicated to the development of guidelines and best practices is also noteworthy. One of the primary strategies outlined is the implementation of detailed emergency protocols to address the inherent risks of using psychoactive substances in ceremonial contexts (Chacruna Institute for Psychedelic Plant Medicines and

[18] "In consideration of the DEA's analysis of membership, a plant medicine church may decide to include a description of its religious beliefs to regular and occasional members, and it may ask that congregants review, understand, and, in some cases, affirm core beliefs in writing to ensure that participation in ceremony is for sincere religious purposes and to prevent any appearance of diversion" (Chacruna Institute for Psychedelic Plant Medicines and Hoots, 2021, p. 27).

Hoots, 2021, p. 65). This includes requiring medical disclosure forms, informed consent, and liability waivers to mitigate both legal and ethical vulnerabilities. The Guide emphasizes that these measures serve both as harm reduction strategies and protective mechanisms for the institution. However, the authors caution that relying on formal documentation may create an inherent tension: while enhancing safety, these measures can also impose an additional administrative burden on the organization.

The Guide further advocates for clear communication about the potential physical, emotional, and psychological risks associated with plant medicine ceremonies. Another significant focus is the recommendation of pre-screening participants to ensure physical and emotional readiness. Leaders are encouraged to conduct interviews and assessments to gauge individuals' health and intentions. This would minimize risks for all involved while reinforcing the notion that participation in these ceremonies requires preparation and commitment. In addressing the issue of diversion, the authors suggest that churches implement mechanisms to affirm the sincerity of congregants' spiritual commitments. According to the Guide:

> A plant medicine church may decide to require congregants to affirm that either 1) they are members of the church and share the church's religious beliefs, or 2) they are exploring the church's religious beliefs and want to engage in prayer to determine if they want to become a member.[19] (Chacruna Institute for Psychedelic Plant Medicines and Hoots, 2021, p. 69)

This procedure would not only satisfy legal scrutiny—particularly under frameworks like the RFRA—but also protect the church from accusations of misuse. The proposed measures to prevent substance diversion underscore a clear legal concern regarding the risks associated with the religious use of psychoactive substances. It is no coincidence that the document presents this issue as a key area of vulnerability for churches, stressing the need for robust internal policies to mitigate potential misuse. This defensive stance would preempt scrutiny from entities such as the DEA.

Behavioral expectations during ceremonies are another area of focus, with recommendations to establish codes of conduct and clear protocols for addressing emergencies or disruptive behavior. On this matter, the role of leadership is described as critical. The Guide emphasizes the dual responsibilities of guiding participants spiritually and ensuring their physical safety. The document encourages leaders to acquire both theological and practical knowledge, including the ability to determine appropriate dosages and recognize signs of distress. The document also underscores the importance of trained assistants in supporting ceremonies, recommending that helpers be well-versed in emergency procedures and, ideally, certified in CPR. Additionally, post-ceremony integration is presented as a crucial element, with suggested follow-up practices such as group discussions or individual check-ins. However, the Guide cautions that while:

---

[19] In an earlier part of the Guide, the authors suggest churches that they may "ask that congregants review, understand, and, in some cases, affirm core beliefs in writing to ensure that participation in ceremony is for sincere religious purposes and to prevent any appearance of diversion" (Chacruna Institute for Psychedelic Plant Medicines and Hoots, 2021, p. 27).

> Continued support subsequent to a prayer ceremony may be viewed as protecting the health and safety of participants [...] a plant medicine church is not a licensed medical professional, particularly with respect to mental health. Unless any aspect of integration is led by a licensed therapist or psychiatrist, the church should not hold itself out as providing any mental health therapy or psychotherapy (Chacruna Institute for Psychedelic Plant Medicines and Hoots, 2021, p. 76).

The statement highlights a recurring concern in the religious use of psychoactive plants: the necessity of maintaining a clear boundary between spiritual practices and medical care. It reinforces the ongoing need for these groups to avoid any association between religious rituals and medical treatment, ensuring that the church does not unintentionally present itself as a provider of professional healthcare services. Such distinctions are crucial for the legal viability of their claims. In addition to emphasizing the need for clear boundaries, the Guide also tackles another critical issue: the financial aspects of ceremonial participation.

> While it is clear that a plant medicine church should not actively encourage or allow diversion, as it is a compelling government interest, it is also important to consider how church operations may give an appearance of diversion. How a church is paid for prayer ceremonies could be construed as engaging in the profiteering from the distribution of psychedelic plant medicines or condoning recreational use. In other words, a church accepting payments may be scrutinized. A church may decide that payment for attendance at a prayer ceremony does not include any costs associated with the plant medicine. Instead, a church can ask for a suggested donation that helps the church cover other costs, such as for the place of worship and its utilities, food, candles, and toilet paper. A church may also ask for annual or monthly dues to cover church services, excluding the psychedelic plant medicines themselves from ceremonies. (Chacruna Institute for Psychedelic Plant Medicines and Hoots, 2021, p. 80)

Inevitably, the risk of diversion always looms around the religious use of psychoactive plants. Hence, the ways in which an institution presents itself and is perceived by government bodies are vital to the success or failure of a claim. This is not only a matter of what things are but how they appear. This point is further reinforced when the Guide discusses the sensitive issue of advertising, highlighting the risks of promoting ceremonies involving controlled substances—whether through social media, online posts, formal advertisements, or websites. They argue that "depending on the advertising and preparedness of demonstrating RFRA elements of sincere religious beliefs, this public information within advertisements could support or hurt the church's RFRA claim". (Chacruna Institute for Psychedelic Plant Medicines and Hoots, 2021, p. 80).

The final recommendation concerns storage, security, recordkeeping, and importation. To underscore the significance of these issues, the Guide highlights one of the key reasons the DEA denied Soul Quest's exemption request: the fact that their ayahuasca supply came not directly from South America but from a business in the Netherlands. In the authors' view, "the lack of religious connection between the sources for the materials to make Soul Quest's sacrament was problematic" (Chacruna Institute for Psychedelic Plant Medicines and Hoots, 2021, p. 82). This relates to Hartney's observations on the critical role of demonstrating a connection to a South American lineage in successfully claiming legitimacy, particularly in relation to ayahuasca. In this context, the necessity of establishing genealogies and linking oneself to recognized groups and traditions underscores the standards employed to validate an institution as a religion and its practices as authentic. Moreover, it highlights the additional challenges faced by groups lacking these connections in their efforts to be recognized as legitimate religious entities.

The initiative to create a document presenting a highly structured framework aimed at mitigating risks and aligning plant medicine churches with legal standards is notable. The strategies outlined by the Guide reflect a calculated approach to addressing vulnerabilities while exposing the risks surrounding the legal gray area of religious use of psychoactive substances. It also highlights the tensions between establishing safety procedures and the growing constraints they impose. Another interesting insight in the Guide concerns the forms of presentation and how the chances of success depend on how groups navigate this intricate legal landscape and the delicate balance between practices and appearances.

One can see that it is not only a matter of being sincere, but also of demonstrating that sincerity through external markers, such as the establishment of specific procedures, protocols, and norms of conduct. This complex dynamic between religious practices and legal scrutiny makes the Guide a valuable resource for groups seeking exemptions, as it helps them steer through the ever-evolving requirements set by government bodies and courts. The procedures and protocols outlined in such documents not only ensure compliance with legal standards but also serve to demonstrate sincerity and authenticity in the eyes of regulatory agencies. In this context, the legal framework itself becomes a tool through which religious organizations must continuously adapt, balancing their practices with the demands of external validation.

5.4 The DEA's Report on Ayahuasca and Its Repercussions

In February 2021, the Church of the Eagle and Condor (CEC) and the Chacruna Institute launched the Ayahuasca Religious Freedom Initiative to secure legal recognition for CEC as an ayahuasca church in the U.S. and understand how the government handles ayahuasca-related issues. As part of this effort, on March 16, 2021, both organizations filed Freedom of Information Act (FOIA) requests with U.S. Customs Border Protection (CBP) and the DEA. These requests sought detailed information on ayahuasca seizures in 2020, including the number, locations, and procedures involved, as well as communications between agencies about the interception or destruction of ayahuasca. The goal was to better understand how the government viewed and managed ayahuasca, particularly in relation to religious practices (McAllister, 2021). On February 13, 2023, the DEA provided a single document to the legal team representing the CEC. This disclosure came 2 years after the two FOIA requests to the DEA and the Department of Justice seeking records related to ayahuasca (Chacruna, 2023).

The document was a 33-page report titled "Ayahuasca: Risks to Public Health and Safety." It was written by the Drug and Chemical Evaluation Section of the

Diversion Control Division. The document provides a brief background on the use of ayahuasca, emphasizing its use by Indigenous peoples and by "modern syncretic religious groups" abroad and in the United States, and associating the use of ayahuasca with "drug tourism industries." The report underscores the difficulties in assessing the adverse health risks of ayahuasca, since it is a concoction with no standardized formula for its preparation. The DEA argued that the "limited number of relevant and well-controlled scientific studies that evaluate the safety and pharmacological effects of ayahuasca" was also problematic. Considering these challenges, the report proposed a "comprehensive evaluation of ayahuasca" by analyzing not only the brew, but its main constituents (DMT and β-carbolines) (Drug Enforcement Administration, 2020b, p. 1). According to the agency, the lack of standard preparation might lead to variations in concentrations and also to the presence of other psychoactive constituents. The report states that:

> Besides the common components usually found in ayahuasca brews as described above, other psychoactive substances such as nicotine, cocaine, atropine, scopolamine, 5-methoxy-N,N-dimethyltryptamine (5-MeO-DMT), 5-OH-DMT (bufotenine) and caffeine have been found in brews of ayahuasca (Drug Enforcement Administration, 2020b, p. 2).

The report has a section dedicated to the pharmacological effects of ayahuasca and its constituents, highlighting adverse health effects associated with the brew. The agency stated that "despite claims that ayahuasca is safe, the use of ayahuasca has been associated with moderate cardiotoxicity, neurotoxicity, psychopathology, transient disorientation, anxiety, coma, and death" (Drug Enforcement Administration, 2020b, p. 9–10). The report also mentioned other adverse health effects such as nausea and vomiting and underscored the risk of developing psychiatric disorders. The DEA's argument is that since ayahuasca contains DMT and β-carbolines, the results of studies on the health risks of these substances can be applied to ayahuasca. This would allow the agency to equate the effects and risks of intravenous DMT use to the use of ayahuasca, for example.[20] The correlation between ayahuasca and "hallucinogenic substances" such as LSD, and DMT can also be seen in the section addressing "psychological and physical dependency"—a common topic when it comes to psychoactive substances. In the agency's view:

> Although tolerance to hallucinogen substances is rare, it has been observed. For example, daily administration of LSD to individuals has resulted in a complete loss of sensitivity to the effects of the drug on the fourth day of administration (Cholden et al. 1955, Isbell et al. 1956, Nichols 2004). Regarding DMT, Strassman et al. (1996) and Wyat et al. (1974) both concluded from clinical studies that there was no evidence of tolerance to the effects of DMT. Although, there is no definitive evidence that the use of ayahuasca (which DMT is a common ingredient) leads to psychological or physical dependence in those cases, it still is possible that the repetitive nature of using ayahuasca could lead to tolerance and or dependence (Drug Enforcement Administration, 2020b, p.17).

[20] "Overall, ayahuasca exhibits a pharmacological profile similar to that of DMT although other psychoactive constituents like β-carbolines in the ayahuasca brew may have a contributory role. Ayahuasca, similar to DMT and other schedule I hallucinogenic substances, has been reported to produce hallucinogenic effects (visual and auditory hallucinations), spiritual experiences, euphoria, psychospiritual distress, alterations of visual and auditory perception, illusions, and abnormal somatic sensations" (Drug Enforcement Administration, 2020b, p. 9).

The agency also addressed the topic of alleged ayahuasca-related deaths to reiterate that ayahuasca presented a significant risk to public health and safety. Based on an article that did a critical analysis of the media coverage associating ayahuasca with life-threatening adverse reactions (dos Santos, 2013) and a two-page letter to the editor of the Travel Medicine and Infectious Disease Journal on the risks of ayahuasca tourism (Bauer, 2018), the DEA presented a list of several possible ayahuasca-related death cases, including:

> For example, an 18-year-old man allegedly died from an ayahuasca overdose during an ayahuasca ritual in Peru. The shaman buried the individual to hide the death. A 33-year-old man suffered convulsions and died after his third ayahuasca ritual. A 40-year-old Swedish man was hospitalized in a coma after taking ayahuasca in Peru. An 18-year-old man drowned after participating in an ayahuasca event. A 39-year-old-French man was founded dead in a room with many bottles of ayahuasca. A 43-year-old female allegedly died from a heart attack during an ayahuasca ceremony. A 19-year-old male was found dead on the side of the road after feeling unwell at a ceremony. A criminal investigation found that a Shaman had arranged for the 19-year-old man to be taken to the hospital because of feeling unwell during the ceremony but the individual died on route to the hospital and was left on the side of the road. A 35-year-old female felt ill during a ceremony and died. A 41-year-old female was found dead in an ayahuasca ceremony room (Drug Enforcement Administration, 2020b, p. 14).

The report acknowledges the authors' claims that "these media reports were poorly described and did not confirm that ayahuasca played a causal or contributing role indicating that correlation is not causation. However, the fact that ayahuasca may have played a role in these events is noteworthy" (Drug Enforcement Administration, 2020b, p. 14). The document suggests that the use of ayahuasca can result in overdoses and intoxications as well. In the conclusion of the report, it says that everything leads "to the only logical and credible conclusion that can be drawn: Ayahuasca is not safe and is a threat to human health" (Drug Enforcement Administration, 2020b, p. 24).

The report is indicative of the DEA's stance on the use of ayahuasca. Despite the legal losses and the creation of an exemption request process, the agency still sees ayahuasca as a risk and has invested in developing resources to reinforce their claims. This is particularly important considering that the report was one of the sources referenced in the agency's determination letter that denied Soul Quest's religious exemption request. Soon after it became public, the report became news in the media (Leite, 2023) and was heavily criticized in the academic milieu. The Chacruna Institute and several researchers wrote an article criticizing the report and questioning its alleged flaws[21] (Labate et al., 2023). The article starts by condemning the flurry of ayahuasca seizures and attempts to criminalize its use. It also had a clear intention of debunking the DEA's document, as stated in the introduction.

> In the present article, we challenge a number of claims made in the DEA report and highlight significant factual omissions, theoretical biases, and misinterpretations of existing data. We will demonstrate that the DEA report severely downplays the safety profile and therapeutic potential of ayahuasca and overemphasizes the risks. It also fails to include current research on ayahuasca demonstrating its potential benefits (Labate et al., 2023, p. 81).

---

[21] I was one of the coauthors of article. My contribution focused on how the DEA approached the public policy available on ayahuasca.

The article questions several arguments and data presented on the DEA's report, underscoring the importance of government agencies developing policies based not only in the current available data on ayahuasca, but also drawing from international regulatory experiences and self-regulatory practices from ayahuasca religions and indigenous groups. The piece also problematizes several issues present in the report, underlining significant methodological and interpretive shortcomings. The authors emphasize a lack of systematic review of existing literature, underscoring the report's failure to incorporate rigorous scientific studies that explore ayahuasca's safety and benefits in humans.

This critique extends to the omission of relevant pre-clinical research findings and epidemiological data from communities that regularly use ayahuasca, both of which could offer, according to the authors, valuable insights into its long-term safety and therapeutic potential. The article also highlights the DEA's disregard for global legal frameworks, stressing that ayahuasca's legal status in other countries reflects a more nuanced understanding of its cultural significance. Furthermore, the authors suggest that the report presents false claims about the preparation of ayahuasca, including overstated risks associated with "dangerous admixtures," and problematic comparisons to animal toxicology, which may not accurately reflect human effects.

The critique takes issue with the DEA's alleged conflation of ayahuasca's effects—such as its psychoactive properties—with adverse health outcomes, arguing that this oversimplification misrepresents the complex interplay of factors influencing user experiences. Additionally, the report's inaccuracies regarding hospitalization and poisoning statistics are called out for exaggerating risks. The authors also criticized the report's failure to consider the role of setting and informal community-based mechanisms to mitigate risks during ayahuasca ceremonies. Finally, they challenge the DEA's conclusions about ayahuasca's supposed public health risks, portraying them as unsubstantiated and alarmist. Through these critiques, the authors sought to expose what they claimed was a selective use of data and the report's broader failure to engage with the existing body of multidisciplinary research, ultimately suggesting a bias that undermined the credibility of the DEA's assessment.

The article aimed to expose alleged overt biases, omissions, and misconceptions of the DEA's report, while underscoring its neglect or misrepresentation of recent scientific advancements. The main argument is that the report disproportionately amplified the risks of ayahuasca use while diminishing its established safety profile and therapeutic potential. The article accused the report of overlooking the crucial role of context in shaping user experiences and mitigating potential harms by narrowly equating ayahuasca with DMT and conflating their respective risks. In the authors' perspective, this reductive approach by the DEA was particularly problematic given ayahuasca's longstanding role in indigenous traditions and its integration into contemporary religious practices over recent decades. Furthermore, the authors censured the report's disregard for the growing body of research highlighting the substance's potential benefits, presenting an incomplete and skewed narrative (Labate et al., 2023, pp. 86–87). The article concluded by questioning the DEA's willingness and capacity to produce adequate scientific data on the use of ayahuasca and calling for openness regarding traditional forms of knowledge:

> Thus, when considering the report as a whole, it seems clear that it was either written by personnel that lacked the proper knowledge and skillsets to produce a comprehensive report or was written with a predetermined prohibitionist style political agenda. That being said, we suggest that future policy related to ayahuasca should be informed by evidence-based science, including social science and humanities research on the topic [...]. Lastly, we advocate for the inclusion of and respect for Indigenous traditions, which is a challenge for governments, universities, and practitioners. Since there are no conclusive studies showing that ayahuasca is harmful to public health, we continue to rely on the immemorial traditional uses and their reports on the safety of ayahuasca, as well as on its key value as a medicine, strongly supported by a growing number of rigorous clinical studies (Labate et al., 2023, p. 87).

The aim here is not to dissect the DEA's assessment of ayahuasca or to analyze the experts' critique point by point, but rather to illuminate the broader tensions between government agencies and scholars in evaluating ayahuasca's risks. These evaluations are especially significant given their frequent use in government reports and legal cases to justify or challenge the prohibition of ayahuasca. Nevertheless, certain key points merit attention. The DEA has focused on equating ayahuasca with substances like DMT and LSD, emphasizing risks derived from clinical studies and highlighting alleged incidents and deaths associated with its use. In contrast, the experts have drawn on recent research on ayahuasca's therapeutic potential, anthropological insights into its traditional use, and examples of successful regulatory frameworks for its religious use to advocate for its safety. Overall, these tensions reveal, as I will explore in the next section, the DEA's stance regarding the accommodation of ayahuasca's religious use within the country.

5.5 The Government Accountability Office's Report on the DEA

In May 2024, the Government Accountability Office (GAO)[22] published a public report for the Congressional Committees titled, "Drug Control: DEA Should Improve its Religious Exemptions Petition Process for Psilocybin (Mushrooms) and Other Controlled Substances" (Government Accountability Office, 2024). This report analyzed the Drug Enforcement Administration's existing process that allows petitions for religious-based exemptions from the Controlled Substances Act (CSA) for the use of psychedelic substances for religious purposes (Antunes, 2025). One of the focus points of the document was to examine the "reported barriers to the

[22] The Government Accountability Office (GAO) is an independent, non-partisan agency that works for Congress. It examines how money is spent and provides Congress and federal agencies with information to help the government in terms of resources and efficiency. The agency's work is done at the request of congressional committees or subcommittees or is required by public laws or committee reports (https://www.gao.gov/about).

legal access and use of psilocybin for religious practices under the Religious Freedom Restoration Act" (Government Accountability Office, 2024). According to the GAO, the agency analyzed data from DEA related to enforcement and religious exemption processes. They interviewed officials at professional associations, and representatives from the DEA and FDA. The agency also consulted research institutions, attorneys and associated advocacy groups, and officials from two states that legalized psilocybin use. Since the agency was asked to clarify their procedures on the matter, the report provides interesting insight on how the DEA examines religious exemptions requests. It states that the DEA's Diversion Regulatory Section reviews petitions, checking for the following information:

> The nature of the religion (e.g., its history, belief system, structure, practice, membership policies, rituals, holidays, organization, leadership, etc.); each specific religious practice that involves the manufacture, distribution, dispensing, importation, exportation, use or possession of a controlled substance; the specific controlled substance that the party wishes to use; and the amounts, conditions, and locations of its anticipated manufacture, distribution, dispensing, importation, exportation, use or possession (Government Accountability Office, 2024, p. 35–36).

In addition to the usual procedures of manufacture, distribution, importation, etc., the report emphasized that the DEA looked for belief systems, rituals, holidays, and structure. However, it specified that there were no details on the type of agent or expert who assessed the request, except that they were evaluated by the section devoted to the diversion of controlled substances. Unlike the ayahuasca groups, lawyers and activists, the GAO did not raise the question of whether the DEA had the legitimacy and competence to attest to one's sincere exercise of religion. Nevertheless, the agency pointed out several problems with the DEA's measures for examining exemption requests.

Nine of the consultants from law firms and advocacy organizations told the GAO that the DEA's religious freedom exemption review process was difficult to navigate and lacked clear guidance on some issues. Specifically, they found that the process could be overly burdensome, and it lacked transparency related to processing time, showing a general lack of faith in the DEA's review process. One of them stated that it was not clear how much and what type of information DEA would consider to be proof of religious sincerity. In this regard, the report highlighted that the DEA guidelines did not provide the standard the agency would use to assess "religious sincerity" or other aspects of the application. It also critiqued the fact that "the DEA guidance requires petitioners to provide documentation on a belief system, structure, and practice, but the guidance does not explicitly state what type of documentation would sufficiently address this requirement" (Government Accountability Office, 2024, p. 37–38). The DEA's capacity or lack thereof to assess the sincerity of non-western religious beliefs was also considered an important issue.

Beyond the agency's stance on determining the sincerity of belief, there was also concern regarding the DEA's unwillingness to answer questions after a petition had been submitted, leaving petitioners unaware of their petition's status, potentially for years. The absence of a clear benchmark for processing was seen as a problem, since it enabled the petitioning process to become a lengthy procedure. To illustrate this, the report reveals that over an 8-year period—from 2016 to early 2024—the DEA reported that 24 petitioners requested a religious exemption under the RFRA. Until the publication of the report, no exemptions were granted, and 2 of the 24 petitioners were denied a religious exemption.[23] The report also highlighted that some petitions related to controlled substances have been pending a DEA determination for an extensive period, including one of almost 4 years and one of 7 years.[24] The experts argued that the regulatory hurdles imposed by the DEA have led groups to withdraw their submitted petitions, sue DEA to receive a determination, or continue their practices without going through the petitioning process. In its conclusion, the report reiterates that the DEA guidance:

> [...] does not include information that clearly defines the types of information the DEA requires of petitioners to evaluate their religious sincerity, nor the standards or relevant factors that the DEA will consider in making a threshold determination on evaluating a petition. This guidance also does not inform petitioners of review processing timeframes for a petition for an exemption from the Controlled Substances Act. In addition, the guidance lacks information for petitioners to be able to inquire about the status of any petitions that have been submitted. As a result, stakeholders and petitioners have limited transparency and may continue experiencing long petition review times without any mechanisms in place to obtain status updates from the DEA. DEA officials stated that its website guidance is meant to clearly outline the Religious Freedom Restoration Act process and requirements for petitioners, and to ensure messaging is consistent (Government Accountability Office, 2024, p.44).

The GAO also made four recommendations to the DEA, suggesting that the agency communicate the types of information that petitioners should provide to allow DEA to evaluate petitions for religious sincerity, and also the standards and relevant factors in making a determination related to religious sincerity. It recommended the establishment of timeframes for the DEA to make determinations on religious exemption petitions. The GAO also proposed that petitioners be able to receive updates on the agency's progress related to exemption reviews.

The GAO report reinforces the hypothesis that, despite legal losses, the DEA still has reservations regarding the recognition of the religious use of ayahuasca as warranting state protection. The absence of clear protocols points to a broader reluctance to engage with these matters. This situation suggests that the tensions between

[23] According to the report: "There are also 14 petitioners that are pending a determination related to a religious exemption and 8 petitioners that withdrew from consideration, according to DEA's information. Of the 24 petitioners requesting a religious exemption, DEA reported that 6 petitioners requested a religious exemption related to psilocybin—three withdrawing and three pending a determination from DEA. Based on DEA's information, the 'date of receipt' to 'date of action(s)' for petitioners that withdrew their requests related to psilocybin ranged from about 7 months to over 4 years. Additionally, petitioners' exemption requests related to psilocybin that are pending a DEA determination ranged from about 8 months to over 3 years from the date of receipt" (Government Accountability Office, 2024, p. 39).

[24] The report mentions the Soul Quest Church, which filed a complaint against the DEA in federal district court and an accompanying motion seeking declaratory and injunctive relief after waiting 3 years without a response from the DEA about a requested religious exemption from the CSA (Government Accountability Office, 2024, p. 41).

ayahuasca groups and the DEA may intensify, leading to further disputes over the intersection of religious practices and regulatory frameworks. Ultimately, the report illustrates the paradox of government agencies determining the legitimacy of religious beliefs and practices, a fundamental challenge in U.S. drug policies.

5.6 The Legal Battle of the Church of the Eagle and the Condor

> The Church is a religion rooted in Indigenous spirituality whose essential sacrament is the use of ayahuasca tea, which is a mixture of sacred plants used for thousands of years by Indigenous people in South America in accordance with ancestral culture. The Church considers ayahuasca to be a sacred being, which is referred to as Grandmother Ayahuasca, a Divine Spirit of Nature. […] The Church is a religious community dedicated to the spiritual reunification of humanity in fulfillment of the Prophecy of the Eagle and the Condor (*Church of the Eagle and the Condor v. Garland*, 2022, p. 2).

The CEC was founded in 2018 in Arizona. The church's leader and co-founder is Joseph Tafur, a Colombian-American physician whose work focuses on integrating modern medicine with Indigenous spiritual healing practices. Tafur's trajectory began by exploring complementary approaches to health in 1997 at the Pacific College of Oriental Medicine and continued this focus during his medical education at the University of California, San Diego (UCSD). He completed a Family Medicine residency at the University of California, Los Angeles (UCLA), followed by a Post-Doctoral Research Fellowship at UCSD's Department of Psychiatry, where he studied mind-body medicine.[25]

In 2011, Dr. Tafur co-founded the Nihue Rao Centro Espiritual, a traditional healing center in the Peruvian Amazon. There, he became familiar with the practices of Peruvian *curanderismo* (folk healing). His experiences at Nihue Rao are described in his book, *The Fellowship of the River: A Medical Doctor's Exploration into Traditional Amazonian Plant Medicine* (Tafur, 2017). The book is both a personal memoir and a claim for the integration of Indigenous spiritual healing practices into modern healthcare. Through the lens of his dual roles as a Western-trained physician and apprentice in Amazonian plant medicine practices, Tafur crafts a narrative that seeks to challenge the boundaries of contemporary medicine while also legitimizing Indigenous practices within a scientific framework. The book's structure and tone reflect this dual purpose, oscillating between deeply personal accounts of healing and broader critiques of the Western medical system. Tafur positions

[25] Tafur is also the co-founder of Modern Spirit, a nonprofit dedicated to integrating spiritual healing into healthcare. Modern Spirit initiated the Modern Spirit Epigenetics Project, a substudy of the MAPS MDMA-assisted psychotherapy research trial. In 2023, he completed an Integrative Medicine Fellowship at the University of Arizona and currently consults in Arizona and California, specializing in ketamine-assisted therapy. He also organizes educational trips to Peru and Colombia, introducing participants to Amazonian plant medicine (https://www.drjoetafur.com/about).

himself as a bridge between two worlds: the empirical biomedical paradigm of Western medicine and the holistic spiritually oriented approach of Indigenous healing traditions. He establishes his authority through his double trajectory, with his medical credentials—describing his education, residency, and research in psychiatry—and his experiential learning as a *curandero* (healer) in the Peruvian Amazon.

The narrative is structured to build a case for the efficacy of traditional forms of healing with plant medicines through anecdotes and patient stories. Tafur's use of personal stories is a deliberate rhetorical choice. These accounts, often deeply emotional and dramatic, are strategic to illustrate Tafur's arguments on the limitations of Western medicine in addressing chronic illness and trauma. These anecdotes, however, are integrated into a broader narrative that advocates for the inclusion of spiritual healing in modern healthcare and critiques the reductionism of Western medicine. Despite covering the period in Tafur's life before the foundation of the CEC, the *Fellowship of the River* presents us insights into the physician ayahuasquero's background and can help us understand the CEC's work.

The CEC presents itself as a multicultural spiritual community committed to fostering unity, holistic healing, and environmental stewardship. According to the church's website, the CEC's mission and values emphasize inclusivity, cross-cultural integration, and spiritual activism. It has a stated goal of uniting people and of becoming a bridge between Indigenous and non-Indigenous traditions. Its narrative is grounded in the Prophecy of the Eagle and the Condor, an archetypal story that frames the institution's mission as a response to the global need for reconciliation between rational, technological ways of knowing (the Eagle) and intuitive, spiritual wisdom (the Condor).

> The Prophecy of the Eagle and the Condor has been told among many communities of North, Central, and South America and there are several versions. In a version rooted in the Incan tradition, the prophecy first speaks of a diaspora of Indigenous peoples who, in the distant past, separated into two paths: that of the Eagle and that of the Condor. The Way of the Eagle is often understood as the path of the mind, materialism, science, and technology. The Eagle Path is embodied in "Western" culture and the European colonization of the Americas and many parts of the world. The Path of the Condor is often understood as the path of emotion, spirit, nature, community, and intuition. The Condor Path is embodied in Indigenous culture and people who continue to resist colonialism by protecting their land and preserving their traditions, languages, and ceremonies.[26]

The Prophecy of the Eagle and the Condor is integral to the CEC's narrative, serving both as the foundation for its creation and as a legitimizing framework for its mission. This duality presents a historical and spiritual division, with the prophecy foretelling a period of discord following European colonization, driven by an overemphasis on intellect and the neglect of emotional and spiritual connection. According to the CEC, its purpose is to reconcile these two paths, fulfilling the prophecy by resolving the world's discord—caused by the excesses of the Eagle path—through a reunion with the Condor path, which emphasizes unity, compassion, and a return to holistic values. This foundational narrative, which centers on

[26] https://www.churchofeagleandcondor.org/about.html

the encounter between two worlds, provides the CEC with its *raison d'être* while resonating with contemporary concerns about ecological and societal imbalance.

In 2020, federal agents intercepted ayahuasca being sent to the CEC from Nimea Rao Centro Espiritual in Peru. After the seizure, Joseph Tafur received a small note from the U.S. Department of Homeland Security with the following text:

> Notice: Narcotics and/or other contraband prohibited from entry into the United States have been seized and removed for appropriate action under 19 CFR 145.509.[27] You will be receiving correspondence from our Fines, Penalties, and Forfeitures Branch in the near future. (*Church of the Eagle and the Condor v. Garland*, 2022, p. 20)

The CEC sought specific information about the seizure and destruction of its ayahuasca by filing in conjunction with the Chacruna Institute for Psychedelic Plant Medicines two FOIA requests to the DEA and the Department of Justice for all records pertaining to ayahuasca (Chacruna Institute for Psychedelic Plant Medicines, 2023). According to the CEC, the DEA persistently refused to provide responsive documents to these FOIA submissions, ignoring their legal obligations for nearly 2 years.[28] Given these circumstances, the CEC decided to file a complaint against the Attorney General of the United States, the U.S. Department of Homeland Security; the U.S. Drug Enforcement Administration, and the U.S. Customs and Border Protection. In the document, the CEC argued that "these increased seizures of ayahuasca, the prosecution of individuals devoted to its religious use, and the specific seizure of the Church's sacrament have all imposed a substantial burden on Plaintiffs' exercise of their religious beliefs." To repair this "intolerable burden," the CEC requested that "the Court protect their sincere religious practices of worship and those of other members of the Church, and safeguard their statutory and constitutional rights" (*Church of the Eagle and the Condor v. Garland*, 2022, p. 2) which included their rights under the Constitution and the RFRA. The church also sought the right to import, possess, and consume ayahuasca in their religious ceremonies.

In the complaint, the CEC presents itself as a religious organization rooted in indigenous traditions and centered on the sacramental use of ayahuasca. In framing its identity and practices, the CEC strategically aligns itself with South American lineages of ayahuasca use. The church's assertion of religious sincerity is grounded in its adherence to these traditions and its deliberate structuring as a religious community. Moreover, the CEC did not attempt to minimize or conceal its use of ayahuasca. Rather, it openly acknowledged the legal risks, presenting its continued use of the sacrament as evidence of the strength and sincerity of its religious

[27] The reference to 19 CFR 145.509 within the Code of Federal Regulations refers to Title 19, addressing Customs Duties. Specifically, Part 145 regulates mail importations, and Section 509 authorizes U.S. Customs and Border Protection (CBP) to seize prohibited items, including contraband, restricted imports, or items noncompliant with U.S. laws. Recipients are typically notified and may contest such seizures. In the case of the CEC, CBP confiscated ayahuasca under this provision, citing its psychoactive properties and classification as a controlled substance under U.S. drug regulations.

[28] As discussed in the section on the DEA report on Ayahuasca, the agency took 3 years to disclose the documents.

commitment. This deliberate defiance is framed not as lawlessness but as an exercise of constitutionally protected religious freedoms—an assertion that fidelity to their spiritual beliefs takes precedence over compliance with laws that they deem unjust and incompatible with their faith.

According to the CEC, the "Church is a faith-emerging belief system incorporating time-honored ways of life in the Americas, as ordained by the ancient and widespread prophecy known as the 'Prophecy of the Eagle and the Condor'" (*Church of the Eagle and the Condor v. Garland*, 2022, p. 15). The church claimed that their members "believe that, in fulfillment of the Prophecy, the Shipibo have begun to share their spiritual tradition of the ayahuasca ceremony. The Shipibo are regarded in Peru as one of the cultures with the most profound understanding of the ayahuasca sacrament" (*Church of the Eagle and the Condor v. Garland*, 2022, p. 16). The core of their argument is that ayahuasca emerged from the Amazon Rainforest and converged with Native North American teachings and principles in fulfillment of the prophecy. The prophecy thus provides a narrative that legitimizes the CEC's use of ayahuasca, presenting the emergence of the church as an encounter between different traditions of Indigenous peoples from the South and North Americas.

The Church further strengthens its claims of sincerity and legitimacy through the backgrounds and roles of its key leaders, Dr. Joseph Tafur and Belinda Eriacho. By presenting Dr. Tafur as both a trained physician and an ayahuasquero (a ceremonial guide), the Church highlights his dual credibility: he is a bridge between traditional Indigenous healing systems and contemporary spiritual seekers, making him a unique figure in the Church. He is described as one of the most experienced practitioners in the country, being trained to serve ayahuasca in partnership with Maestro Ricardo Amaringo in South America. Similarly, Belinda Eriacho, a Diné (Navajo) and Ashiwi (Pueblo of Zuni) healer, brings North American Indigenous traditions into the Church's foundation. Through her leadership role in the CEC, alongside her professional credentials in public health and community service, the church reinforces its image as a sincere and well-structured spiritual organization (*Church of the Eagle and the Condor v. Garland*, 2022, p. 7).

The CEC description of ayahuasca as a sacrament is integral to its religious identity, and the church employs specific arguments to justify its use. Ayahuasca is described not as a recreational drug but as a profound spiritual tool with transformative and purifying effects. The CEC emphasizes that the sacrament is not pleasurable in a conventional sense; it has an unpleasant taste, often induces nausea and vomiting, and leads to physical discomfort. These effects are understood as part of a "purge" or spiritual cleansing process, which they refer to as "La Purga" (*Church of the Eagle and the Condor v. Garland*, 2022, p. 10). For the Church, this physical and emotional discomfort is presented as beneficial and necessary, as it aids in the removal of "spiritual material" from the body and mind. Ayahuasca is also described as a "sacred medicine." In that regard, the CEC clarifies that:

> The term "medicine," as it is used by Indigenous people, is not employed in the same manner as in Western cultures. In this Complaint, "medicine" refers to anything that can be used for healing, including spiritual healing, and may refer to plants, songs, prayers, and personal experiences. In Indigenous worldviews and that of the Church's members and leaders,

> there is no meaningful distinction between medicine and sacrament, as plant medicines are sacred and address the interconnected realms of physical and spiritual health. The Church does not claim that the use of ayahuasca, even when called medicine, can cure or treat specific disorders or indications (*Church of the Eagle and the Condor v. Garland*, 2022, p. 9).

As previously discussed, the association of ayahuasca with the notions of therapy and medicine can be a complicating factor for groups seeking religious exemptions. Still, the discourse surrounding ayahuasca often involves these categories which can blur its religious identity. For ayahuasca-based practices to fall within the desired legal protection they must therefore undergo a process of "religionization"—that is, they must adopt a religious framework in order to be recognized as part of protected religious practices. The religionization is essential for ayahuasca groups because, in legal terms, substances and practices that are primarily therapeutic or medicinal might not be afforded the same constitutional or statutory protections as those grounded in religious beliefs. While the use of ayahuasca is often presented as a form of healing or therapy, it must be understood as a religious act in order to navigate the complex intersection of law, therapy, and religion. Hence, ayahuasca groups tend to emphasize the sacred, spiritual dimensions of their practices, ensuring that they are recognized not as a therapy, in the medical sense of the term, but as an integral part of their religious rites and beliefs, in order to qualify for the legal protections associated with religious freedom.[29]

Moreover, the CEC argued that ayahuasca is physiologically safe, countering the government's claims about its risks and presenting it as a sacrament used for spiritual healing rather than recreational purposes. For instance, the framing of the physical discomfort and challenges associated with ayahuasca consumption as part of a ritualistic and spiritually transformative process dissociates its consumption from recreational drug use, thus reinforcing its position that ayahuasca has a sacramental role. They also sought to strengthen the argument of sincerity by stating that the church has established comprehensive systems and procedures, including bylaws, a Code of Ethics, and Ceremonial Guidelines, to ensure the safety and structure of its operations, particularly regarding the use of ayahuasca. The CEC highlighted that, to prevent misuse, only designated board members were authorized to handle the sacrament, and that strict measures were in place, such as logs of ayahuasca quantities received, used, and stored in a secure, locked, and refrigerated location (*Church of the Eagle and the Condor v. Garland*, 2022, p. 18).

Additionally, the CEC claimed to have implemented rigorous participant screening to safeguard well-being, assessing medical and psychological conditions that might contraindicate ayahuasca use or interact with prescription medications.

[29] A similar dynamic can be observed in Brazil, where many ayahuasca groups incorporate healing rituals into their ceremonies. However, the Brazilian National Council for Drug Policies recognizes these practices primarily as acts of faith rather than therapeutic interventions. In this regard, healing practices performed in ayahuasca ceremonies are not seen as part of a scientifically based medical protocol, but rather as integral components of religious rituals. This distinction ensures that the use of ayahuasca in Brazil is protected under the legal framework of religious freedom and as part of a religious and cultural tradition of the Amazon, and excluded from the medical domains.

Participants have to provide informed consent, agreeing to follow ceremonial guidelines designed to ensure health and safety. However, the Church explicitly states that it does not make medical claims regarding ayahuasca's ability to treat specific health conditions (*Church of the Eagle and the Condor v. Garland*, 2022, p. 18). The church's legal argument is rooted in the recognition of ayahuasca's established religious use in the United States, particularly through the practices of the UDV and Santo Daime churches. By referencing the legal cases of UDV and Santo Daime, the CEC sought to draw a parallel between their use of ayahuasca and the practices of these churches, both of which have been recognized as legitimate religious uses of a controlled substance under U.S. law.

The CEC also highlighted the broader historical and cultural context of ayahuasca's use. The complaint asserted that the church's ayahuasca's religious use had evolved from its origins in the Amazon Rainforest to its contemporary practice in the United States, with roots in the indigenous traditions of the Shipibo people of Peru. These practices, they argue, are comparable to those of other Indigenous peoples, such as those in Brazil, whose spiritual practices have influenced the development of Santo Daime and UDV. This argument emphasizes the continuity of ayahuasca's use as a sacred plant across cultures and geographies, reinforcing its legitimacy as a sacrament within the CEC. By aligning their practices with indigenous and established religious traditions, the church asserted that their use of ayahuasca was not only a cultural and spiritual continuation of recognized traditions but also a legitimate expression of faith (*Church of the Eagle and the Condor v. Garland*, 2022, p. 11). Not only did they establish genealogical connections and similar paths to Santo Daime and UDV, the CEC also compared itself legally to those churches. According to the complaint:

> There is no appreciable difference between the Church in the instant case and the operations of the UDV and Santo Daime. Plaintiffs herein represent a Church and a ritual community arising out of indigenous beliefs, rituals, and pathways blending with other cultures to give rise to an emergent religion. Like the UDV and Santo Daime, the elders of the Church have received what they experience as divine guidance and direction with respect to the establishment of this church and its mission. Like the UDV and Santo Daime, the tenets of the Church encompass spiritual matters as well as guidance on how to live a sacred life. Like the UDV and Santo Daime, the Church regards ayahuasca as the quintessential sacrament that helps to connect each of its members to the Divine and guide them toward a harmonious and spiritual relationship with all of Creation. Like the UDV and Santo Daime, the elders of the Church care for its sacrament with impeccability and respect. Like the UDV and Santo Daime, the Church protects its sacrament from sacrilege, from desecration, and from diversion. Differences in theology are a tenuous basis for selectivity in governmental accommodations. A selective accommodation that excludes the Church would effectively establish the UDV or Santo Daime in comparison to the Church in the religious marketplace of spiritual ideas.

Finally, the CEC resorted to the international context regarding the legal status of ayahuasca to further bolster its case. The complaint points out that the term "ayahuasca" is not mentioned by name in any international drug control treaty, which suggests a lack of global consensus on the legal status of the brew. This omission is used to argue that ayahuasca should not be automatically classified as a controlled substance under U.S. law, as its international legal status remains ambiguous. By drawing attention to the absence of a clear international prohibition, the CEC challenged the notion that ayahuasca's legality or lack thereof is universally settled, positioning itself within a broader, more nuanced legal debate about the substance's status and use.

In establishing itself as a religion, the CEC emphasized key elements that courts and government agencies commonly use to evaluate the sincerity of religious claims: a defined set of beliefs (*The Prophecy of the Eagle and the Condor*), consistent rituals, recognized leadership, a committed core membership, a demonstrated willingness to endure hardship for the faith, and stringent screening and safety protocols.[30] The CEC's narrative of a connection to Indigenous lineages from South and North America combined with the professional and cultural ties of its leaders, lent weight to its claims of authenticity. By framing its practices with ayahuasca as both ancient and essential, and by invoking legal protections under the RFRA, the church positioned itself as both a religious practice and an indigenous tradition. This dual emphasis allowed the CEC to strengthen its case for recognition as a sincere and legally protected religious organization under the RFRA.

On April 12, 2024, the DEA and the CEC finalized a settlement agreement to regulate the religious use of ayahuasca while addressing the government's enforcement priorities. The agreement permits CEC to import, manufacture, distribute, and use ayahuasca strictly for religious purposes, provided it complies with detailed procedural and security measures. These include maintaining meticulous logs of importation, storage in a locked refrigerator with restricted access, and mandatory health screenings for ceremony participants (*CEC et al. v. Garland*, 2024, pp. 3, 10–11). While import quantities are initially capped at 25 kg per year, divided into smaller shipments, the agreement allows for adjustments based on CEC's legitimate needs, subject to DEA notification (*CEC et al. v. Garland*, 2024, p. 5). Additionally, the DEA waived its standard registration fees and agreed not to conduct administrative inspections during religious ceremonies (*CEC et al. v. Garland*, 2024, pp. 2, 9).

To ensure compliance, the agreement imposes strict record-keeping and security protocols, including detailed logs of all ceremonial uses and the quantities consumed. Ayahuasca must be transported to ceremonial sites in locked containers, and emergency response measures, including the presence of a first-aid-trained individual, are mandatory at all ceremonies. While the agreement does not limit the quantity of ayahuasca required for religious purposes, it reserves the DEA's right to spot-sample imports to verify compliance (*CEC et al. v. Garland*, 2024, pp. 8–10).

---

[30] According to the complaint (*Church of the Eagle and the Condor v. Garland*, 2022, p. 18) "There are currently approximately forty active members belonging to this multicultural congregation. The members have been meeting for more than four years for prayer, ceremonies, gatherings, and sweat lodges conducted by Ms. Eriacho and Drs. Tafur and Garcia. The Church and its members continue, on a regular basis, to use ayahuasca in ceremonies held in Arizona under the supervision and care of Dr. Tafur. Ayahuasca is the Church's only sacrament and, despite the threat of civil and/or criminal sanctions, the Church and its members have chosen to follow the tenets of their religion rather than be coerced to act contrary to their religious beliefs."

Beyond its technicalities, the agreement reflects the intricate balance the government and plaintiffs must navigate between its regulatory priorities and the constitutional protections afforded to religious practice. The DEA's imposition of detailed procedural requirements reveals its ongoing effort to maintain control and oversight, reflecting the agency's mandate to regulate controlled substances and prevent potential abuses. This dynamic underscores the inherent tension between the DEA's regulatory goals and the limits imposed by the courts. For the CEC, this agreement both legitimizes its practices and embeds them within a framework of state oversight, illustrating how regulatory measures can simultaneously safeguard religious freedom while creating bureaucratic hurdles. The case further highlights the complex interplay between religious freedom and regulatory oversight. The mandatory procedures, while framed as safeguards, also impose a degree of standardization to the religious use of ayahuasca. Requirements such as health screenings and emergency response protocols align with public health norms, subtly integrating biomedical priorities into the religious domain (*CEC et al. v. Garland*, 2024, p. 3). Ultimately, this agreement illustrates the broader challenges faced by certain groups and institutions seeking to integrate the use of psychoactive substances into legal frameworks often ill-conceived to accommodate them.

Shortly after the settlement agreement was finalized on April 12, 2024, a significant controversy arose. Several Shipibo organizations issued a public letter denouncing the agreement and questioning CEC's legitimacy to use and represent Shipibo traditions and practices. These organizations, including the Shipibo-Conibo-Xetebo Council (COSHIKOX), the Association of Onanyabo Shipibo-Konibo Ancestral Doctors (ASOMASHK), and others, addressed the letter to various national and international bodies, including the U.S. and Peruvian governments, as well as global institutions like the United Nations. They strongly rejected CEC's use of terms like "Shipibo Tradition" in its public presentation and accused the Church of misappropriating Shipibo knowledge and practices without consultation or consent from the Indigenous community (Shipibo-Conibo-Xetebo Council et al., 2024).

The letter highlighted several demands, including the revocation of CEC's authorization to import and distribute ayahuasca, respect for the intellectual property and sacred knowledge of the Shipibo-Konibo people, and adherence to international protocols for Indigenous rights. It also expressed deep concern over the lack of prior consultation with the Shipibo-Konibo, criticizing both the church and the U.S. government for failing to engage with the indigenous community. Asserting their collective rights, the organizations announced their intention to file an international criminal complaint against CEC and its representatives, as well as the U.S. government.

In response to the criticism from Shipibo organizations, the CEC opened channels of dialogue with proponents of the public letter, engaging directly with key Shipibo organizations in Peru. According to an update on their website titled "Reciprocity" from September 2024, the Church has undertaken efforts to strengthen its relationships with the Shipibo community. During the summer of 2024, Joe Tafur, as a representative of the CEC, traveled to Pucallpa to meet with leaders from Oni Xobo, ASOMASHK, and COSHICOX. The meetings were focused on discussing the CEC's activities, explaining the court settlement, and addressing questions posed by Shipibo representatives. The CEC has also initiated actions to support Indigenous-led initiatives. The church has begun contributing to a reforestation project in Iquitos, Peru, in partnership with the Shipibo nonprofit ADEPIAP (Association for Indigenous Community Development in the Peruvian Amazon). This project promotes environmental sustainability through reforestation and includes the cultivation of ayahuasca and chacruna plants. The initiative is supported by Modern Spirit Organization, Inc., which has acted as a fiscal sponsor to facilitate the transfer of funds to ADEPIAP.

The relationship between the CEC and Indigenous groups from South America underscores some of the difficulties inherent to the issue of Indigenous representation. Indigenous communities are often dispersed, lacking a unified leadership, which complicates the establishment of clear genealogies and connections to specific practices or traditions. In the case of the Shipibo, the decentralized and diverse nature of Indigenous governance makes it difficult to ascertain whether any single entity can claim authority over traditions such as an ayahuasca ceremony. These events highlight the dual pressures facing organizations like the CEC, which must navigate both legal and cultural landscapes. While its settlement with the U.S. government secured the legal framework for its religious practices, the CEC also faced the complex task of negotiating with Indigenous organizations in South America. These negotiations involve addressing concerns about representation, consent, and the ethical use of Indigenous traditions and practices.

The case of the CEC is pivotal as the first non-Christian church to obtain a CSA exemption under the RFRA. This landmark decision provides key insights into how the government and courts interpret religion, sincerity, and risk. It also highlights the unique challenges non-Christian groups face in navigating a legal framework shaped by Christian-centric legal paradigms. Organizations like the CEC must demonstrate the sincerity of their beliefs through well-established features such as sacred texts, defined membership, and institutionalized practices, while proving their use of controlled substances poses no public health or safety risks. In broader terms, this dual burden imposes the need to portray religious authenticity with rigorous safety, security, and anti-diversion measures and protocols, demonstrating a balance between its practices and the compliance with regulatory frameworks.

5.7 Recent Developments in the U.S. Landscape

As I finalized this manuscript in the first half of 2025, three important developments occurred that may significantly alter the legal and regulatory landscape surrounding the use of psychoactive substances for religious purposes in the United States.[31] The

[31] Given the recent nature of these developments and the constraints of this manuscript's timeline, a comprehensive analysis falls beyond the scope of this chapter.

first concerns a notable case that began in 2023, when the Church of the Celestial Heart (CCH)—a religious group inspired by Santo Daime and incorporating elements of Indigenous traditions, Umbanda, and others—had its ayahuasca seized and destroyed by the U.S. government. In response, CCH filed a lawsuit under the RFRA seeking protection from government interference (*Church of the Celestial Heart v. Garland*, 2023). The case became one of the most recent in a growing legal battle over the religious use of ayahuasca in the United States, raising critical questions about the boundaries of religious freedom, state authority, and the evolving landscape of religious practice. By April 2025, the lawsuit reached a settlement: the government granted CCH permits to import, manufacture, and distribute ayahuasca for religious use. In doing so, it effectively conceded that prohibiting the sacramental use of ayahuasca does not serve a compelling state interest (McAllister, personal communication, 2025). With this outcome, CCH became only the fourth religious institution in the U.S. to receive a formal exemption to the use of ayahuasca in its ceremonies. While the long-term implications remain uncertain, the case marks another pivotal moment in the ongoing tensions between religious rights and state regulation, reflecting broader debates over the legal status of these practices.

In May 2025, in a historic shift, the DEA granted the Church of Gaia a religious exemption to serve ayahuasca—the first time such approval was granted without litigation. This decision stands in stark contrast to the experiences of other churches, such as the CEC, and CCH, which opted to pursue legal action to obtain exemptions. The Church of Gaia succeeded by strictly following the DEA's petition process, adopting a cooperative, non-confrontational legal strategy. This included agreeing not to serve ayahuasca during the review period, a condition many view as unconstitutional and a violation of religious freedom. However, the church maintained firm positions on certain practices, such as refusing to destroy unused ayahuasca,[32] while negotiating acceptable storage and tracking procedures.

This exemption highlights the ever-changing relationship between religious freedom and the DEA's authority over psychedelics. Critics still argue that the agency lacks the competence and legitimacy to assess the sincerity of religious beliefs. The Church of Gaia's case may indicate a subtle shift in the DEA's posture, potentially shaped by legal pressure, public scrutiny, and the strategic efforts of religious freedom advocates. Still, the broader system remains fraught with risk and uncertainty, as churches continue to navigate a bureaucratic framework that can jeopardize their legitimacy, safety, and continuity.

A third key development occurred in June 2025, when the Sacred Plant Alliance (SPA)—a coalition of U.S.-based churches that use psychedelics as sacraments—announced its intention to sue the DEA over what it claims is an illegal and

[32] In a recent article published in *DoubleBlind Magazine*, Taylor Loyden—the Church of Gaia's lawyer—stated that the DEA suggested all unused ayahuasca be destroyed after the ceremony. The Church of Gaia refused. "We said absolutely not. This is a sacrament. [...] It is sacred. It is not something we're willing to sacrifice or compromise on. But we are willing to work with you on storage and tracking protocols so that you feel comfortable with our system, and we can demonstrate that it's secure" (Carreon, 2024).

unconstitutional religious exemption process (Hoots, 2025). According to SPA, the DEA's current "Guidance" for religious exemptions under the Controlled Substances Act (CSA) violates both RFRA and the Administrative Procedure Act (APA). Although the Guidance purports to provide a non-litigious pathway for sincere religious organizations to gain legal recognition for the use of substances like ayahuasca and psilocybin, the SPA argues that it has, in practice, served as an obstacle rather than a facilitator of religious freedom. Notably, the SPA points out that the Church of Gaia had never conducted ceremonies in the U.S. prior to its petition and did not represent an active congregation, a fact that, according to the SPA, underscores the system's bias against functioning religious communities.

The SPA's legal strategy draws on established precedent in administrative law. The organization has enlisted attorneys Shane Pennington and Sean McAllister to argue that the DEA's Guidance functions as de facto legislation, despite never having gone through the public rulemaking process required by the APA. Moreover, the SPA contends that forcing petitioners to suspend their religious practices indefinitely—often without a timeline or substantive feedback—constitutes an unlawful "substantial burden" on religious exercise, in violation of the RFRA. According to Hoots (2025), the SPA provided the DEA with ample notice, submitting a formal letter in April 2025 and receiving a vague, non-committal response the following month. While the DEA acknowledged the possibility of future rulemaking, it declined to offer a concrete timeline or commitment, leaving the current Guidance in place.

This initiative has the potential to reshape the regulatory landscape for churches that use psychoactive substances as part of their religious practice in the United States. If successful, it could compel the DEA to establish a new administrative process, one that offers a clearer, more functional pathway for churches to obtain exemptions. At stake is the future of psychedelic churches in the U.S., and the broader question of whether the state should have the power to determine what constitutes a religion or to assess the sincerity of belief.

5.8 The Paradox of Defining and Safeguarding Religion

The current moment for ayahuasca groups reflects both a watershed in institutional recognition and an inflection point fraught with complexities. While these recent developments may signal a significant shift in the struggle for legal protections under the RFRA, they also illuminate the tensions and paradoxes inherent in this evolving landscape. On the one hand, regulatory frameworks designed to safeguard religious freedom also impose bureaucratic oversight that standardizes—and, in some ways, transforms—the very practices they aim to protect. Requirements such as health screenings, strict security protocols, and emergency measures inevitably incorporate biomedical and legal priorities into the religious use of psychoactive plants, reshaping certain practices in the process. As ayahuasca gains global prominence, disputes over its rightful use are also likely to intensify. Given its South

American roots, controversies involving Indigenous peoples further raise issues such as legitimacy, authenticity, and representation.

Despite recent legal victories and the first exemption granted by the DEA, ayahuasca groups still face an uncertain path. Legal recognition, while a milestone, is not a panacea; it introduces new challenges. As more groups seek regulatory exemptions under the RFRA, the precedents set by current cases will likely shape the discourse of emerging groups. Ayahuasca communities must also grapple with tensions between safeguard and surveillance, religious freedom and legal compliance. How these groups navigate such tensions will play a pivotal role in shaping the broader legal framework for the religious use of psychoactive substances in the United States.

The question of whether courts and government agencies should be tasked with defining religion and determining the sincerity of religious exercise highlights a fundamental issue in the regulation of religious practices. These institutions are compelled to enter sensitive territory, setting criteria for what qualifies as religion and distinguishing it from domains such as therapy, philosophy, and commerce. This process entangles the state in contentious matters, potentially privileging certain traditions while marginalizing others that do not conform to established frameworks.

These cases attest to the growing interest in establishing legally recognized churches centered on psychoactive plants. This rise in religious claims is fueled by ongoing efforts to decriminalize and regulate their use. States like Oregon and Colorado have taken steps to regulate forms of psychedelic-assisted therapy and decriminalize ceremonial use, while cities such as Santa Cruz and Oakland have decriminalized psychedelic plants altogether, signaling a potential transformation in how these substances are understood and governed. This evolving legal landscape raises complex questions, particularly regarding the sincerity of religious belief. While state-level protections may offer a degree of legal security, the fragmented nature of U.S. drug policy means that federal law still poses significant risks, as seen in the DEA's continued oversight of religious exemptions. As more cases challenge traditional legal definitions of religion and seek formal recognition, the broader debate over religious freedom, public health, and drug policy will continue to shape the future of psychoactive plant use in the United States.

References

Anonymous. (2011). Ayahuasca manifesto: The spirit of ayahuasca and its planetary mission. *Door of Perception*. https://doorofperception.com/wp-content/uploads/Ayahuasca-Manifesto_Anonymous_May-1st-2012.pdf

Antunes, H. F. (2025). DEA Under Fire: Inefficiency or Resistance? Chacruna Institute for Psychedelic Plant Medicines. https://chacruna.net/dea-religious-exemption-process-questioned/

Appeal. Soul Quest Church of Mother Earth, Inc. v. U.S. Drug Enforcement Administration, No. 22-11072 (11th Cir. 2022).

Asad, T. (1993). *Genealogies of religion*. Johns Hopkins University Press.

Bartlett, B. (2019). *The U.S. Drug Enforcement Administration's problematic process for religious exemption for use of prohibited psychoactive substances.* Chacruna Institute for Psychedelic Plant Medicines. https://chacruna.net/the-u-s-drug-enforcement-agencys-problematic-process-for-religious-exemption-for-use-of-prohibited-psychoactive-substances/

Bauer, I. L. (2018). Ayahuasca: A risk for travelers? *Travel Medicine and Infectious Disease, 21*, 74–76.

Burwell v. Hobby Lobby Stores, Inc., 573 U.S. 682 (2014).

Carreon, M. (2024, June 4). Here's how Church of Gaia beat the DEA to serve ayahuasca. *DoubleBlind Magazine*. https://newsletter.doubleblindmag.com/p/here-s-how-church-of-gaia-beat-the-dea-to-serve-ayahuasca

CEC et al. v. Garland et al. (2024). Settlement Agreement, No. 22-cv-01004-SRB (D. Ariz.).

Chacruna. (2023). *FOIA brings to light DEA's problematic report, "Ayahuasca: Risks to public health and safety"*. Chacruna Institute for Psychedelic Plant Medicines. https://chacruna.net/foia-brings-to-light-deas-problematic-report-ayahuasca-risks-to-public-health-and-safety/

Chacruna Institute for Psychedelic Plant Medicines, & Hoots, A. (2021). *Guide to RFRA and best practices for psychedelic plant medicine churches*. Chacruna Institute for Psychedelic Plant Medicines.

Church of the Eagle and the Condor v. Garland, 2022.

dos Santos, R. G. (2013). A critical evaluation of reports associating ayahuasca with life-threatening adverse reactions. *Journal of Psychoactive Drugs, 45*(1), 67–78.

Drug Enforcement Administration. (2020a). *Guidance regarding petitions for religious exemption from the Controlled Substances Act pursuant to the Religious Freedom Restoration Act.* https://www.deadiversion.usdoj.gov/GDP/(DEA-DC-5)(EO-DEA-007)(Version2)RFRA_Guidance_(Final)_11-20-2020.pdf

Drug Enforcement Administration. (2020b). *Ayahuasca: Risks to public health and safety*. Drug and Chemical Evaluation Section, Diversion Control Division.

Drug Enforcement Administration. (2021). *Letter of determination U.S. Department of Justice*.

Government Accountability Office. (2024). *Drug control: DEA should improve its religious exemptions petition process for psilocybin (mushrooms) and other controlled substances*. https://www.gao.gov/assets/gao-24-106630.pdf

Hartney, M., & Bartlett, J. (2020). *DEA and the religious exemption: A fox guarding the henhouse*. Chacruna Institute for Psychedelic Plant Medicines. https://chacruna.net/dea-prohibition-religious-freedom-ayahuasca-ceremonies/

Hoots, A. (2025). *Sacred Plant Alliance to sue DEA over religious exemption process*. Chacruna Institute for Psychedelic Plant Medicines. https://chacruna.net/sacred-plant-alliance-to-sue-dea-over-religious-exemption-process/

Janik, T. (2023). *Soul Quest Church of Mother Earth: Ayahuasca decriminalization and the struggle of an institution to become a church*. Doctoral dissertation, Anthropology, University of Wisconsin-Milwaukee.

Labate, B., Ermakova, A. O., Sloshower, J., Galvão-Coelho, N., Palhano-Fontes, F., Antunes, H. F., Loures de Assis, G., Cavnar, C., de Araújo, D., & Ribeiro, S. (2023). The DEA report on ayahuasca risks: "Science" in service of prohibition? *Journal of Psychedelic Studies, 7*(2), 81–89. https://doi.org/10.1556/2054.2023.00279

Leite, M. (2023). *DEA is guided by a myopic view of ayahuasca.* Chacruna Institute for Psychedelic Plant Medicines. https://chacruna.net/dea-is-guided-by-a-myopic-view-of-ayahuasca/

Levy, A. (2016). *The drug of choice in the age of kale: How ayahuasca, an ancient Amazonian hallucinogenic brew, became the latest trend in Brooklyn and Silicon Valley*. New Yorker Magazine.

Litman, V. (2023). Psychedelics, the DEA, and regulating religion. *Regulation, Spring*, 8–10. https://www.cato.org/regulation/spring-2023/psychedelics-dea-regulating-religion

McAllister, S. (2021). *Ayahuasca FOIA requests reveal increased ayahuasca seizures, lack of due process, and government secrecy.* Chacruna Institute for Psychedelic Plant Medicines. https://chacruna.net/ayahusca_religious_freedom_information_act_church_of_the_eagle_and_condor/

Shipibo-Conibo-Xetebo Council, et al. (2024). *Pronouncement on the case of the Church of the Eagle and the Condor in the United States.*

Soul Quest Church of Mother Earth, Inc. v. U.S. Drug Enforcement Agency. (2022).

Tafur, J. (2017). *The fellowship of the river: A medical doctor's exploration into traditional Amazonian plant medicine*. Espiritu Books.

The Church of the Celestial Heart v. Garland, No. 23-cv-00545-SAB (E.D. Cal. 2023).

United States v. Meyers, 95 F.3d 1475 (10th Cir. 1996).

United States v. Quaintance, 608 F.3d 717 (10th Cir. 2010).

Young, C. (2024). *Soul Quest Closure: A message to our beloved community from Soul Quest Church of Mother Earth's Founder*. https://www.ayahuascachurches.org/

Chapter 6
On Drugs and Cults: The Ayahuasca Ban in France

As seen in previous chapters, the use of ayahuasca is often accompanied by legal issues. There are frequent episodes in which ayahuasca groups and Indigenous peoples encounter legal restrictions, such as the confiscation of ayahuasca shipments, imprisonment and prosecution. The reaction of national states to the unprecedented expansion of this phenomenon—which until the last decades of the twentieth century remained relatively unknown and geographically confined to certain parts of South America—has often been one of distrust and repression. In most cases, government reactions are usually based on accusations of illicit drug use and trafficking (Labate & Feeney, 2012) and public health and safety risks.

This is the case in Europe, which has shown strong resistance to ayahuasca. The case of the Netherlands is one of the most notable. Almost 20 years after the legal decision that authorized the practices of a Santo Daime group in the country in 2001, the Dutch courts decided in 2019 to ban the use of the brew, relegating hitherto legitimate and legal institutions to the underground overnight. In Italy, in March 2022, the Ministry of Health banned not only ayahuasca, but also the plants used in its making and its active ingredients. This decision took the country's Santo Daime group—one of the largest in Europe—by surprise, forcing its members to drink water instead of daime in their ceremonies as a form of protest.

In Spain, there was a notorious recent case of a YouTuber, Carles Tamayo, who secretly infiltrated a Santo Daime group in 2022, taking part in four ceremonies in which he made video recordings with a hidden camera without the group's knowledge. At the last ceremony he attended, Tamayo was discovered and fled the scene. The YouTuber handed over all his material to the Spanish police and filed a complaint against the group for attempted kidnapping. The case had huge repercussions, as a video published by the YouTuber—who has 743,000 subscribers to his channel—has so far over 800,000 views.[1] At the time, he was invited to a series of

[1] https://www.youtube.com/watch?v=Y1WC28neTVM

H. Fernandes Antunes, *Religion, Drug, or Cult?*, Law and Religion in a Global Context 5, https://doi.org/10.1007/978-3-032-04368-9_6

TV shows in which he presented accounts with sensationalist overtones, accusing Santo Daime of being a destructive cult that distributes dangerous drugs to its members without providing adequate health or safety measures. Shortly afterwards, the Spanish police arrested members of two neoxamanic ayahuasca groups in the country. Their homes were raided in the early hours of the morning by police officers, treating them as members of a dangerous international drug trafficking organization (Labate et al., 2023). Between 2021 and 2023, the police raided six ayahuasca ceremonies in the country. Despite these initiatives, on July 10, 2025, the High Court of Justice of Madrid issued a landmark ruling confirming that ayahuasca is neither controlled nor prohibited under Spanish or international law. The court emphasized that ayahuasca, as a plant preparation, cannot be classified as a narcotic or psychotropic substance under Article 368 of the Spanish Penal Code, citing international treaties and reports by the International Narcotics Control Board. A month earlier, on June 11, 2025, the Madrid Provincial Court had also ordered the return of seized ayahuasca, rejecting its confiscation and destruction. Together, these rulings provide unprecedented legal safeguards and establish jurisprudence in Spain, reinforcing that ayahuasca use cannot be criminalized in the country (Navarro, 2025).

In the midst of these complex scenarios, the case of France is one of the most peculiar. Like other European countries, such as Italy, France has a "zero tolerance" policy towards ayahuasca. However, the French case is also unique in that not only is ayahuasca classified as a prohibited drug, but ayahuasca groups are also portrayed as dangerous cults.[2] To understand the legal framework for ayahuasca in France and its consequences, we focused on a wide range of documents such as court decisions, pharmacological reports, the academic literature available on the French case, decisions and reports from governmental agencies, letters sent to the French government questioning the ban on ayahuasca, institutional documents from ayahuasca groups, as well as media reports and interviews with key players involved in the process.

The analysis of these materials shows that the ban on the use of ayahuasca in France goes beyond the debate about psychoactive substances and their possible risks. Moreover, the French government's ban on ayahuasca cannot be reduced simply to a question of public health, entering the debate about "cults" and "religions" and the alleged threat that minority groups pose to the country. A critical issue addressed here is not just the question of defining whether a substance presents health risks, but whether or not the groups that consume it can be recognized as religions, or criminalized as sectarian movements and dangerous cults.

---

[2] Following Introvigne (2023), I opted to translate the French term *secte* as "cult," since the term serves a derogatory function, while "sect" is a milder term in English.

6.1 The Introduction of Ayahuasca in France and the First Legal Problems

The use of ayahuasca has been known in France for decades. As Novaes and Moro (2023) point out, the drink began to gain notoriety mainly because of the work of French doctor Jacques Mabit, who founded the Takiwasi Centre (*La Maison Qui Chante*) in Peru in the early 1990s, an institution that provides treatment with ayahuasca and other plants for people who suffer from substance abuse.[3] Ayahuasca also reached the French public through the films, books and lectures of French filmmaker Jan Kounen, whose work focused mainly on the context of Shipibo-Conibo shamanism.

However, the drink's introduction in France, as in many other countries, came about through Brazilian groups. In 1997, two Frenchmen and a Brazilian graduate student created a small Santo Daime branch in Paris. During the group's early years, they received the daime without any problems through the Brazilian student, who was also a member of a Santo Daime church in Brazil. However, in 1999, problems began for the Paris group. According to Claude Bauchet, leader of the Parisian Santo Daime branch, the troubles in Europe started with the Dutch case. In 1999, the Santo Daime church in Amsterdam was accused of using illegal drugs, in this case, DMT. Following the complaint, the Dutch police launched an investigation into the use of ayahuasca in the country, and alerted all European police agencies (Bauchet, personal communication 2022).

Bauchet's group was the subject of investigations for 8 months, until his arrest in December 1999. On the day of his arrest, the police went to his company in the morning. The officers then took him to his home. After searching his home, the officers found approximately 10 L of Santo Daime, which were seized. In addition to Bauchet, other members of the group were arrested and held in pre-trial detention for 3 weeks, before being released on bail to await their trials. In total, seven members of the group stood trial and were charged with a series of offenses, the main charge being international drug trafficking (Bauchet, personal communication 2022).

Another case that attracted the attention of the French authorities regarding ayahuasca concerns a trial related to the Takiwasi Center. The center became notorious after a complaint in June 2000 from a father whose 25-year-old daughter underwent psychotherapeutic treatment with a French psychologist and a psychiatrist. The father, who believed that his daughter had suddenly changed her behavior, hired a private detective to investigate the people responsible for his daughter's treatment. The investigation took 2 and a half years, from early 1998 to mid-2000, during which time it was established that the psychologist and psychiatrist made regular trips to the Takiwasi Center in Peru. The father, convinced that his daughter was a victim of a hallucinogenic cult that recruited patients to send them to Peru to take drugs, wrote a 60-page report full of allegations. The report was sent to a series of

[3] For a detailed analysis of the practices and controversies surrounding Takiwasi, see Dupuis (2016).

institutions, such as the *Mission interministérielle de vigilance et de lutte contre les dérives sectaires* (Interministerial Mission for Monitoring and Combating Cults—MIVILUDES),[4] the Ministry of the Interior, the Catholic Church, and the *Union nationale des associations de défense des familles et de l'individu* (Association for the defense of the Family and Individuals—UNADFI). The alarmist tone of the document caught the eye of the French authorities and reverberated in the media (Bourgogne, 2011, p. 356).

Headlines such as "A hallucinogenic therapy," "Connections with a cult investigated for psychic manipulation and fraud," "Group of obscure psychologists," "The strange Doctor Mabit," illustrate the sensationalist tone with which the issue was covered in the French media. The impacts of the complaint, fueled by the media coverage, led to accusations of mental manipulation, potential suicides, abuse and fraud. The repercussions for the accused were significant. In addition to the social stigma and loss of clients, the psychiatrist was temporarily suspended by the French Medical Association (Bourgogne, 2011). Due to the repercussions of the case the Takiwasi Center published in 2002 a 30-page document denouncing the "smear campaign" that had been launched against the institution, addressing a number of issues, including the accusation that they were a cult (La Maison qui Chante, Takiwasi, 2002). The document provides an overview of the center, its legal status, public recognition, therapeutic approach, seminars, and other activities. It addresses funding sources, external evaluations, and the use of ayahuasca, detailing its botanical and psychoactive properties, potential hallucinogenic effects, and associated risks. It concludes with a defense against all the allegations made by the media and government agencies, situating them within a broader context of misinformation. In a section titled "Is Takiwasi a cult?", the document states:

> Whether it is the Takiwasi center, the association La Maison Qui Chante or the people who have visited us, there has never been any issue of any kind of mental manipulation, a fact which is characteristic of the sectarian phenomenon. In no way can our action be compared

---

[4] Originally called the Observatoire interministériel sur les sectes (Interministerial Observatory on Cults), the MIVILUDES was created in 1996 following a report by a parliamentary commission investigating alleged cults that mentioned 172 groups, most of them linked to the New Age universe, which were heavily stigmatized after its publication. Between 1996 and 2001, there were a series of parliamentary commissions and reports on the subject and, in 1998, it became possible to bring civil actions against sectarian movements or cults. One of the main organizations in this debate was the *Union nationale des associations de défense des familles et de l'individu* (Association for the defense of the Family and Individuals—UNADFI), a French anti-cult association founded in 1974, which played an important role in the media campaign against Santo Daime and Takiwasi (Bourgogne, 2011, pp. 360–361). The creation of the MIVILUDES reflected growing concerns over "cult deviations" (*dérives sectaires*), particularly in the wake of high-profile cases like the Order of the Solar Temple suicides in the 1990s. Nonetheless, the MIVILUDES has been heavily scrutinized for its broad and ambiguous definitions of what constitutes a "cult," which, critics argue, allow excessive state interference in religious practices. The lack of a clear legal definition has led to accusations of stigmatization, particularly from minority religious groups, alternative health movements, and international organizations such as the U.S. State Department and the United Nations, which have raised concerns about potential violations of religious freedom.

> to a cult, as one of the determining criteria for this qualification comes from its Latin etymology "*sectare* = to cut". All the people who have come into contact with our center or association have never been asked to leave their family or environment, or to cut ties with their loved ones or culture. For the minors (less than a dozen), there was always the agreement of both parents, or even their direct presence for two of them. All these people can testify that they have never been pressured into therapy or donations of any kind. They are free to leave the center at any time during their stay. Seminar participants are independent in terms of accommodation, food and air travel. [...] On the contrary, Takiwasi strives to remove drug-addicted patients from the pernicious ties they may have had with the world of delinquency, various mafias and initiatory pseudo-societies, and to discourage any compromise with occultism, magic, spiritism, "*ouija*" and other divinatory or alienating practices (La Maison qui Chante, Takiwasi, 2002, p. 14).

The Takiwasi Center further argued that its openness to the outside world contradicted the characteristics of a sectarian group, emphasizing that it welcomed an average of a thousand visitors annually, including journalists, patients and their families, students, researchers, and trainees, thereby demonstrating transparency rather than secrecy. The group also pointed to its academic connections as evidence against accusations of sectarianism. In 2000, Takiwasi was invited to present its work at a seminar on ethnopsychiatry led by Professor Tobie Nathan at the Université de Paris 7. The document also mentions one member's recent affiliation with a doctoral program in Ethnology at Paris 8 under the supervision of Professor Patrick Deshayes, a specialist in Amazonia. According to Takiwasi, both professors, who directed a university program dedicated to supporting individuals leaving cults, were familiar with Takiwasi and had seen no evidence of sectarian practices. The document states that Deshayes had visited the center multiple times as part of his research and had not identified any sectarian phenomena within its activities.

It is noteworthy that Takiwasi did not object to the idea of cultish movements or the framework of mental manipulation. On the contrary, the group acknowledged that such practices existed and posed a genuine risk. Their argument was not a rejection of the broader concerns about sectarianism but rather a clarification that Takiwasi's activities did not align with the defining characteristics of cults. By emphasizing its legal recognition, transparency, and engagement with academic institutions—including experts specialized in identifying sectarian movements—Takiwasi framed its defense within the very discourse used by governments to regulate and delegitimize certain organizations. In doing so, despite refuting the accusations, the center inadvertently reinforced the state's framework for distinguishing between acceptable and unacceptable religious or therapeutic practices.

Despite Takiwasi's initiative, this scenario resulted in two trials of the health professionals involved in the case, who were accused of participating in a cult and of circumventing French drug law. The accused were acquitted in both trials. With regard to the first case, the accusation was based on the 2001 *About-Picard* law,[5] a controversial piece of legislation aimed at preventing sectarian abuses. The law emerged from a series of government commissions that framed the practices of

[5] The law was named after its proponents, Senator Nicolas About and Member of Parliament Catherine Picard.

certain groups as forms of mental manipulation, exploitation of vulnerable individuals, and financial fraud. It introduced an unprecedented legal mechanism allowing for the criminal prosecution of individuals and organizations accused of sectarian coercion, with potential penalties ranging from fines to prison sentences. While the French government justified the measure as a means of safeguarding human rights and fundamental freedoms, critics have argued that it grants excessive discretion to authorities in defining what constitutes a cult, leading to concerns about religious discrimination and the repression of alternative practices.

Eventually, the health professionals in question were acquitted of the cult-related charge because the young woman involved had no direct connection to the Takiwasi Center, had never traveled to Peru nor had she consumed ayahuasca. The second charge, which concerned alleged violations of French drug law, was also dismissed, as Takiwasi operates in Peru and has no legal presence in France. Additionally, at the time, ayahuasca's legal status in the country remained ambiguous (Bourgogne, 2011, p. 361). Regardless of these acquittals, the case heightened scrutiny of ayahuasca by French authorities in a markedly negative manner. Moreover, the *About-Picard* law's broad and ambiguous definitions of sectarian influence contributed to the stigmatization of ayahuasca practices, fueling media portrayals that framed it as a potentially dangerous tool of manipulation. The growing public visibility of ayahuasca—coupled with the case's legal repercussions—positioned it as an object of state concern, reinforcing efforts to regulate and restrict its use in France.

6.2 Ayahuasca and Chemical Submission: The First Pharmacological Reports

In June 2001, the *Commission nationale des stupéfiants et des Psychotropes* (National Commission on Narcotic Drugs and Psychotropic Substances—CNEP)[6] issued its first report on ayahuasca. The document was the result of a request made by the commission the previous year, months after the arrest of the Santo Daime group in Paris. The aim of the report was to assess the addictive potential of ayahuasca, as well as to propose its possible regulation in order to limit its abusive and recreational use. In addition to the technical aspects, such as composition, active ingredients, toxicology, effects, etc., the report addresses a series of issues relating to the practices surrounding the use of ayahuasca. It mentions the traditional use of ayahuasca by shamans in South America and also by "neo-Christian religious movements" that emerged in Brazil in the first half of the twentieth century, Santo Daime and União do Vegetal. Despite recognizing the religious nature of the groups in question, the commission

[6]The National Commission on Narcotic Drugs and Psychotropic Substances is a government agency attached to the French Ministry of Health that has the power to decide on the regulation or prohibition of psychoactive substances in France. In addition to the full members belonging to various government agencies, the commission also includes a number of experts from various fields of health.

warns of the risks of non-traditional uses that tend to develop into "cults" or as "ethnomedicine," as in the case of Takiwasi, becoming a public health problem. The document also mentions the imprisonment of Santo Daime members in France in 1999, Spain in 2000 and the Netherlands in 2001. The commission clearly showed a sense of unease about ayahuasca and its users, recommending that the MIVILUDES be informed about the use of the brew in France, and requesting that the *Centres d'Évaluation et d'Information sur la Pharmacodépendance* (Center for Evaluation and Information on Drug Addiction—CEIP) monitor the use of ayahuasca in its branches for the presence of ayahuasca users (Commission Nationale des Stupefiants et des Psychotropes, 2001).

Three years later, two pharmacological reports on ayahuasca were published in France. The first one was developed by the Toxlab laboratory and written by pharmacology and toxicology experts Gilbert Pépin and Gaëlle Duffort. The report's introduction mentions that hallucinogenic plants have been used by "primitive societies" since protohistoric times. According to the authors, until recently, the use of such plants was limited to a restricted circle of South American Indigenous peoples, associated with mystical, religious and therapeutic practices, and also used during exceptional circumstances, such as the initiation of young people at the end of puberty. After this brief mention of the "archaic uses of hallucinogens," the report turns to the contemporary urban scene, highlighting the emergence of new natural hallucinogens on the recreational drug market as part of a growing movement of return to nature. Among these natural hallucinogens, the report says, ayahuasca is experiencing a new boom in Europe.

After this initial analysis, the report explored the question of the possible risks of ayahuasca, indicating that "to date, there have been no cases of acute toxicity linked to ayahuasca" (Pépin & Duffort, 2004, p. 82). With regard to the medium or long-term toxicity of ayahuasca, the experts mention the findings of the Hoasca Project. Despite acknowledging that the project found no evidence of health risks in relation to the prolonged use of ayahuasca, the report argued that, in addition to the psychological and psychiatric disturbances that ayahuasca can cause—such as nausea, vomiting, diarrhea, vertigo, sweating, euphoric or aggressive states, intensified perception, visual hallucinations, etc.—its consumption outside of its traditional framework, understood by the authors as the practices of certain indigenous Amazonian populations, could lead to fraud and manipulation. Undoubtedly, the most obvious danger, according to the report, was the risk of "chemical submission." Despite not presenting a specific case, the report emphasizes that cases have been observed in Europe of "cults" that have drugged their followers with ayahuasca, without providing the psychological and physical preparation necessary to reduce the drug's toxic effects in the short and medium term (Pépin & Duffort, 2004).

It is worth noting that the *Agence française de sécurité sanitaire des produits de santé* (French Health Products Safety Agency—AFSSAPS) defines "chemical submission" as "the administration for criminal (rape, pedophilia, violence, robbery) purposes of psychoactive substances without the victim's knowledge" (Commission Nationale des Stupefiants et des Psychotropes/CEIP-Paris, 2005, p. 5). According to the National Report on Chemical Submission, carried out by the CEIP-Paris in

2005, of the 260 complaints, almost half were considered to be proven cases of chemical submission. The victims were mainly women with an average age of 30. The most frequent case was sexual assault, whether or not it was associated with robbery. On the other hand, the majority of men were victims of robbery, with or without physical aggression. The report states that the acts took place mainly in the victim's or perpetrator's home, as well as in entertainment venues.

In view of the French agency's definitions and data, it is clear that the issue of "chemical submission" goes beyond the limits of pharmacology, entering the realm of the motivations and intentions of the actors who offer certain substances to their victims in order to commit crimes or offences. In other words, the core of the definition of an act of "chemical submission" does not lie in the pharmacological component, the active ingredient, the effects or the toxicology of the psychoactive substances, but in the motivations of the actors, more precisely, in the act of inducing an altered state of consciousness without the victim's knowledge in order to commit a robbery or sexual abuse.[7] In contrast, the use of the notion of "chemical submission" in pharmacological and toxicological reports on ayahuasca takes on an entirely new guise. Ayahuasca is associated with cult movements that practice a different form of "chemical submission" that resembles brainwashing practices, supposedly drugging their followers without proper psychological and physical assistance, and creating a possible public health problem (Pépin & Duffort, 2004, p. 83). Recently, during an online event in 2024 discussing the legal framework of ayahuasca in France, ayahuasca researcher Helle Kasik strongly criticized the report. According to Kasik:

> Natalia Rebolo, the lawyer who coordinates the Ayahuasca Defense Fund program in ICEERS, contacted me about the case of Santo Daime in France. She asked about my opinion about the lab report of so-called "toxicological expertise" from an organization called Toxlab that they had received for Claude (Bauchet)'s case from French authorities. I found that according to the lab report the concentrations of psychoactive compounds in the samples taken from Claude's case were very low in comparison to published results in scientific literature on the chemical composition of ayahuasca. However, the authors of the document described the use of ayahuasca as dangerous, for example, because the use of ayahuasca causes schizophrenic symptoms and aggression. Their description of the effects of ayahuasca was absolutely incompatible with published scientific evidence and with my own fieldwork observations. Surprised, I looked for the source of this information and what I found is that the authors of the document had copied this inadequate description of effects from an article that describes the effects of another plant without giving the reference to that other article. I found that their interpretations contained serious factual errors, plagiarism and falsification. [They were] neglecting this large amount of high-level research on the safety of ayahuasca, so I wrote a detailed report about my observations demonstrating, based on solely published scientific evidence that the practice of Santo Daime is not a threat to public health. [...] I was surprised to see that the scientific and ethical level of presenting

[7] According to the 2019 report by the *Agence Nationale de Sécurité du Médicament et des produits de Santé* (National Agency for the Safety of Medicines and Health Products), by far the most used substance in cases of chemical submission in France is alcohol, which accounted for 96% of cases (Agence Nationale de Sécurité du Médicament et des produits de Santé, 2019).

> legal evidence to the court can be so low in a civilized country like France that is considered to have advanced science and culture.[8]

Kasik's accusations of "errors, plagiarism and falsification" are noteworthy especially considering that the Toxlab report was used as scientific evidence on the Santo Daime trial (see next section) in order to claim that ayahuasca presented a risk to public health. As stated earlier, the report also reshaped the meaning of the legal category "chemical submission" into a notion that associates ayahuasca with "cultish" mind control techniques. The notion that psychedelic substances can be used to brainwash people, hindering their free will and becoming automatons devoid of personal autonomy and agency was originally developed by American psychologist Margaret Thaler Singer (Dupuis, 2021, p. 3). That theory is based on the notion that people remain members of so-called cultish groups against their will, due to the group's control over the member's mind. As a result, "cult" members are thus allegedly not liable as social actors and may be coerced in order to restore their autonomy.

Dupuis (2021, p. 3) argues that despite the lack of scientific evidence, this idea has played an important role in legal cases and has formed the basis of the controversial practice of "deprogramming" used from the 1970s onward by some American anti-cult movements. The French anthropologist recalls that, since the 1980s, there have been intense public, scientific and legal debates about the notions of "cult" and "brainwashing" and critics have pointed out the unscientific and subjective nature of these concepts, denouncing their use as a justification for persecuting unpopular movements and for violating the constitutional rights of their members. After years of debates, as Dupuis (2021, p. 3) reminds us, an academic consensus had emerged, considering theories on brainwashing pseudoscience. Nevertheless, in the anthropologist's view, the association of psychedelics with the notions of "mental manipulation" and "brainwashing" contributed significantly to the social stigmatization of psychedelics and to the legitimization of their prohibition in Europe.

This can be illustrated by the fact that the risk of "chemical submission" associated with ayahuasca is also present in a report published by the CNEP, which was produced by the CEIP Bordeaux. Like the Toxlab report, the CEIP Bordeaux also categorized Santo Daime and the União do Vegetal as "cults" stemming from neo-Christian movements. Unlike the previous report, however, the document in question did not typify chemical submission, but rather described three alleged cases related to ayahuasca consumption. The first one only mentions the case of a woman who took ayahuasca regularly in a Santo Daime group and lost 15 kilos. The second mentions a psychologist who wanted to write an article on pseudo-shamanism. She infiltrated an ayahuasca group, not identified in the report, and took part in two sessions. According to the document, the psychologist had bad experiences and psychiatric issues that lasted for months after her participation in the ceremonies. The third deals with a potential case of chemical submission that could be related to ayahuasca. A 32-year-old man claimed that his credit card had been stolen by a woman. He reported having vision problems, fatigue and memory loss half an hour after

[8] https://www.youtube.com/watch?v=MNNRxW2NJnM&t=21s

consuming alcohol. His urine sample showed the presence of cannabis, nicotine, codeine, caffeine and harmine. The latter is one of the active ingredients in ayahuasca. The test did not, however, find any traces of DMT, a substance present in ayahuasca.

Despite not mentioning the term "chemical submission" on their website, the MIVILUDES has also incorporated the argument of mental manipulation when addressing ayahuasca and "the example of 'neo-shamanic' narco-tourism." The agency mentions that some ayahuasca centers, which have branches in France, operate as "therapeutic communities," entrusting the organization of their trips to agencies specializing in "spiritual tourism" or "psycho-tourism." According to the MIVILUDES, initiatory rituals are offered through travel organizations as a form of "narco-tourism," and during these trips, the consumption of hallucinogenic substances classified as narcotics in France such as ayahuasca and iboga is often recommended. The agency stresses that the consumption of these substances, "can be extremely effective in the process of mental manipulation exercised by a guru over his followers, and can lead to physical, psychological and even fatal risks." The MIVILUDES goes further, suggesting that, "in reality, their only purpose is to strengthen the hold exerted over group members and definitively sever ties with their loved ones, likely to divert them from joining the movement."[9]

Beyond the controversial debate about ayahuasca's suggestibility potential or the question of whether or not it lends itself to chemical submission, in the sense of mental manipulation, the recurring mention of this possibility in the pharmacological reports and government agencies' documents attests to the growing concern of the French public authorities, especially the Ministry of Health, as well as various specialists on the possible impacts of a growing use of ayahuasca in the country. These initiatives were extremely important for the legal sphere and for the framework given to the use of ayahuasca, considering that these reports became evidence in the trial of the Santo Daime members in 2004 and were often cited by French authorities not only to justify the stance that ayahuasca poses a serious threat to public health and safety, but to portray ayahuasca groups as dangerous sectarian movements and criminal organizations.

6.3 The Trial of the Santo Daime Members in Paris

On January 15, 2004, the Paris court ruled on the case of the Santo Daime members arrested in 1999. All the members were charged with the following crimes: importation, acquisition and possession of narcotics, use of narcotics, and drug trafficking. The group's defense was based on three points: the preeminence of religious freedom as a major constitutional right; the fact that neither France nor international

[9] https://www.miviludes.interieur.gouv.fr/quest-ce-quune-d%C3%A9rive-sectaire/o%C3%B9-la-d%C3%A9celer/international

treaties included ayahuasca in their list of controlled substances; and, finally, that the doses of DMT were derisory and not capable of producing the effects alleged by the prosecution. In addition, the defense argued that ayahuasca posed no health risks.

In his decision, the judge emphasized the testimony of Dr Pépin, one of the authors of the Toxlab report on ayahuasca, highlighting its hallucinogenic effects and the risk of unwanted psychological disorders. Despite recognizing the superiority of the principle of religious freedom, the court argued that it could not override the maintenance of public order. In the words of the judge: "It is clear that legislation on the consumption or supply of drugs cannot be refuted under a religious cover whose sole purpose could be to circumvent legality" (Tribunal de Grande Instance de Paris, 2004, p. 16). The court recognized, as the defense claimed, that ayahuasca is not on the list of proscribed substances, either in France or international law.

However, based on Pépin's testimony, the court emphasized that ayahuasca was a preparation containing DMT, adding that "people who [...] extract the active and hallucinogenic substance, DMT, cannot take advantage of the fact that this substance is found naturally in many plants" (Tribunal de Grande Instance de Paris, 2004, p. 17). In the judge's view, Santo Daime members brought foreign plants into France with the aim of extracting an illegal substance. Based on this position, the court handed down its judgement: the accused were found guilty and sentenced to 18 months' probation.

It should be noted that the term "cult" appears only twice in the 23-page ruling and is related to a random statement by a mother whose son had allegedly been kidnapped by the Santo Daime "cult." She argued that her son had suffered mental and physical deterioration, without providing any further details or evidence. When referring to Santo Daime, the judge defines it as a religious practice that has its origins in a syncretic religion. The question of whether Santo Daime was a cult or a religion was not of interest to the court, nor were the practices of the group's members scrutinized. On the contrary, the conviction was based solely on the procedure of extracting a substance classified as illegal (DMT) in the country.

This last point is particularly relevant, as it played a decisive role in the appeal. After being found guilty, the Santo Daime members contacted a pharmacist member of the CNEP, who wrote a brief report on the pharmacology and legal framework of ayahuasca according to the country's drug legislation (Beauverie, 2004). His report attested that the decree of February 22, 1990, which established the list of substances classified as narcotics, included DMT as a raw material, as well as preparations made from it. However, the pharmacist emphasized that the drug legislation excludes animals and plants containing DMT or preparations made from them from the list. According to the expert, ayahuasca was not a preparation made from the extraction of DMT, but a decoction made from plants. Beauverie pointed out that the making of ayahuasca consists of soaking the plants in 30–40 L of water and reducing this volume to 4 or 5 L. This procedure, he said, is a decoction followed by a reduction and cannot be compared to an extraction technique for producing DMT. The pharmacist concluded his report by stating that ayahuasca had not yet been classified as illegal in France (Beauverie, 2004).

This two-page document presented by the defense played a crucial role in the group's acquittal in the appeal. The decision by the Paris Court of Appeals emphasized that, according to Dr Pépin's testimony, ayahuasca could be used for "chemical submission" purposes. However, the court recognized that, in France, ayahuasca had not been classified as a narcotic and was not on the Ministry of Health's list of controlled substances. The judge argued that the toxicity of a product alone does not allow the state to classify it as a narcotic. As for DMT, the ruling relied on the report submitted by the defense, pointing out that DMT obtained by extraction, in other words, by separating it from the compound it is part of to obtain a substance in its pure state, is undoubtedly prohibited. In contrast, the court stated that "the operations of 'decoction', 'infusion' or 'maceration' could not make it possible to obtain a 'substance', [...] since they do not make it possible to isolate 'the chemical elements and their compounds present in their natural state or produced by industry'" (Cour d'appel de Paris, 2005, p. 17). The court then acquitted the Santo Daime members and closed the case for lack of a legal basis.

It should be highlighted that the court did not acquit the Santo Daime members because it recognized the prominence of religious freedom over French anti-drugs legislation. It was a decision based exclusively on technical criteria, given that the procedure of producing ayahuasca was not typified in the country's legislation. It is also noteworthy that in the initial trial and appeal, the allegations of "cult" and "chemical submission" played a minor or even insignificant role. The core of the debate was the question of the classification of ayahuasca as a narcotic and not the practices of the groups that consume it.

By overturning the lower court's decision, the Court of Appeals set a legal precedent so that ayahuasca would not be considered illegal in France. The impact of this decision, however, was short-lived, as 3 months after the group's acquittal, the French government issued a decision banning ayahuasca. The measure was a major setback for the members of Santo Daime, as the legal framework that claimed ayahuasca was not covered by the country's drug legislation fell apart. As a result, the group went from freedom to illegality just 100 days after the court decision that acquitted them (Bourgogne, 2011).

6.4 The Commission on Narcotic Drugs and the Ban on Ayahuasca

On December 16, 2004, the CNEP convened a meeting, and its report was released in February 2005. One of its key resolutions was the classification of all plants and active ingredients found in ayahuasca as illicit. The document noted that the AFSSAPS, through the CEIP network, had been monitoring ayahuasca use in France for several years. It also highlighted that an evaluation of its potential for abuse and addiction was first presented to the Commission in 2001 (Commission Nationale des Stupefiants et des Psychotropes, 2005, p. 18). The report also introduced a typology of ayahuasca use, distinguishing several contexts in which it is consumed. It described "traditional use" as a longstanding practice among Indigenous peoples across the Amazon basin in Peru, Ecuador, Colombia, Bolivia, and Brazil, where ayahuasca plays a central role in religious, initiatory, and therapeutic rituals. It also highlighted its adoption by "neo-Christian cults," particularly the Brazilian religious movements Santo Daime and União do Vegetal (UDV), which emerged in the early twentieth century and have since expanded across South America. The report identified "recreational use" as a rare phenomenon and pointed to "ayahuasca tourism" as a growing industry, with tour operators organizing retreats and seminars featuring Amazonian shamans. It also noted the rise of "therapeutic use" outside traditional settings, particularly within the "ethnomedicine" movement for addiction treatment, exemplified by the Takiwasi center in Peru, led by Jacques Mabit, a French doctor initiated into shamanism and traditional medicine. Finally, it referred to "psycho-spiritual use" as collective rituals centered on ayahuasca consumption (Commission Nationale des Stupefiants et des Psychotropes, 2005, p. 20).

In this typology, Santo Daime and the UDV are not only seen as "cults," but are excluded from the rubric of "traditional use." In other words, they are framed as cults originating from the only tradition recognized by the French government, the Indigenous use of ayahuasca restricted to the Amazonian context. Another noteworthy feature of the report was the intervention by the MIVILUDES representative—who acted as a rapporteur for the meeting—on the use of ayahuasca in cults. According to his presentation, incorporated into the committee's report, there was no legal definition of a cult or sectarian group, but some characteristics could be outlined: a cult has an exclusive structure; it can have religious or other objectives (not specified in the report); it presents itself in the form of an association, or a professional training organization; it can display characteristics of psychotherapy; it practices financial and economic exploitation, psychological dependency and takes advantage of the chronic or temporary weakness of individuals; it is a movement that operates clandestinely in organized but invisible sleeper cells; its financial organization is built up and regularly remodeled to prevent forms of control; the movements are stable but evolving, able to change their leadership, their names and their geographical location; education, health, professional training are their spheres of predilection, but they also operate in strategic areas such as youth protection, social assistance for children, the elderly and the disabled; and finally, they seek to present an air of respectability in the eyes of the public (Commission Nationale des Stupefiants et des Psychotropes, 2005, p. 22).

The breadth of the features—some of them contradictory—highlighted by the MIVILUDES about sectarian movements is noteworthy. These groups can operate across religious, therapeutic, professional, and educational spheres, sometimes adopting clandestine, extremist structures while also engaging in social welfare, healthcare, and the protection of marginalized communities. They remain elusive yet actively cultivate a positive public image. Their organizational frameworks are exclusive but highly adaptable, capable of sudden transformations that redefine their appearance and areas of influence. Though they may seem stable, they are in a constant state of evolution. With specific regard to ayahuasca, the MIVILUDES representative argued that its promotion and consumption is based on groups focused on psychiatry and the "spiritual dimension," offering courses and training sessions. His presentation emphasized this network's association with the Takiwasi center in Peru. In addition, the representative mentioned the alleged case of a psychotherapist (not identified in the report) who attended religious communities and allegedly took control of young people through psychiatric treatment.

Vincent (pseudonym), a member of the CNEP at the time, recalls that the MIVILUDES representative stated that there was a dangerous new cult on French territory called Santo Daime that promoted the use of ayahuasca and that the commission should intervene in the case. In response, Vincent argued that the discussion of whether Santo Daime was a cult or a religion was not a matter for the CNEP, which should limit itself to analyzing the chemical, toxicological and pharmacological aspects of ayahuasca (Vincent, personal communication 2022). Despite his position, the commission approved the ban on ayahuasca with a score of 15 votes in favor, one against and 5 abstentions. According to the report, the commission decided that, because of its composition, ayahuasca had hallucinogenic effects and had an obvious potential for abuse and addiction. The document underlines in its conclusion that "its use in a sectarian context makes it a particularly sensitive product." The commission decided that "all these elements make it possible to propose the application of stricter control measures, in particular a classification on the list of narcotics" (Commission Nationale des Stupefiants et des Psychotropes, 2005, p. 23). The report highlights thus a central issue for understanding the ban on ayahuasca in France, namely that the commission's focus was not limited to a pharmacological evaluation, but also to the debate about cults and their risks to French public order. There was therefore not only a fear of the ayahuasca brew, but above all a suspicion regarding the practices of ayahuasca groups.

The ban on ayahuasca resulted from an unprecedented collaboration between the Ministry of Health and the Ministry of the Interior, represented by MIVILUDES. As in Brazil and the United States, a drug agency responsible for regulating the potential and risks of substances from a pharmacological and toxicological perspective asserted its authority to determine which practices and groups qualified as legitimate religions and which posed a potential threat. Unlike court rulings that relied strictly on pharmacology and legal frameworks governing ayahuasca, the Ministry of Health moved beyond the domain of pharmacology and into the debate on cults and religions. As a result, the CNEP's decision created a legal problem for Santo Daime members. That same year, members of the group and representatives of Takiwasi asked the Ministry of Health and later the Council of State[10] to remove ayahuasca from the list of plants and substances classified as narcotics (Bauchet

[10] The Council of State is France's highest administrative court and also serves as an advisor to the government on legal matters. It reviews the legality of administrative decisions and ensures that public authorities comply with the law.

et al., 2005). The request was written by Francis Caballero, a famous French lawyer who specializes in drug cases. Caballero argued that the Health Ministry's decision was based on unscientific toxicology reports (Bourgogne, 2011, p. 358). In addition, the lawyer claimed that the ban on ayahuasca constituted a violation of religious freedom in accordance with Article 10 of the *Déclaration des Droits de l'Homme* (1789 Declaration of Human Rights), Article 2 of the 1958 Constitution, Article 9 of the European Convention on Human Rights, and Articles 18 and 19 of the International Covenant on Civil and Political Rights.

The request was rejected initially by the Ministry of Health and a second time after an appeal to the Council of State. On the question of the health risks of ayahuasca, the Ministry of Health's decision mentioned the three alleged cases of chemical submission with ayahuasca presented by the CEIP Bordeaux report. With regard to the accusation of violating the principle of religious freedom, the Ministry of Health claimed that the "strict regulation of the narcotics trade is necessary to meet the essential requirement of protecting public health," arguing that "the classification of a substance as a narcotic drug does not in any way infringe the principles laid down in Article 9 of the ECHR and Article 4 of the 1789 Declaration of Human Rights" (Ministère de la Santé et des Solidarités, 2006, p. 3). Similarly, the Council of State stated on the toxicity of ayahuasca that:

> In order to classify these plants as narcotics, the Ministry of Health, citing the work of specialists, indicates that [...] Ayahuasca or Daime, can constitute a factor in the psychological destructuring of the individual and also lead to a form of chemical submission of the users of this drink; [...] that Ayahuasca consumption can cause cardiovascular complications, such as increased blood pressure and heart rate; [...] that Ayahuasca, by virtue of its composition, has proven psychoactive effects, that it causes significant somatic effects and that it is neurotoxic in animals (Conseil d'État, 2007, p. 3).

On the issue of religious freedom, the Council of State stated that "the violations caused by the decision are neither excessive nor disproportionate to public health concerns" (Conseil d'État, 2007, p. 3). However, it should be noted that on other occasions, the Council of State has endorsed requests to remove psychoactive substances from the list of narcotics. One of the most emblematic cases is undoubtedly the decision to annul twice the ban on "poppers,"[11] in 2009 and 2013, after strong pressure from the LGBTQI+ community. The removal of poppers in two consecutive occasions from the list of narcotics shows that the Council of State's decisions in the name of the public health of the French population are often subject to pressure and lobbying from social movements and civil society, and may go against the guidelines of the health ministry.

[11] "Poppers" is the common name given to alkyl nitrites. They are usually inhaled to intensify sexual experiences or to produce a short euphoria. Poppers are especially popular among the LGBTQIA+ community (Beck et al., 2014). In France, between 1999 and 2001, the ANSM reported 6 deaths and 146 cases of serious intoxication linked to their use (https://poppers-pascher-blog.com/poppers-mort/).

6.5 Santo Daime on Trial Again

CNEP's decision relegated the Santo Daime members in France to the underground. After almost two decades of practicing Santo Daime in secret without incidents, Claude Bauchet was arrested again in 2019. He spent 4 days in custody and was released on bail. In June 2024, the Santo Daime leader, alongside other members of the church, faced their second trial. He and other members were charged with having illegally imported, transported, possessed, offered goods dangerous to public health, in this case, ayahuasca, and also for using ayahuasca and cannabis, substances classified as narcotics (Tribunal de Grande Instance de Paris, 2024, p. 7). The investigation started due to an anonymous letter denouncing Bauchet and other Santo Daime members:

> On February 08, 2019, a preliminary investigation was opened by the Paris public prosecutor's office following an anonymous letter denouncing four individuals (Claude Bauchet, [...][12]) who were allegedly orchestrating private ceremonies for a fee linked to the "Santo Daime" (a syncretic belief made up of Christian and Amerindian elements, with the consumption of the aforementioned products, to achieve a state of hallucination and delirium under the control of shamans), the consumption of ayahuasca (a psychotropic plant classified as a narcotic), marijuana (cannabis herb), as well as extracts of frog (Phyllomedusa) (Tribunal de Grande Instance de Paris, 2024, p. 7).

According to the ruling, these ceremonies were organized around Amazonian Indigenous peoples (mainly from the state of Acre, in north-western Brazil), in which the shaman would lead a process combining the consumption of ayahuasca, rapé and sananga, in preparation for trances lulled by songs and melodies. It stated that the ceremonies were organized in France by a coordinator in charge of the Indigenous guests' tours, in conjunction with local people. The court describes ayahuasca as a hallucinogenic listed as a narcotic which causes a profound alteration in consciousness, either of a mystical or schizophrenic nature, with significant digestive effects (nausea, vomiting, and diarrhea), dizziness with hyper-sudation, euphoria, = aggressiveness, magnification of sounds, colors, contours, and smells. It also mentions that there is evidence of greater capacity for introspection, suggestibility, body awareness, with visual hallucinations, especially of animals, confusion, agitation, intense excitability followed by depression, loss of consciousness, so that ayahuasca proves to be an important factor in psychological destructuration, without acute toxicity or addiction, despite a few reported cases of death (Tribunal de Grande Instance de Paris, 2024, p. 7).

The judge stated that Bauchet presented himself as the manager of Conjonction-Amazonie (marketing products from the Amazon rainforest), and as the French representative of Santo Daime, a "Christian-Shamanic cult," highlighting that he "had already been investigated by the justice system for similar offences, and in an

[12] Given that I only had the chance to interview Claude Bauchet, who agreed to disclose his personal information, I opted to leave out the names and personal information of the other people involved, focusing mainly on the allegations faced by Mr. Bauchet.

interview published online, he considered that the inclusion of ayahuasca on the list of narcotic substances, in 2005, infringed his religious freedom" (Tribunal de Grande Instance de Paris, 2024, p. 8). The ruling also describes the investigations in detail. According to the document, the investigation, coordinated through intercepted communications, concluded that the organization of Santo Daime ceremonies in France and Belgium was arranged via text messages, with logistics managed for South American shamans, and participation costs ranging from €80 to €120 per person. It mentions that advice was given on avoiding explicit mentions of ayahuasca or kambô to evade legal risks. The investigators also mentioned financial records, indicating regular cash withdrawals, along with money transfers to individuals in Brazil linked to Santo Daime, often using specific identifiers associated with an Indigenous group. They surveilled an event at a rural lodge in which they stated they had confirmed ritualistic practices, with the presence of Amazonian shamans, participants consuming a "burgundy-brown liquid resembling ayahuasca," and the use of rapé. Authorities tracked the comings and goings of the group. In this regard, the document mentions a police and fire department intervention that had been carried out on January 1, 2019, with "people unconscious after consuming drugs, but the intervention was not followed up due to the party organizer refusing access to his property because of a religious festival" (Tribunal de Grande Instance de Paris, 2024, p. 10).

Judicial wiretaps and invoice analyses have reportedly uncovered a series of ritual gatherings at Bauchet's residence between May 2018 and February 2019. These ceremonies, allegedly linked to the Santo Daime, took place on at least nine documented occasions, often involving the consumption of ayahuasca and rapé. Despite Bauchet's extended travels to Brazil between May and October 2018, the investigators suggested that the rituals continued in his absence, resuming with regularity upon his return. Further surveillance in 2019 indicated that the ceremonies persisted, occurring roughly three times per month and drawing around 20 participants per gathering. The investigators claimed that to maintain discretion, Bauchet employed encrypted messaging applications, such as WhatsApp, and used coded language—referring to the ceremonies as "choirs." Beyond these ritual activities, authorities also pointed to Bauchet's involvement in cannabis cultivation, suggesting he oversaw two annual harvests (Tribunal de Grande Instance de Paris, 2024, p. 10–11).

Several participants in ceremonies linked to Claude Bauchet were interviewed, having described gatherings that ranged from 15 to 50 attendees, with entry fees varying between 35 and 100 euros. These events involved the consumption of ayahuasca, rapé, and, on occasion, cannabis. The ruling stated that, while similar ceremonies were reportedly held across France and Belgium by other facilitators, Bauchet's activities appeared to be confined to his own residence. According to statements from witnesses, Bauchet did not pressure anyone to partake in ayahuasca; rather, participants knowingly consumed it, fully aware of its legal status. Bauchet's wife indicated that he sourced ayahuasca from Brazil via parcels and distributed it to participants, sometimes free of charge, asking only for food contributions. She emphasized that Bauchet was deeply immersed in the Santo Daime tradition, to the extent that she doubted whether he could forgo the practice. One individual suggested that ayahuasca was central to their rituals, and another claimed that the payment for the brew was not seen as a highly lucrative venture, it was rather perceived as an act of sharing, with generous provisions and household upkeep provided in return.

Testimonies also indicated that no serious health incidents were reported during these ceremonies, including a gathering on January 1, 2019, at Bauchet's residence. Moreover, one of the members provided 20 declarations from participants testifying to the benefits of ayahuasca, its voluntary and unforced use, and Bauchet's generosity in organizing the ceremonies (Tribunal de Grande Instance de Paris, 2024, pp. 11–12). One participant in the ceremonies described Santo Daime as having a profound impact on his physical and spiritual well-being, stating that he felt compelled to share its benefits with others. He likened an ayahuasca ceremony to 10 years of psychoanalysis and claimed that any emotional difficulties experienced during rituals were addressed through traditional cleansing techniques using breathing techniques and incense. He asserted that no psychological breakdowns had occurred at the ceremonies he attended (Tribunal de Grande Instance de Paris, 2024, p. 13).

According to the judge, Bauchet and the other members were arrested at their respective homes on October 1, 2019, as part of an investigation into Santo Daime ceremonies. A search of his residence led to the discovery of several bottles of ayahuasca, totaling 14.8 kg, along with 3.5 kg of a viscous black paste of similar composition. Authorities also seized vials of yellowish powder believed to be rapé, a liquid suspected to be sananga, six cannabis plants, and a small quantity of dried cannabis. A designated growing area equipped with lamps and air extractors was also found, which Bauchet admitted using for cultivation. Toxicological analysis confirmed that the seized ayahuasca samples contained DMT, tetrahydroharmine, and harmine—substances classified as narcotics. The rapé samples primarily contained nicotine, caffeine, and traces of THC, while other vials included coronaridine and dibogamine. Investigators also uncovered handwritten records detailing expenses, participation fees, and transportation costs. Financial estimates suggested a net income of approximately €200–400 per ceremony, amounting to around €12,550 between 2017 and 2019. Bauchet acknowledged that these funds helped cover his living expenses and trips to Brazil (Tribunal de Grande Instance de Paris, 2024, pp. 12–13).

The document stated that, during police custody, Claude Bauchet admitted to regularly hosting Santo Daime ceremonies at his home, where participants consumed ayahuasca in measured doses. He described himself as an "officer or leader of the ritual" rather than a guru or shaman. According to his estimates, around 40 regular participants attended these gatherings, contributing approximately 40–50 euros per ceremony, primarily to cover the costs of ayahuasca and lodging. Bauchet stated that he sourced his ayahuasca from Rio Branco, Brazil, stressing that it was not illegal there. He acknowledged being aware of its classification as a narcotic in France and admitted to importing it by mail. He claimed to have been practicing for about 20 years and had cultivated cannabis since 2018, mainly for personal use to help him "come down" from ceremonies or to relieve joint pain (Tribunal de Grande Instance de Paris, 2024, p. 14).

Bauchet upheld before the judge that his activities were religious in nature, arguing that ayahuasca was not dangerous within the controlled setting of his rituals. He emphasized its therapeutic value and stated that religious practice took precedence over legal restrictions in his view. He also noted that ceremonies were contraindicated for individuals with psychosis, schizophrenia, or those taking antidepressants. To ensure participant safety, he claimed to have trained with a psychotherapist to screen for such conditions. Additionally, he asserted that no deaths had ever been linked to ayahuasca use and that a lethal dose was unlikely due to the body's natural response of vomiting in cases of excessive ingestion. He stated that he had sought legal recognition for ayahuasca within his religious practice by appealing to the Council of State for an exemption, though his request was denied. In his view, the classification of ayahuasca as a narcotic was unjustified, asserting that it was neither toxic nor addictive. Additionally, he claimed to have lost money since becoming involved with Santo Daime (Tribunal de Grande Instance de Paris, 2024, pp. 14–16).

Bauchet and the other defendants requested that they be acquitted on the grounds that neither the toxicity nor the dependence of ayahuasca had been demonstrated, following the opinions of scientists who studied the substance's active ingredients. They also claimed that the consumption of ayahuasca was inseparable from their religion, and that its classification as a narcotic would impede them from practicing their religion. However, the court argued that the mere fact that ayahuasca is listed as a narcotic makes it illegal to supply, import, offer or possess, and that the text does not set a threshold above which this substance is removed from the list (Tribunal de Grande Instance de Paris, 2024, pp. 16–17).

According to the judge, the investigation was supported by physical surveillance, telephone interceptions, and witness testimonies, in which was established that he had been organizing gatherings since January 2018, during which ayahuasca was consumed. The judge also stated that the evidence indicated that Bauchet was responsible for acquiring the substance, which contained DMT, harmine, harmaline, and tetrahydroharmine—compounds classified as narcotics. In the court's view, the fact that these substances were consumed in a religious rather than a recreational context did not alter their legal status. Bauchet was therefore found guilty of transporting, possessing, acquiring, and distributing narcotics and was sentenced to 10 months' probation (Tribunal de Grande Instance de Paris, 2024, p. 20).

Regarding Bauchet's sentence, the court presented him as a retired telecommunications worker, who had dedicated himself to the dissemination of ayahuasca, both through his spiritual practice and his business, "Amazonvie," which specialized in the online sale of Brazilian products. The judge stated, however, that his involvement with ayahuasca had placed him under judicial scrutiny, culminating in legal proceedings that questioned the legitimacy of his religious practices in the eyes of the state. The court recognized that, although Bauchet had no prior criminal record, authorities placed him under judicial supervision in 2019. The court also noted that while he had adhered to the legal restrictions imposed on him, he continued to advocate for the therapeutic and spiritual benefits of ayahuasca, emphasizing its lack of addictive properties and rejecting any association with sectarian movements. The judge stated that Bauchet's insistence on framing his use of ayahuasca as a matter of religious freedom became a central theme in his legal battle, positioning his case within a broader discourse on the right to spiritual autonomy. The court, in its ruling, however, claimed that it sought to balance the enforcement of drug laws with the particularities of Bauchet's situation.

The case highlights once again the complexities surrounding the recognition of certain uses of psychoactive substances as religious practices within contemporary legal and cultural frameworks. While Bauchet and the other defendants presented their practices as a matter of religious conviction, the legal system addressed it through the regulations governing controlled substances, treating it as a risk to public health and safety. The description of the group's activities, along with the surveillance conducted by authorities, contributed to a portrayal of Santo Daime members as criminals. Their discretion in organizing ceremonies was framed as evidence of clandestine and illegal activity, reinforcing the perception of an underground network operating outside the law. One could argue, however, that the group's justified fear of imprisonment for their practices pushed them further into secrecy, making their activities more vulnerable to legal scrutiny. In the end, the court reaffirmed the state's role in regulating these practices and determining the legal boundaries of religious expressions involving psychoactive substances. Two days after the verdict, Bauchet published a letter questioning the court's ruling:

> At the time of this trial, we fell into a trap, that of a speedy justice... The law, nothing but the law, the context did not interest them... Next case! I was stunned to hear the sentence: 10 months' probation for […] and me. […] My lawyer had warned me that this court (*14e chambre correctionnelle*) only tries drug traffickers, and its judges have a reputation for being very severe. I discovered a cold, heartless, deaf and blind court. […] It's a personal feeling (but also a shared one), that we were doomed in advance. Our scientific reports showing that ayahuasca is non-toxic and non-addictive were swept aside. The decision of the French Constitutional Council to define (in 2022) what a narcotic is […] was swept aside. Our right to religious freedom was swept aside (Bauchet, 2024, p. 1)

In the letter Bauchet refers to two key rulings issued by the French Constitutional Council in 2022 on the definition of narcotics. In its January 7, 2022 decision (n° 2021-960 QPC), the Council defined a *stupéfiant* (narcotic) as a psychoactive substance with addictive potential and harmful health effects. Later, in its February 11, 2022 decision (n° 2021-967/973 QPC), the Council reaffirmed that narcotics are defined by their classification under Article L. 5132-7 of the Public Health Code, managed by the *Agence Nationale de Sécurité du Médicament et des Produits de Santé* (National Agency for the Safety of Medicines and Health Products—ANSM), and ruled that this delegation of classification power was constitutional (French Constitutional Council—Decision n° 2021-967/973 QPC).[13] These initiatives were important given that the classification of a narcotic was not explicitly defined in

[13] https://www.conseil-constitutionnel.fr/decision/2022/2021967_973QPC.htm

French law. This new definition created a legal framework that provided Bauchet and others the opportunity to file a second claim with the Council of State to review the classification of ayahuasca as a controlled substance.

6.6 The Council of State's Second Ruling and the Legal Status of Ayahuasca

> This judgment of people and not of ayahuasca (already classified), as negative as it may be, in no way calls into question the appeal we filed (in August 2023) with the Council of State. Justice applies the law, while the Council of State can change the law. We have very strong arguments in our request. Scientific proof that ayahuasca is not a narcotic, as defined by the French Constitutional Council (neither toxic nor addictive). We have also shown that the reasons for the French ayahuasca classification (in 2005) are flawed, full of untruths and disproportionate, as it undermines our religious practice, of which ayahuasca is the sacrament. We therefore have the weakness to believe that this High Court of Justice (administrative) will carefully study our case and see the deceit/lies in this classification. The subject is an important one: after all, it is a question of Constitutional Law that affects religious freedom! We will put all our positive energy into this request and continue to raise the banner of Santo Daime freedom (Bauchet, 2024, p. 2)

As stated in Bauchet's letter, he and other Santo Daime members, alongside the Spanish NGO ICEERS, filed an appeal for excess of power against the Ministry of Health on its silence regarding the request to review the 2005 decision that classified the ayahuasca brew, and the plants banisteriopsis caapi and psychotria viridis as narcotics (Sevaux & Mathonnet, 2023, p. 4). While the first request was made mostly on the grounds of religious freedom, the second one was mainly based on the 2022 decisions regarding the definition of "narcotics," and invested heavily in presenting scientific evidence that ayahuasca was not toxic or addictive. The document argues that the classification was made in error, as it was based on an opinion issued in 2004 without citing specific medical studies.[14] The request contends that recent scientific research undermines the justification for the prohibition of ayahuasca and that the classification violates religious freedom as protected by both the *Déclaration des droits de l'homme et du citoyen* (Declaration of the Rights of Man and of the Citizen 1789) and the European Convention on Human Rights.

The appeal highlights that ayahuasca has been used traditionally by Amazonian Indigenous communities in shamanic rituals and that its religious use gave rise to syncretic movements in Brazil, such as Santo Daime. It also underscores the Brazilian government's official recognition of Santo Daime as a religion in the 1980s and the Peruvian government's 2008 designation of ayahuasca practices as cultural heritage. The request emphasizes that Bauchet, as a leader of the Santo

[14] "This decision follows an opinion issued by the French National Commission on Narcotic Drugs and Psychotropic Substances on 16 December 2004, which merely asserted the possible dangers of consuming ayahuasca without citing the medical studies on which it relied" (Sevaux & Mathonnet, 2023, p. 5).

Daime movement in France, has been responsible for preparing and sharing the brew as part of religious rituals (Sevaux & Mathonnet, 2023, p. 4–5).

The request challenged the legal classification of ayahuasca by arguing that the criteria set forth in international conventions, such as the 1961 New York Convention and the 1971 Vienna Convention, did not apply to ayahuasca. According to the document, a substance must meet specific criteria—causing physical or psychological disorders, creating dependence, and posing a public health or social problem—to be classified as a narcotic. The document asserts that ayahuasca does not meet these criteria, as recent studies indicate that it has low toxicity, it is not addictive, and does not constitute a significant public health concern (Sevaux & Mathonnet, 2023, p. 13–14).

The document acknowledges that although these international definitions are not binding on the states parties, the Constitutional Council had recently adopted a similar definition. The document references the 2022 decision by the French Constitutional Council which affirms that the classification of substances should be based on evolving scientific and medical knowledge. The Council clarified the definition of narcotics as "psychotropic substances characterized by a risk of addiction and harmful effects on health" (Constitutional Council, 7 January 2022, decision no. 2021-960 QPC). According to the request, the prohibition of ayahuasca disregards this principle and disproportionately affects religious practitioners who rely on the brew for their ceremonies. Based on this new definition, it argues that the classification of ayahuasca constitutes an excessive restriction on religious freedom (Sevaux & Mathonnet, 2023, p. 17–18).

Furthermore, the document cites scientific literature, including a 2021 ICEERS report, which states that ayahuasca is physiologically safe and does not lead to neuropsychological alterations. The report also references research showing that the lethal dose of ayahuasca is significantly higher than typical ceremonial doses, implying that its risk of overdose is minimal compared to legal substances like alcohol. The ICEERS report is based on a 2012 study that concluded that ayahuasca does not produce tolerance and therefore does not imply the need to increase the dosage over time to continue to experience the desired effects. The report also underlines that ayahuasca consumption does not activate the areas of the brain linked to the reward system, unlike addictive drugs, so the risks of abuse or addiction are limited. On the contrary, the document states that, according to a number of studies, ayahuasca can combat addiction on other substances (alcohol, tobacco, etc.). The ICEERS report emphasizes the "psychotherapeutic potential" of ayahuasca to "reduce panic and despair scores in experienced users." According to the document, "the ICEERS report states, on the basis of several studies carried out between 2001 and 2012, that ayahuasca is physiologically safe" (Sevaux & Mathonnet, 2023, p. 19). It also mentions that:

> In their 2020 article, the Portuguese researchers [Brito da Costa et al. 2020] state that the lethal dose of ayahuasca for humans, depending on the studies, is between 20 and 50 times the dose usually consumed during religious ceremonies, so "a toxic dose of ayahuasca would correspond to about 7.28 liters for a 70 kg individual, which is unlikely (Sevaux & Mathonnet, 2023, p. 20)."

The appeal reiterated that not only ayahuasca is not toxic to humans, but "that numerous studies indicate that there is no risk of addiction associated with ayahuasca consumption" (Sevaux & Mathonnet, 2023, p. 22). Their claim laid emphasis on several key arguments regarding the safety and therapeutic potential of ayahuasca. It asserted that ayahuasca does not contain any addictive components and that there is no physical toxicity associated with its use. It also highlighted, referencing a study by Bernard Jean-Charles (2016), that the only medical contraindications associated with ayahuasca are related to individuals undergoing treatment with certain antidepressants or those with a psychotic-type psychological structure.

Furthermore, the appeal underscores that the risk of overdose from ayahuasca is significantly reduced due to the unpleasant taste of the brew and its emetic properties, which induce vomiting after consuming an effective dose. It argues that these physiological effects act as a safeguard for consumers. In addition to its safety profile, the document claims that ayahuasca offers potential therapeutic benefits, particularly in the treatment of depression, anxiety, and substance abuse disorders. Although acknowledging that the research into the therapeutic effects of ayahuasca is still in its early stages, the appeal cites initial studies that suggest promising results, indicating that the brew holds considerable therapeutic potential (Sevaux & Mathonnet, 2023, p. 23). It also mentions a 2022 article from Brazilian researchers (Maia et al., 2023) that concludes:

> […] that while the evidence for the therapeutic benefits of ayahuasca is most consistent for depression, with numerous and varied studies (preclinical, observational, clinical), a growing number of preliminary studies suggest its potential for the treatment of other disorders, such as anxiety, mourning, eating disorders, post-traumatic stress, personality disorders, Parkinson's and Alzheimer's disease, and serious physical illnesses (cancer, chronic diseases) (Sevaux & Mathonnet, 2023, p. 24)

Based on the testimonies of Dr. Helle Kaasik and Professor Fabio Antierio Pedalino Costa, the document claims that no public health or social problems can be attributed to the consumption of ayahuasca. The appeal emphasizes that ayahuasca is consumed by a small, specific group of individuals, primarily within the context of the Santo Daime religious ritual, which is conducted under a well-defined framework. In addition, it states that the consumption of ayahuasca in this context is carefully managed by individuals who possess thorough expertise in its preparation, consumption, and the handling of its effects. It is stressed that the consumption takes place in designated locations where participants remain until the effects of the brew have completely worn off. This controlled environment minimizes any potential risks, particularly regarding the safety of individuals who are not part of the ritual. This structured setting, the appeal claims, ensures that the use of ayahuasca does not result in any harm or disturbances to third parties (Sevaux & Mathonnet, 2023, p. 25). The document also presents a lengthy quote from Bernard Jean-Charles (2016, pp. 96–97 apud Sevaux & Mathonnet, 2023, pp. 26–27):

> […] one of the fears relating to the issue of psychedelics is that these substances may be used for sectarian purposes. Could ill-intentioned people create a "negative" framework for taking ayahuasca, leading to sectarian aberrations? We have shown that the setting in which the psychedelic is taken is crucial to the experience, so this danger seems to exist, particu-

> larly for people who are potentially vulnerable to a sectarian hold. However, the legislative prohibition—based on moral and political criteria that are worthy of discussion—is an element that encourages the emergence of this "negative" framework: beyond the anxiety-inducing effect of an illegal psychedelic experience, the accompanying person [i.e., the guide/facilitator] becomes uncertain, as his or her intentions cannot be controlled or verified by third parties. The accompanying person's interpretations may become the only ones available, and the person's subjective experience cannot be shared further because of the illegal nature of the experience. Conversely, if the law were to propose positive frameworks for such use (e.g. control of the substances ingested, possible accreditation of supervisors and compliance with contraindications), it would reduce both accidents and traumatic experiences, but also the risk of sectarian aberrations, which seem to be encouraged by this total ban. In addition to the policy of total prohibition of narcotics, [...] the legal prohibition of the use of psychedelics encourages their potential danger by creating an insecure framework, increasing the risk-taking contexts—both on a personal and societal level. The legislative stance on psychedelics should therefore be reexamined [...] in an intelligent way.

They also reiterate that ayahuasca is consumed exclusively as part of specific rituals, and as such, it does not and cannot serve any recreational purpose. This point is significant: the claimants argue that since ayahuasca is used by a small group of people within a strictly defined context, and with a religious purpose, the consumption of ayahuasca is unlikely to pose any public health or safety issue. The request further argues that the inclusion of Banisteriopsis caapi and Psychotria viridis in the list of narcotic substances, despite the fact that these plants are non-toxic, do not pose any risk of addiction or abuse, and are not likely to result in public health or social problems, constitutes a legal error. Specifically, the appeal contends that the Order of April 20, 2005 is flawed due to an incorrect legal characterization of the facts surrounding the substances' safety and use (Sevaux & Mathonnet, 2023, p. 27). According to the document:

> Above all, it should be remembered that the classification of a substance as a psychotropic is not based solely on its allegedly psychoactive effects on the consumer, but also on other criteria, including its impact on society due to the risks of addiction and abuse that its use can generate. In this respect, it is clear from the above that the consumption of ayahuasca does not present any risk, either to its users or to society as a whole (Sevaux & Mathonnet, 2023, p. 28).

Despite the main focus on questioning the classification of ayahuasca as a controlled substance, the appeal reiterated that the ban of ayahuasca constituted a violation of Santo Daime members' right to religious freedom and violated the right to private and family life. The document argues that the ban on ayahuasca institutes a disproportionate infringement on religious freedom, as protected by both Article 10 of the Declaration of the Rights of Man and of the Citizen of 1789 and Article 9 of the European Convention for the Protection of Human Rights and Fundamental Freedoms.

In the appeal, the legal scholar Jean Carbonnier's definition of religion is referenced, which emphasizes the dual criterion of religion: a subjective element (faith) and an objective element (a community united in that faith). The text cites a legal argument that public law does not distinguish between religions based on their size, age, dogma, or observance, and private law should similarly recognize any religion when faith is combined with a community, regardless of its size. The document asserts that creating distinctions between religions would reintroduce an outdated hierarchy, which conflicts with modern legal principles (Sevaux & Mathonnet, 2023, p. 29). The appeal also draws on legal precedents that apply this definition to both long-established religions, such as certain Hindu groups, and newer movements, like Jehovah's Witnesses. The request states that this body of jurisprudence would support the claim that the legal recognition of a religious community should not be determined by its size or history.

Regarding Article 9 of the European Convention, the appeal highlights that individuals are entitled to freedom of thought, conscience, and religion, which includes the right to manifest their religion publicly or privately. Although this right can be limited under specific circumstances—such as public safety, health, morals, or the protection of others' rights—the document argues that the restrictions imposed by the ban on ayahuasca are lopsided. By classifying ayahuasca and its plants as narcotics, the document contends that the state is unlawfully restricting the Santo Daime community's ability to practice their beliefs, thereby violating these fundamental freedoms (Sevaux & Mathonnet, 2023, p. 30). Ultimately, the appeal concludes that both the 1958 Constitution and the European Convention for the Protection of Human Rights and Fundamental Freedoms safeguard religious freedom. It claims that this protection extends not only to the right of individuals to choose their beliefs freely but also to express and practice them. While the free exercise of religion may be subject to limitations for reasons of public safety, the appeal stresses that such restrictions must be strictly proportionate to the objective they aim to achieve (Sevaux & Mathonnet, 2023, p. 31).

In this context, the Santo Daime is presented as a religious movement that blends elements of Christianity with certain Indigenous spiritual traditions. The document underlines that this movement, particularly prevalent in Brazil, unites a community of believers around a shared faith in Christ and the Virgin Mary. It emphasizes that the Santo Daime practice is exclusively conducted through spiritual services, known as "works," during which sacred hymns are sung after participants consume ayahuasca. The appeal aims to clarify that ayahuasca is not merely a religious symbol, nor is it a ritual tool like the rosary in Catholic worship. Instead, it serves as the central sacrament upon which the Santo Daime faith is founded, and its consumption is indispensable for the conduct of spiritual services. In other words, they claim that by categorizing the plants that comprise ayahuasca as narcotics and imposing a complete ban on their consumption, the decree of April 20, 2005 not only deprives the Santo Daime members of an essential ritual element but also entirely obstructs their ability to practice their religion (Sevaux & Mathonnet, 2023, p. 32).

On December 18, 2024, the Council of State made its decision. The Council rejected the request, asserting that the scientific studies presented did not provide sufficient evidence to overturn the classification of *Banisteriopsis caapi* and *Psychotria viridis* as narcotic substances. The ruling emphasized that maintaining this classification did not constitute a manifest error of assessment, alleging that severe toxic effects—including fatal outcomes—had been reported among individuals who had consumed ayahuasca while also using other narcotic substances or having a personal or family history of psychiatric disorders. Additionally, the decision underscored concerns that increased ayahuasca consumption could lead to misuse, posed health risks, and could potentially result in addiction. According to the council, the presence of a hallucinogenic psychotropic compound in *Psychotria viridis*, already classified as a narcotic, further justified maintaining the prohibition (Conseil d'État, 2024, p. 4).

Regarding the claim that banning ayahuasca infringed on religious freedom as protected by Article 10 of the Declaration of the Rights of Man and of the Citizen of 1789 and Article 9 of the European Convention on Human Rights, the Council of State argued that such an infringement was neither excessive nor disproportionate given the public health concerns outlined previously. The ruling also dismissed the argument that this classification violated the right to private and family life under Article 8 of the European Convention. It asserted that the mere possibility of criminal penalties for using these plants did not, in itself, amount to an infringement of this fundamental right. Based on these considerations, the Council of State concluded that the applicants had no valid grounds for requesting the annulment of the ban on ayahuasca (Conseil d'État, 2024, p. 4).

After the Council of State's ruling Bauchet stated that, although they had initially considered bringing the case before the European Court of Human Rights (ECHR), further analysis led them to conclude that this legal avenue would not allow for a reassessment of ayahuasca's pharmacological aspects. Instead, they chose to continue their efforts through other means, particularly against what they described as the French state's "obscurantist" resistance to an "Indigenous practice." He argued that the prohibition of ayahuasca had broader implications, indirectly infringing on religious freedom for those who regarded it as a sacrament essential to their spiritual practice. Furthermore, he viewed the ban as an insult to Amazonian peoples, whose culture and traditions were being disregarded. Bauchet also denounced the classification of ayahuasca as a narcotic, calling it an arbitrary and politically motivated decision devoid of any scientific or public health justification. He claimed that this classification stemmed from political influence, particularly from organizations such as the MIVILUDES which had raised concerns about the potential for chemical submission and psychological manipulation by so-called "hallucinogenic cults." However, he emphasized that no formal complaints had ever been filed to support these claims. In his view, the classification was purely ideological, based on unfounded assumptions rather than concrete evidence (Bauchet, 2025, p. 2). With the support of ICEERS, Bauchet is preparing to bring his case before the United Nations Committee on Economic, Social and Cultural Rights (CESCR) to challenge what they described as France's refusal to acknowledge scientific evidence.

6.7 The Challenges of Ayahuasca for French Secularism

There is no doubt that the current situation of ayahuasca in France reflects a particular stance regarding drug policies, given that it is considered one of the strictest countries in Europe in this regard (Bourgogne, 2011). However, the French government's position on ayahuasca cannot be reduced solely to the impacts of national drug policies. There is also a clear concern regarding both the health risks associated with ayahuasca and the perception of ayahuasca groups as dangerous cults engaging in new forms of clandestine and criminal activities that pose a threat to public order. To understand the particularity of the French case, it is crucial to examine the historical trajectory of the notion of "cult" and its political implications.

As Introvigne (2023) points out, at the beginning of the nineteenth century, the term "cult" began to be used in official documents and police reports to refer to the activities of freemasonry. During this period, the term took on a new meaning beyond its Catholic reference to heretical movements, becoming associated with organizations considered subversive and suspected of posing a risk to the state. This framework was later extended to a variety of groups in the 1970s and 1980s, eventually categorized by religious studies scholars as "new religious movements." It was precisely during this period that the modern anti-cult movement emerged in the United States. At the time, psychologists adapted the notion of "brainwashing" from American Cold War propaganda against communism, arguing that individuals did not join these groups voluntarily but were manipulated through mind control techniques. Borrowing from this perspective, movements classified as "cults" came to be seen as subversive organizations that stripped members of their agency through coercive persuasion.

Over the decades, the stigma associated with the term "cult" led to its abandonment by most social scientists, as it not only carried a negative evaluative charge but also functioned as a tool for discriminating against minority groups, separating "true religion" from its deviated criminal form (Introvigne, 2023, p. 207). Despite its disuse as an analytical tool in religious studies and in the social sciences, the term "cult" remained central in the agenda of the state and public opinion in some parts of the world, particularly in France. The ban on ayahuasca in France therefore cannot be fully understood without considering the country's official stance on surveillance and control of "sectarian groups" or "cults" within its territory. A key institution in this surveillance apparatus is the MIVILUDES, a government agency responsible for surveilling alleged sectarian movements that has been at the center of controversy for its broad and ambiguous mandate, as it operates without providing a precise definition of what constitutes a "cultish deviation." This lack of a clear framework has led to criticism that the institution arbitrarily targets certain minority movements, reinforcing a narrative that criminalizes and pathologizes alternative practices. By conflating the notion of religious minorities with dangerous manipulation, the MIVILUDES plays a crucial role in shaping public image around groups such as Santo Daime, framing their use of ayahuasca as both a health risk and a form of ideological coercion.

The regulation of religion in France is also justified through the discourse of individual freedom and human rights. Paradoxically, Santo Daime members also invoke human rights language to argue that the prohibition of ayahuasca violates their individual freedoms. This dual use of human rights illustrates how it has become a contested language through which the limits and definitions of religion can be established. While the state deploys human rights discourse to restrict practices deemed incompatible with French republic, religious groups use the same framework to claim legitimacy and protection under the law. The ayahuasca case highlights thus France's difficulty in accommodating practices that do not conform to national values and ideals. Any form of practice perceived to undermine the French *laïcité* is framed as a potential threat to the Republic's foundational principles. Ayahuasca is portrayed thus as a substance that induces altered states of consciousness and fosters communal religious experiences, which is seen as particularly disruptive to the republican values of the country.

It should be noted that the French government's approach to regulating practices such as ayahuasca use is also deeply intertwined with the transformation of the concept of public order in the country. Historically, public order was considered a limiting framework for religious freedom, with the state ensuring that religious expression did not disturb social harmony or security (Dieu, 2020, p. 14). However, recent shifts in French policy have expanded the scope of public order, transforming it from a boundary to individual freedoms into an essential, overarching value that takes precedence over religious expression. This shift reflects broader concerns about public safety and the integration of practices perceived as non-conforming to the values of the Republic, particularly certain forms of Islam and, more recently, the practices of ayahuasca groups. Public order, once seen strictly through a lens of security, is now understood as a social and civil value that can override religious freedoms in the name of preserving societal cohesion (Dieu, 2020, p. 15).

This transformation of the notion of public order parallels debates about the role of secularism in French society, particularly as it relates to the regulation of religious expression. As Asad (2006, p. 497) has argued in his analysis of the Islamic veil ban, the French state asserts the authority to define the acceptable boundaries of religious expression, framing it as a matter of both individual rights and the secular public good. In the case of ayahuasca, the French state similarly seeks to define and regulate practices that it perceives as incompatible with republican values, using public order as a key justification for limiting such practices. The shift towards a more expansive understanding of public order, which now includes social norms and the protection of societal identity, has significant implications for certain minorities. As Dieu (2020, p. 34) notes, this form of public order seeks to impose behavioral norms on individuals wishing to participate in public life, potentially leading to more restrictive regulations on practices that deviate from the national ideal. In this context, the state's stance on ayahuasca can be seen as part of a broader effort to regulate religious practices through the lens of national identity, societal values, and public order.

The French government and courts operate under the assumption that some forms of religious agency and individual freedom, like oil and water, do not mix. The tension between state intervention and religious freedom is not simply about legal definitions but about deeper ideological commitments. While France presents itself as a defender of individual liberties, its regulatory apparatus often functions to discipline expressions that challenge the state's normative vision of selfhood and autonomy. It is noteworthy that the strategy from the Santo Daime group to overturn the French government's decision appears to be shifting away from appeals to religious freedom and human rights, as these arguments have been consistently overridden by concerns framed in terms of public health and order. In response, they have opted for an alternative approach: challenging the scientific validity of the government's claims that ayahuasca poses a public health and safety risk. Their new strategy aims to prove that the data presented to justify the prohibition lacks robust scientific support. The existing biomedical research on ayahuasca—including studies on its therapeutic potential—has thus far failed to sway French authorities. Whether such scientific data will have greater influence in transnational arenas, such as the United Nations, remains to be seen.

References

Agence Nationale de Sécurité du Médicament et des Produits de Santé. (2019). *Soumission chimique: Résultats de l'enquête 2019.*.

Asad, T. (2006). Trying to understand French secularism. In H. Vries & L. E. Sullivan (Eds.), *Political theologies: Public religions in a post-secular world* (pp. 194–215). Fordham University Press.

Bauchet, C., Bourgogne, G., Bourgogne, C., Mabit, J., Vaillant, C., & Vacandare, J. P. (2005). *Recours pour excès de pouvoir: Mémoire introductif et ampliatif.* https://www.bialabate.net/wp-content/uploads/2008/08/AyahuascaAppealCouncilStateFrance2005.pdf

Bauchet, C. (2024). *Letter to my dear sisters, brothers, and friends.* Saint Prix.

Bauchet, C. (2025). *Le déni scientifique de la France, face à l'ayahuasca: Une prohibition injustifiée: Rétrospective d'une histoire inachevée.*

Beauverie, P. (2004). *Lettre au juge d'instruction du 20 octobre 2004.* Établissement Public de Santé Paul Giraud.

Beck, F., Guignard, R., & Richard, J. B. (2014). Poppers at the top: Usages of alkaline nitrites in France. *MedSci (Paris), 30*(10), 916–921. https://doi.org/10.1051/medsci/20143010015

Bernard, J.-C. (2016). Ayahuasca : L'importance du cadre et de l'intention lors de prise de psychédéliques. *Psychotropes, 22*(2), 81–100. https://doi.org/10.3917/psyt.222.0081

Bourgone, G. (2011). One hundred days of ayahuasca in France: The story of a legal decision. In B. C. Labate & H. Jungaberle (Eds.), *The internationalisation of ayahuasca* (pp. 353–363). Lit Verlag.

Commission Nationale des Stupéfiants et des Psychotropes. (2001). *Plantes hallucinogènes et leurs principes actifs.* No. 46 du 19 avril 2001. Procès-verbal adopté à la réunion du 27 juin 2001. https://www.bialabate.net/wp-content/uploads/2018/02/CommissionNationaleStupefiantsPsychotropesMinutesMeeting2001.pdf

Commission Nationale des Stupéfiants et des Psychotropes. (2005). *Procès-verbal de la 62ème réunion du 16 décembre 2004.* Adopté à la réunion du 24 février 2005. https://archiveansm.integra.fr/var/ansmsite/storage/original/application/f79919183626ba37e421a535f9b9dca6.pdf

Commission Nationale des Stupéfiants et des Psychotropes/CEIP-Paris. (2005). *Soumission chimique, enquête nationale.*. https://archiveansm.integra.fr/var/ansmsite/storage/original/application/2aa3678860194f894fc6fb43525da8b5.pdf

Conseil d'État. (2007). *République Française au Nom du Peuple Français.* No. 282100. https://www.bialabate.net/wp-content/uploads/2008/08/AyahuascaRulingCouncilState2007.pdf

Conseil d'État. (2024). *République Française au Nom du Peuple Français.* No. 487157.

Cour d'Appel de Paris. (2005). *Dossier n° 04/01888, arrêt du 13 janvier 2005, 10ème Chambre, Section B.* https://www.bialabate.net/wp-content/uploads/2008/08/versao2.pdf

Dieu, F. (2020). L'ordre public et les religions: ordre public, ordre laïque? *Revue du droit des religions, 9.* https://doi.org/10.4000/rdr.1107

Dupuis, D. (2016). *The murmurs of ayahuasca: Ritual paths and cultural transmission in Takiwasi*. Doctoral Dissertation, Anthropology, École des Hautes Études en Sciences Sociales, Paris.

Dupuis, D. (2021). Psychedelics as tools for belief transmission: Set, setting, suggestibility, and persuasion in the ritual use of hallucinogens. *Frontiers in Psychology, 12*, 730031. https://doi.org/10.3389/fpsyg.2021.730031

Introvigne, M. (2023). Mystics or criminals? "Cults," religion, and drugs. In B. C. Labate & C. Cavnar (Eds.), *Religious freedom and the global regulation of ayahuasca* (pp. 301–318). Routledge.

La Maison Qui Chante, Takiwasi. (2002). *Argumentaire face à la campagne de diffamation lancée en France contre les dirigeants de l'association "La Maison qui Chante" et du "Centre Takiwasi"*.

Labate, B., Antunes, H. F., Loures de Assis, G., & Cavnar, C. (2023, January 5). *A call for public support against the current demonization of ayahuasca practices in Spain*. Chacruna Institute. https://chacruna.net/a-call-for-public-support-against-the-current-demonization-of-ayahuasca-practices-in-spain/

Labate, B. C., & Feeney, K. (2012). Ayahuasca and the process of regulation in Brazil and internationally: Implications and challenges. *International Journal of Drug Policy, 23*, 154–161.

Maia, L. O., Daldegan-Bueno, D., Wießner, I., Araujo, D. B., & Tófoli, L. F. (2023). Ayahuasca's therapeutic potential: What we know—and what not. *European Neuropsychopharmacology, 66*, 45–61.

Ministère de la Santé et des Solidarités. (2006). *Requête no. 282100 formée par M. Bauchet et autres demandant l'annulation de l'arrêté du 20 avril 2005 modifiant l'arrêté du février 1990 fixant la liste des substances classées comme stupéfiants*.

Novaes, C., & Moro, M. R. (2023). The landscapes of ayahuasca in contemporary France. In B. C. Labate & C. Cavnar (Eds.), *Religious freedom and the global regulation of ayahuasca* (pp. 106–121). Routledge.

Navarro, S. S. (2025, July 17). La justicia española aclara que la ayahuasca no está fiscalizada ni prohibida en España y ordena su devolución: Una sentencia histórica que sienta jurisprudencia. Cannabis Magazine. https://www.cannabismagazine.net/el-tribunal-superior-de-justicia-de-madrid-confirma-que-la-ayahuasca-no-esilegal-en-espana/

Pépin, G., & Duffort, G. (2004). Ayahuasca: liane de l'âme, chamanes et soumission chimique. *Annales de Toxicologie Analytique, 16*(1), 76–84.

Sevaux, J., & Mathonnet, P. (2023). *Recours pour excès de pouvoir*. Conseil d'État.

Tribunal de Grande Instance de Paris. (2004, January 15). *Jugement du 15 janvier 2004*, No. 9828602936. https://www.bialabate.net/wp-content/uploads/2017/12/High-Court-of-Paris-15-January-2004-Bauchet-case.pdf

Tribunal de Grande Instance de Paris. (2024, June 4). *Jugement du 04 juin 2024*, No. 18211000246.

Chapter 7
Conclusion

Is ayahuasca a sacrament, a cultural phenomenon, a drug, or a tool for psychological manipulation? After examining how this Amazonian brew has become an object of public interest and state intervention in three different countries, we are no closer to a definitive answer than when this journey began. As stated in the introduction, the goal of this book was never to define what ayahuasca is, but rather to explore how it has become the center of disputes over religious freedom, cultural rights, drug policies, and the contested boundaries between legality and illegality. One of the key challenges—and advantages—of this study is that ayahuasca resists strict classification. Its meanings and uses vary widely, not only across legal frameworks but also among the actors engaged in these disputes. It is described as a "divine being," a "sacrament," a "medicine," a "cultural heritage," a "way of life," a form of "therapy," a "tool for personal transformation," a "dangerous drug," or a "powerful hallucinogen," and the list of terms goes on.

When it comes to regulation—or the lack thereof—these competing classifications reflect broader debates about how different nation-states define what constitutes religion, culture, therapy, or drugs. These definitions, in turn, require the establishment of boundaries between such domains, boundaries that are neither random nor static. They emerge from the interactions of diverse actors who contest and negotiate the characterization and limits of certain practices. The use of ayahuasca has become both a battleground and a lens for examining the intersections of law, religious freedom, heritage and drug policies, academia, and activism, revealing how the frontiers of legality and legitimacy are constantly being disputed and redrawn. The debates surrounding its regulation are far from settled. If anything, they are becoming increasingly complex as new actors, legal battles, and cultural shifts continue to shape its trajectory. Yet, despite these changes, certain core issues remain central: the disputes around religious and cultural recognition, the reach of state intervention, and the ongoing negotiation of legitimacy within various legal and social frameworks.

H. Fernandes Antunes, *Religion, Drug, or Cult?*, Law and Religion in a Global Context 5, https://doi.org/10.1007/978-3-032-04368-9_7

The legal, historical, and political trajectories explored in this book reveal the complexities of regulating ayahuasca. The cases of Brazil, the United States, and France illustrate the diverse ways in which states define, legitimize, or restrict its use. By tracing how ayahuasca has been positioned within different legal and bureaucratic frameworks, this book has not only examined specific regulatory mechanisms but also explored the underlying historical and political assumptions that shape these disputes. In Brazil, ayahuasca has undergone a significant transformation, from being framed within drug policies to being increasingly recognized as cultural and religious heritage. This shift, however, took decades to consolidate. In 1985, ayahuasca was temporarily banned, only to be decriminalized and regulated for religious purposes 2 years later. Since then, the discourse has gradually moved toward recognizing it as a cultural expression linked to Indigenous and Afro-Brazilian traditions, which are entitled to state protection. Over time, terms such as "drug," "narcotic," and "hallucinogen" lost their relevance and were eventually abandoned in official narratives surrounding it. Anthropological discourse—and anthropologists themselves—played a crucial role in legitimizing ayahuasca use in Brazil. By challenging the framework of medical science and its alleged limitations, and by characterizing it as a social practice that promotes integration and community values embedded in a Christian background, anthropologists contributed to the recognition of groups such as Santo Daime, Barquinha and UDV as cultural expressions that promote religious and social values cherished in Brazilian society. This framework allowed ayahuasca use to be incorporated into the broader landscape of Brazilian religions. However, similar to Afro-Brazilian religions, ayahuasca groups came to be understood as expressions of racial and ethnic minorities whose traditions deserve safeguarding due to their historical and cultural significance.

This framework laid the foundation for a significant shift in Brazil's public debate: the ongoing recognition of ayahuasca's religious use as part of the country's intangible cultural heritage. While the transition from drug to heritage policies marks a milestone in the public acknowledgment of ayahuasca, the process has been far from smooth. Various actors—including religious groups, Indigenous communities, state institutions, and activists—have contested its scope, limits, and criteria. Santo Daime groups and the UDV have successfully positioned themselves within the heritage discourse, but Indigenous groups have increasingly challenged this narrative, asserting their role as ayahuasca's original stewards. These tensions have sparked complex negotiations over authenticity, legitimacy, and the balance between tradition and innovation. Central to these debates are questions of authority: Who has the right to speak for ayahuasca, and who can claim to be its legitimate bearer? The changing boundaries of legitimacy in Brazil reveal that recognition is not a top-down institutional process but a contested arena where different actors mobilize to advance their claims.

Moreover, these disputes highlight broader concerns about the state's ability and willingness to craft policies that accommodate the diverse voices within the ayahuasca landscape. Indigenous peoples, in particular, have questioned the legitimacy of certain legal instruments, exposing the limitations of state-driven approaches in addressing Indigenous political and cultural demands. The Brazilian case illustrates how ayahuasca regulation extends beyond drug policy, intersecting with broader national debates on pluralism, affirmative policies, and the state's role in recognizing and legitimizing cultural and religious practices. While Brazil has gradually moved toward acknowledging ayahuasca as a legitimate religious and cultural tradition, this recognition remains fraught with tensions and disputes.

In contrast, in the United States, ayahuasca is primarily framed in legal debates about religious exemptions for controlled substances. This distinct sociopolitical context has produced its own complex dynamics of legitimacy, restriction, and contestation. The legal battles over ayahuasca in the country expose a fundamental paradox at the heart of its legal system: while the law ostensibly protects religious practice and belief, it simultaneously requires courts and government agencies to define what counts as religion, what constitutes sincerity, and what level of risk justifies state intervention. Furthermore, the cases of ayahuasca churches highlight the uneasy intersection between two legal paradigms—the commitment to religious freedom and the regulatory framework of drug prohibition—each of which claims a totalizing authority. The government's insistence on framing ayahuasca as a controlled substance reveals an underlying assumption: that risk, particularly the potential for harm or misuse, is a more legally operative category than belief. It is not just about controlling substances; it is about controlling the terms under which religious legitimacy is granted or denied.

While the victories of UDV, Santo Daime, and the settlements between the CEC, the CCH, and the US government mark significant milestones, they have not resolved the deeper controversies surrounding ayahuasca's religious use. Instead, they illustrate how legal recognition is a double-edged sword, securing exemptions while simultaneously subjecting religious practices to bureaucratic oversight, standardization, and surveillance. Regulatory requirements such as health screenings, strict security protocols, and emergency measures inevitably incorporate biomedical and legal priorities into religious use, subtly reshaping these traditions. The exemption from drug laws comes at the cost of increased state intervention, making legal recognition both a safeguard and a mechanism of control. Moreover, these cases reveal the courts' reliance on a Protestant-inflected understanding of religion, where the notions of belief and sincerity are prioritized. This framework allowed the ayahuasca churches to claim legitimacy but left open the question of whether non-Christian or less formally structured groups could do the same. While new decisions can expand the scope of religious protection, it does not dismantle the state's authority to define religion. Rather, it reaffirms that the boundaries of religious legitimacy remain fluid, contested, and ultimately subject to legal interpretation.

This intricate scenario has led lawyers, NGOs, and activists to develop legal and advocacy initiatives to navigate the legally fraught terrain of ayahuasca regulation. Faced with the challenge of religious freedom constrained by state-imposed definitions, these actors have sought to secure legal protections for ayahuasca churches through litigation, policy reform, and public engagement. At the same time, their efforts have gone beyond securing exemptions, raising fundamental questions about the government's legitimacy and capacity to determine what constitutes a religion. By challenging the state's authority to define religious sincerity and regulate religious practices through biomedical and legal frameworks, these initiatives expose the limitations of existing legal paradigms and demand a broader, more inclusive recognition of religious diversity. In doing so, they not only contest current interpretations of the law but also push for a reconfiguration of the relationship between religious freedom and state intervention.

These disputes also reflect broader shifts in the legal and cultural landscape. The increasing prominence of ayahuasca and psilocybin mushrooms use in the country, alongside the decriminalization of psychedelics in states like Colorado, signals a transformation in how these substances are understood and governed. Yet, the tension between religious freedom and regulatory control persists. While state-level protections may offer some security, federal law still poses significant risks, as seen in the DEA's continued oversight of religious exemptions. As more groups seek recognition, the struggle over ayahuasca is becoming less about a single plant or tradition and more about the role of the state in adjudicating religious authenticity. If religious freedom depends on legal recognition, and legal recognition depends on state-defined categories, then the very notion of religious exemption becomes a site of perpetual negotiation, one in which risk, sincerity, and legitimacy remain unsettled and deeply contested.

France, in contrast, stands out as the most prohibitive case among the three. Unlike Brazil, where ayahuasca has been incorporated into cultural and religious heritage policies, or the United States, where religious groups can petition for legal exemptions for the religious use of ayahuasca, France has taken an entirely repressive stance, presenting a unique intersection of drug policy and public order. France is known for its strict drug policies, and the French government's stance on ayahuasca reflects this rigid approach. The legal prohibition of ayahuasca in the country is primarily based on concerns about public health and safety, but it also encompasses broader social and political considerations, particularly regarding the classification of ayahuasca groups as "cults." This framing is not merely about regulating psychoactive substances but about controlling practices that are seen as potentially disruptive to the established order.

The categorization of ayahuasca groups as dangerous cults is rooted in the history of the term "cult" in France, where it has been associated with subversive organizations deemed a threat to public order. This historical framework is reinforced by the government's surveillance apparatus, particularly the MIVILUDES, which monitors groups it deems sectarian. By labeling ayahuasca groups as "cults," the French state not only criminalizes their practices but also creates a public narrative that associates these groups with coercion and ideological manipulation, further stigmatizing them as dangerous organizations.

Hence, not only is ayahuasca classified as an illicit drug, but ayahuasca groups are framed as criminal organizations subject to state surveillance and criminal prosecution. The criminalization of ayahuasca in France reflects a model where the state actively polices certain practices that pose challenges to the ideals and values that sustain their notion of public order. The association of ayahuasca with "chemical submission" and brainwashing narratives further illustrates how state institutions mobilize specific forms of expertise to justify the ban on ayahuasca, demonstrating that legal restrictions are often intertwined with broader political anxieties about certain practices and groups.

Central to the French case is the tension between secularism and religious freedom. While the state invokes secular principles and the discourse of protecting individual freedoms and the public order to justify its prohibition of ayahuasca, the groups involved argue that their practices are a form of religious expression protected by human rights. This tension highlights the difficulties of accommodating practices that fall outside the mainstream or challenge national values. The French legal system thus finds itself caught between protecting individual freedoms and upholding a republican model that narrowly defines acceptable forms of religious expression.

In this regard, the issue of ayahuasca is also affected by shifting stances on public order in the country. In recent years, this legal principle has expanded beyond concerns about security to encompass social norms and the protection of national identity. This shift has profound implications for certain groups, especially for those like the Santo Daime, whose use of a psychoactive substance is viewed as incompatible with republican values. The state's approach to regulating such practices is framed as an effort to preserve societal cohesion, but this increasingly expansive view of public order undermines the rights of those whose practices do not align with the dominant national ideal. In response, the Santo Daime group in Paris has shifted its strategy, moving away from religious freedom arguments, which have consistently been overridden by concerns about public health and order. Instead, they are now focusing on challenging the scientific basis for the government's claims about the risks of ayahuasca. Whether this new strategy will lead to a change in France's position remains uncertain, but it highlights the deep entanglement of legal, scientific, and political forces in the regulation of ayahuasca in the country.

Despite their glaring differences, the regulation of ayahuasca across different national contexts reveals a shared concern for balancing religious freedom against state interests. While the specifics of these cases differ, they all involved efforts to assess whether ayahuasca posed a risk to public safety or social stability. In all cases, these concerns were not just about the health risks associated with ayahuasca consumption, but also about the role of the state in regulating and controlling certain practices and expressions.

Mahmood's (2015) analysis of "public order" within political secularism offers a valuable lens for understanding these dynamics. She argues that secular states, while affirming private religious belief, often restrict public religious expressions deemed threatening to national identity or social cohesion. The concept of public order thus serves as a mechanism for state intervention, drawing a distinction between protected private belief and regulated public practice. Rooted in nineteenth-century European jurisprudence, this rationale has historically justified limitations on the public expression of certain practices that challenge dominant moral and legal frameworks. In the case of ayahuasca, state regulation reflects not only concerns over health and safety but also anxieties about its potential to unsettle established norms and values.

Whether in France, Brazil, or the United States, the state's intervention in ayahuasca practices can thus be seen as part of a broader political-legal framework aimed at preserving public order, safeguarding public morals, and asserting the sovereignty of the state in defining the limits of public expressions of certain groups. In this context, the legal issues surrounding ayahuasca exemplify the ways in which national states define the boundaries of acceptable religious practice, often invoking principles such as public health, safety, and order to classify, regulate, safeguard, protect, to scrutinize, restrict, or even ban practices deemed incompatible with their historical trajectory or legal framework.

In contrast to a top-down imposition, however, the regulation of practices like ayahuasca use is often a complex process involving numerous actors, negotiations, and disputes. These actors are not limited to state representatives but also include scholars, religious leaders, Indigenous peoples, politicians, activists, and NGOs, and they occupy unequal positions of power and bring different skills, competences, and resources to the table (Montero et al., 2023). This myriad of actors and their varied capacities for influencing public policy highlight the dynamic nature of law and policymaking. The involvement of scholars as experts, the mobilization of NGOs, and the growing engagement of ayahuasca groups and activists demonstrate that the regulation of religious practices involves a broader social negotiation, extending beyond the state's formal decision-making processes.

The role of rights discourse in this process is particularly significant. As stated in a previous work (Montero et al., 2023), the language of rights has become central in these quarrels, serving as a key tool for actors to assert their demands and frame their claims in a way that resonates in the public sphere. The mastery of rights language and the strategic use of legal discourse have become essential for actors to gain visibility and advocate for their causes. This is particularly evident in the case of ayahuasca, where activists, Indigenous peoples, religious leaders, and scholars alike utilize rights discourse to challenge the state's position and to promote new understandings of religious freedom, cultural recognition, public health, and cultural heritage.

This expansion of legal discourse beyond the institutional arena of law means that it is no longer seen as exclusive domains of lawyers, judges, or legal experts; it has become part of the repertoire of a wide range of actors who are engaged in social and political struggles. This shift has expanded the reach and interpretation of legal concepts, allowing for new claims and contested meanings to emerge. As these actors mobilize within public and legal debates, they not only engage with the law but also shape its application, contesting interpretations and advancing new understandings of rights and legal frameworks. The current landscape of rights discourse reflects thus a diversification of legal language, where a wide array of social actors contributes to unsettle established legal grammars. This broadens the scope of legal disputes, challenging the traditional notion that law is confined to the expertise of legal professionals and expanding its reach into the realm of public activism and collective mobilization.

The cases explored in this book have thus far-reaching implications for the issue of pluralism and its impacts in contemporary democracies. These cases pose significant challenges in understanding how legal disputes emerge and the broader effects they have, not only at the institutional level but across various other arenas, such as the media and academia. These are multifaceted processes that defy easy categorization, yet they offer valuable insight into the governance of difference and the regulation of practices and bodies within the boundaries of national states. They reveal the underlying mechanisms and devices that are mobilized in the process of defining and delimiting the limits of key concepts such as religion, culture, drug use, freedom, safety, and risk. Such categorizations are not merely semantic; they carry profound implications for legal recognition, state intervention, and the boundaries of acceptable practice. Ultimately, these cases illustrate how classification systems shape the conditions of legitimacy and action, influencing not only regulatory outcomes but also broader societal understandings of what constitutes religious freedom, cultural heritage, or drug use. By examining these processes, we gain a deeper understanding of how definitions are established and contested, and how such definitions shape the regulation and public discourse surrounding them.

Looking ahead, the future of ayahuasca regulation will likely be shaped by ongoing transformations in drug policy, religious freedom jurisprudence, and global discussions on religious, cultural, and Indigenous rights. The increasing decriminalization and medicalization of psychedelics, particularly in the United States, may open new legal pathways for ayahuasca. However, these developments also raise critical government concerns about commercialization and its potential shift toward recreational uses. In contrast, the rising visibility of Indigenous claims to ayahuasca sovereignty in South America introduces both opportunities and tensions. On one hand, it has the potential to strengthen affirmative policies that recognize Indigenous rights and traditional governance structures. On the other hand, it disrupts existing legal paradigms and challenges established religious groups, as it questions the frameworks that have historically privileged non-Indigenous actors in regulatory negotiations. As Indigenous communities assert greater control over ayahuasca, there may be increasing demands for policies that acknowledge Indigenous governance models rather than simply extending legal frameworks originally designed in dialogue with religious organizations.

By placing the cases of Brazil, the United States, and France side by side, one can see how national histories, legal traditions, and political cultures produce divergent regulatory landscapes. In Brazil, ayahuasca is moving toward cultural heritage recognition, but tensions persist around claims of tradition and authenticity. The U.S. case, while allowing religious exemptions, subjects groups to bureaucratic scrutiny and legal uncertainty, while government bodies and courts establish definitions and attributes for "religion" and "sincerity." France, however, presents a unique approach, where ayahuasca is not only criminalized but also entangled in the country's broader policies against cults. This adds an extra layer to the problem, as the French state must not only regulate psychoactive substances but also navigate the delicate distinction between legitimate religious practices and sectarian movements. These contrasts reveal that ayahuasca's legal status is not just a matter of drug policy but also an expression of deeper struggles over the nature and limits of religion, the challenges of national identity, and the constraints of state authority.

To conclude, it should be reiterated that these classifications have significant repercussions on people's lives. After being a member of Santo Daime for two decades and researching the debates on ayahuasca for 15 years, I cannot define what ayahuasca is. Nevertheless, from my personal and academic perspective, I can unequivocally state that the practices by ayahuasca groups described in this book do not resemble the hallmarks of criminal organizations or drug cartels. There are no firearms involved, no large-scale money laundering operations, and no intricate criminal networks. What one typically encounters are small groups—usually fewer than 50 people—composed of individuals from diverse professional and personal backgrounds who come together to consume ayahuasca in a ceremonial context. The rise in arrests, seizures, and legal cases demonstrates a growing discrepancy between scientific research and the legal framework surrounding ayahuasca. While anthropologists highlight its historical and cultural significance, and the medical field is increasingly enthusiastic about its therapeutic potential, ayahuasca groups often find themselves awakened in the middle of the night at gunpoint by police officers who treat them as if they were dangerous drug traffickers.

It is not up to this book to present a roadmap or a definitive solution for ayahuasca's predicament, far from it. Still, if history teaches us anything, it is that the war on drugs is a failed war. Criminalization fosters stigmatization, persecution, and incarceration, forcing practices and groups underground, where it becomes difficult to promote accountability and transparency. This is not about proposing a single, universal regulatory path. As I have shown, each nation navigates issues such as drug policy, religious freedom, and public order through its own legal and cultural lenses. However, one cannot fail to mention that, in most cases, criminalization is the worst possible policy choice.

References

Mahmood, S. (2015). *Religious difference in a secular age: A minority report.* Princeton University Press.

Montero, P., Nicácio, C., & Antunes, H. F. (2023). Introduction: Religious pluralism and law in contemporary Brazil. In P. Montero, C. Nicácio, & H. F. Antunes (Eds.), *Religious pluralism and law in contemporary Brazil. Law and religion in a global context* (Vol. 4). Springer. https://doi.org/10.1007/978-3-031-41981-2_1

MIX
Papier aus verantwortungsvollen Quellen
Paper from responsible sources
FSC® C105338

If you have any concerns about our products,
you can contact us on
ProductSafety@springernature.com

In case Publisher is established outside the EU,
the EU authorized representative is:
Springer Nature Customer Service Center GmbH
Europaplatz 3, 69115 Heidelberg, Germany

Printed by Libri Plureos GmbH
in Hamburg, Germany